A GREAT GIFT FROM THE PROUD PEOPLE

"I am still tied to the Barrens, not by the simple web of memories alone, but by something more powerful. There is an abiding affection in my heart for the men and women of the plains who lent me their eyes so that I was privileged to look backward through the dark void of years and to see not only the relics of forgotten times, but also to see into the minds and the thoughts of the men of those times. It was a great gift I had from the People and one that deserved repayment . . ."

PEOPLE OF THE DEER

"The most powerful book to come out of the Arctic for some years. It traces with a beautiful clarity the material and spiritual bonds between land, deer and people."

—*Times Literary Supplement*

"This is a fascinating and beautiful book."

—*St. Louis Dispatch*

"A continuously stirring account of one of the least known regions of the North American continent."

—*The New York Times*

"It is not often that a writer finds himself the sole chronicler of a whole human society . . . Mowat has done marvelously well at the job."

—*The New Yorker*

Bantam Books by Farley Mowat
Ask your bookseller for the books you have missed

THE BOAT WHO WOULDN'T FLOAT
THE DESPERATE PEOPLE
THE DOG WHO WOULDN'T BE
NEVER CRY WOLF
PEOPLE OF THE DEER
THE SNOW WALKER
A WHALE FOR THE KILLING

PEOPLE OF THE DEER

Farley Mowat

With Drawings by Samuel Bryant

BANTAM BOOKS
TORONTO • NEW YORK • LONDON • SYDNEY

To Frances,
Ohoto's friend

PEOPLE OF THE DEER

*A Bantam Book / published by arrangement with
Little, Brown & Company in association with
The Atlantic Monthly Press*

*The author wishes to thank the Atlantic Monthly
for permission to use some material
that first appeared in its pages.*

PRINTING HISTORY

*Little, Brown edition published February 1952
19 printings through May 1975
Bantam edition / September 1981*

*Bantam Books are published by Bantam Books, Inc. Its trade-
mark, consisting of the words "Bantam Books" and the por-
trayal of a bantam, is Registered in U.S. Patent and Trademark
Office and in other countries. Marca Registrada. Bantam
Books, Inc., 666 Fifth Avenue, New York, New York 10103.*

PRINTED IN THE UNITED STATES OF AMERICA

0 9 8 7 6 5 4 3 2

Contents

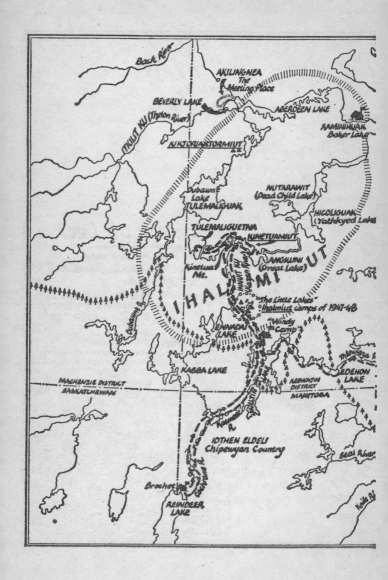

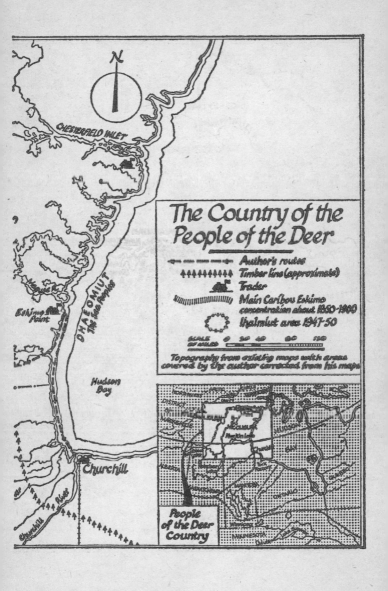

N

CHESTERFIELD INLET

The Country of the
People of the Deer

- - - Author's routes
+++++++ Timber line (approximate)
Trader
Main Caribou Eskimo
concentration about 1880-1900
Ihalmiut area 1947-50

SCALE
OF MILES 0   20   40   80   120

Topography from existing maps with areas
covered by the author corrected from his maps

DHAEOMIUT
The Sea People

Eskimo
Point

Hudson
Bay

Churchill

Churchill River

People
of the Deer
Country

Foreword

On an evening when the sun hovered above the horizon's lip, I sat beside a man who was not of my race, and watched a spectacle so overwhelming in its magnitude that I had no words for it.

Below us, on the undulating darkness of the barren plains, a tide of life flowed out of the dim south and engulfed the world, submerged it so that it sank beneath a living sea. The very air was heavy with the breath of life itself. There was a sound of breathing and of moving that was like a rising wind. It was as if the inanimate and brutal crust of rock had been imbued with the essential spark and had risen from its ageless rigidity to claim the rights of life.

The man who sat beside me stared over the rolling hordes that swept in upon us, and it was as if he stretched the hands of his soul out to the flood—the eddying, turbulent and all-embracing flood.

I felt afraid. The man beside me was no longer there. In some way that I could not fathom he had gone from me and had flung himself into that living torrent. There was an ecstasy upon him then. The man was gone, his spirit had sought and found a union with the amorphous, living entity which had possessed his land.

I could not understand, for I was a stranger in that place, but the man who had been beside me was of the land. He was more that that. He was of this profound, incredible thing I was beholding.

Darkness was full upon us before the man returned to me. There was no light left upon the plains, but the unseen shadows still held the faint murmur of ten thousand vital hearts beating with strength and power on every side of us. It was too dark to see and yet I knew the man had turned his face toward me, fixed his eyes on mine. He spoke so quietly it might have been that I heard words spoken from the divided voice of the monstrous visitation I had witnessed.

"*Tuktu-mie* . . ." The words came slowly. . . . "This is the Host—the Legion of the Deer. . . ."

Foreword to the New Edition

At the time *People of the Deer* was published, in 1952, it was impossible for me to obtain documentary corroboration for much of the story. The book dealt harshly with the Old Empires of the North—the missions, the R.C.M.P., the trading companies, and the federal government—who between them possessed all of the official "evidence." They were not about to give me access to the documentary proof of their errors of omission and commission. I was therefore forced to be somewhat circumspect. Some of the names used had to be pseudonyms. Furthermore, I was sometimes forced to refrain from correctly identifying events in terms of time and locale.

By 1959, when I wrote *The Desperate People,* conditions had altered drastically and I was able to obtain the requisite documentation—the paper "proof" of the truth. Consequently, in *The Desperate People* all names used were the correct ones and the events were presented in their actual spatial and temporal contexts. Where apparent discrepancies occur between the two books, the version given in *The Desperate People* is the correct one.

In the Foreword to *The Desperate People*—my 1959 sequel to *People of the Deer*—I wrote: "There are now belated signs of a lightening on the somber horizon of the Canadian arctic; but this may be no more than the illusion of a false sunrise in a polar winter . . ."

It is now fifteen years since those words were written and the sunrise has proved to be an illusion in all truth. The physical disruptions which our society inflicted on the Eskimos during the first half of this century have been ameliorated to the extent that few Eskimos now die of physical neglect. Since about 1960 we have made considerable efforts to ensure that they will survive in the flesh; but at the same time we have pursued a policy which is very efficiently destroying them psychically. We have made a ruthless and concerted effort to dispossess them from their own age-old way of life and thought and to force them into the mold of our modern technological society. Assimilation has been our goal . . . and it has failed disastrously. In 1974 almost all Canadian Eskimos have been broken away from the support of their land (which is theirs no longer) and live clustered in modern slums—many of them hardly better than ghettos—in not many more than a score of artificial settlements along the rim of the Canadian North. Here they exist for the most part on welfare payments of one kind or another—no longer taking sustenance from the land and the sea. Effectively they live in unguarded concentration camps, provided with the basic requirements for mere physical survival, but deprived of the freedom to shape and control their own lives. We have salved our national conscience by ensuring that they do not die anymore of outright starvation, but we have resolutely denied them the right to live according to their own inherent needs—the right to *function* as viable human beings according to their own desires and capabilities.

Genocide can be practiced in a variety of ways.

The Desperate People, of whom I wrote in 1952 and 1959, are desperate still. But *now* they include *all* the native peoples of Canada—Indian, Eskimo and mixed bloods. They are making what may be their last convulsive effort to achieve survival apart from, and despite, a society which will accept them only if they transform themselves into second-class simulacrums of Western man. They are fighting what may well be their ultimate battle to exist in the world according to their own concept of what their lives should be. They are making what is probably their final effort to achieve the freedom to be themselves.

We have long prided ourselves on being a democratic nation, dedicated to the altar of freedom. Freedom for whom? If it is only freedom for ourselves to do as we please at the expense of others, then our pious stance is even more abhorrent than that of any overt tyrant—for ours is based upon a vile hypocrisy.

To have freedom one must give freedom. Let us put our vaunted belief in freedom to the test. Let us give back the freedom that we have taken from the native peoples of this land. If we cannot do this, then not only are they doomed, but we will have doomed ourselves as well.

Because the time is short, and the time is now, and that time will not come again, I am re-issuing this book in the hope that it may help us to understand and to acknowledge the crimes against humanity we have perpetrated here, *in our country*, under the aegis of a free democracy . . . crimes which we are perpetrating still in a more subtle guise.

F.M.

Port Hope, Ontario
March, 1974

I

The Why and Wherefore

In the spring of 1935, when I was an undersized youth of fifteen, I made my first journey into arctic lands, under the tutelage of a great-uncle who was an amateur but fanatical student of birds. My Uncle Frank's consuming interest in wild things had been perpetuated in me, for from the age of six I too had been passionately interested in all the animals that haunted the rolling prairies near my home in Saskatoon. Our house in that western city had for long years been shared with pet skunks, coyotes, crows, gophers and rattlesnakes of uncertain disposition. Even my human friends were chosen almost exclusively from the half-wild and suitably ragged children at the Dundurn Indian Reserve, for I shared with those sons of nomads a strange devotion to the illusory freedom of the broad prairie plains. That restless longing to find affinity with primordial things was a legacy from my father, but it took shape and gained direction under the influence of Great-uncle Frank. He, at my mother's request, undertook to take me with him on one of his yearly pilgrimages to the ancient tundras of the arctic, where we were to spend a summer among the curious Northern birds whose very names were mystery in my ears, and whose ways of life were old before ours were begun.

1

In the first week of May 1935, the meadowlarks brought spring to Saskatoon—and Uncle Frank was close behind. Tall, gaunt and weather-worn, he was still filled with the indestructible energy which had carried him through arduous years of struggle with the tough sod of an Alberta wheat farm. He had acquitted himself well in that long battle against hail and blight, and now in his late sixties he was able to indulge his lifelong hobby, and so each new spring saw him voyaging to some distant place to watch birds whose lives he longed to know and understand.

To my young eyes, Uncle Frank was a somewhat dusty Olympian and beside him I felt as insignificant as a blade of twitch grass. Yet when he looked down upon me from his great, spare height, he seemed to be vaguely satisfied with what he saw and so, on the day following his arrival at Saskatoon, we two set off together for Winnipeg, the central gateway to the arctic lands. It was the beginning of an Odyssey.

From Winnipeg the railroad sweeps westward in a wild curve over the flat, rich wheatlands which are the bed of ancient Lake Agassiz, a mighty lake that died with the last glacier. Then the steel bends northward and the train passes through the flat farmlands, and little villages go by—each marked by the bulge of an orthodox steeple and the square monument of a grain elevator. Slowly the forests extend their rough fingers into the black soil of the farms, until the fingers close tightly. The prairies are gone, and only the matted disorder of forests remains.

The train runs more cautiously now, for it is entering a land that is hostile to strangers. It makes its way northward through the low forests which are the home of the Cree Indians, and at last it draws up with gusty relief at the frontier town of The Pas. Here, in a decaying cluster of buildings, the Winnipeg train turns gratefully back to the south and hurries to leave behind it the anonymous tangle of forests and muskegs.

But The Pas, that seedy settlement which has been left behind to wither and rot as the frontier has pushed north, is not yet the end of the steel. Instead, it is the southern terminus for a cockeyed political shenanigan that is proudly known in Canada's capital as "the Hudson Bay Railway" but is better known in the land where it lives as "the Muskeg Express." A rebellious and contrary railway that may have an equal in the wilds of Siberia, the Muskeg Express has no relatives on this continent. It stretches northward for five hundred desolate miles to the shore of Hudson Bay. It thinks nothing of running a hundred miles at a time without curves and without bends to relieve the heavy-footed pace it maintains.

For part of the way its roadbed is built on blocks of ancient peat moss, and this moss in turn sits uneasily on the perpetual ice of the muskegs and swamps, whose black depths hold the last dominions of the old, vanished glaciers.

The only passenger accommodation on the train was in the caboose. So Uncle Frank and I lived there for the three days and two nights that the journey consumed. I amused myself by keeping track of the little white-painted signboards which marked off each mile and by counting the number of rail spikes per mile that flew out of the ties and went buzzing off through the air like bullets, as the train passed along. I was grateful to the mile-boards, and to the spikes, for the monotony of that northward journey through the unchanging and somber forests was almost unbroken by anything else.

But at Mile 410 something *did* happen, something that was to lead me into an undreamed-of world in the years which still lay far ahead. Near Mile 400, I had noticed that the maddening succession of stunted and half-drowned spruce trees was beginning to be pierced by long, finger-like openings running down from the northwest. When I pointed them out to my Uncle Frank, he explained that these were the slim tentacles which were being thrust southward by those great arctic plains we call the Barrens, and the presence of these fingers of the plains marked the passing of the dominion of forests.

I climbed up to the high bench of the caboose cupola to have a better look at the new lands which were appearing, and I was there when the marker for Mile 410 came into view, and simultaneously the rusty whistle of the old engine began to give tongue. It was to continue sounding for a full half-hour, with a reckless disregard for steam pressure. But at the first blast I looked forward over the humped backs of the freight cars—and noticed the whistle no more!

A brown, flowing river had appeared and was surging out of the edge of the dying forests and plunging across and over the snow-covered roadbed ahead. A broad, turbulent ribbon of brown ran out of an opening to the southeast and traced its sinuous course northwest over the snows of a land that was still completely gripped by the frosts—for this was no river of water, but a river of life. I had my binoculars to my eyes in the instant, and through the lenses I saw the stream dissolve into its myriad parts and each part of that river was long-legged shape of a deer!

"C'est la Foule!" The French-Canadian brakeman stood beside me, and at the sound of his words I understood what it was that I was beholding. "It is the Throng!" Those were the words that the first of the early French explorers wrote in his journal when he beheld what is perhaps the most tremendous living spectacle that our continent knows—the almost incredible mass migration of the numberless herds of caribou—the reindeer of the Canadian North.

The train whistle continued to blow with increasing fury and exasperation but the rolling hordes of the caribou did not deviate from their own right of way, which took precedence over man's. They did not hurry their steady lope and, as we drew up to them, the engine gave up its futile efforts to intimidate the Throng, and with a resigned whiffle of steam we came to a halt. It was a long halt. For the next hour we stayed there, and for an hour the half-mile-wide river of caribou flowed unhurriedly north in a phenomenal procession, so overwhelming in its magnitude that I could hardly credit my senses. Then, abruptly, the river thinned out and in a few moments was gone, leaving behind it a broad highway beaten into the snow. The old train gathered its waning strength; the passengers who had alighted to brew up some tea climbed aboard, and we too continued into the north.

The stunted trees closed in again and the white mileboards flickered past as if the sight of the Throng had been only an illusion in time and in space. But it was no illusion, for every detail of that sight remains with me now, with a clarity that does not belong to illusions. It was a sight that a boy—or a man—does not forget. And the sight I beheld at Mile 410 was, many years later, to draw me inexorably back to the land of *la Foule*.

In its own good time, the Muskeg Express brought us out of the forests and within sight of the ice-filled waters of Hudson Bay, and to the end of a journey. I spent that summer at Churchill in a fly-haunted search for birds' eggs, under the untiring direction of my uncle. The spectacle of *la Foule* faded to the back of my mind, for on the sodden muskegs there were too many strange birds calling—the Hudsonian curlews with their haunting whistles; the godwits, and the snow buntings and longspurs. There was too much for me to see, there on the south verges of the arctic, and too much to hear.

With the last summer days of 1935 I again climbed back aboard the Muskeg Special and left the tantalizing borders of the Barrens behind me for a decade. I returned home with a large box of birds' eggs, a tin can containing six live lemming-mice, and a crate holding a queer bird called a jaeger (a hunter), which looks like a gull and acts like a hawk.

In addition to these things I brought back many memories, both varied and vivid. Yet, as time passed, it was the memory of the great herd of caribou at Mile 410 that emerged as the strongest of all. And that particular memory was kept alive, and grew more powerful as I grew older because of an intangible longing that the arctic had implanted so deeply in my heart that its fever could not be chilled even by the passing years.

It is, I suppose, a sort of disease—an arctic fever—and yet no microscope can discover its virus and it remains completely unknown to the savants of science. The arctic fever has no effect on the body but lives only in the mind, filling its victim with a consuming urge to wander again, and forever, through those mighty spaces where the caribou herds flow like living rivers over the roll of the tundra. It is a disease of the imagination, and yet it attacks men whom you would not normally accuse of being imaginative. It is this unknown disease that drives taciturn white men back to their crude log shanties year after year, back to the desperate life of the interminable winter night, and back to the wind and the search through the gray snow for the white fox and ermine. The disease is one of great power indeed, for it does not leave such victims as these until life itself leaves them.

The infection lay dormant in me for many years. From 1935 until 1939 my life held so many things that the call of the bleak lands to the north was never strong enough to take command of my will. During those years I went on with my schooling, spending my holidays on the prairies, in the mountains to the west, and in the forests to the east—but never completely forgetting the stark plains to the north. In those years I was particularly engrossed in the study of birds and mammals, for I had decided that I would become a zoologist and spend my life at that study.

But then, when I was nineteen years old, I had to exchange my old shotgun for a Lee-Enfield rifle, for I became a soldier in the Hastings and Prince Edward Regiment. I exchanged the prairies and mountains for the close confines of an infantry regiment, and the world that now lay outside those narrow bounds suddenly became a mad, nightmare creation which I feared and could not understand. 1941 came, and I was part of the phony war in southern England and on my brief leaves I watched without comprehension as the walls of great cities crumbled over the dismembered bodies of men. I began to know a sick and corroding fear that grew from an unreasoned revolt against mankind—the one living thing that could deliberately bring down a world in senseless slaughter. The war drove inexorably on. My regiment moved through Italy, then up through France into Belgium and Holland, and at long last into the Reich. And one day there were no more crashes of shellfire in the air—and it was done.

In the spring of 1946 I returned to my own land—but it was a far cry from my return to my home in 1935. I wished to escape into the quiet sanctuaries where the echoes of war had never been heard. And to this end, I at once arranged to become what is called a "scientific collector" who would go into far places and bring back rare specimens for science to stare at. Desperately seeking for some stable thing rooted deep in reality, I grasped the opportunity to labor in what I thought was the austere pursuit of knowledge for its own sake.

So it was that at the end of 1946 I found myself far up in the forests of northern Saskatchewan at a place called Lac La Ronge. Nominally I was there to collect birds for a museum, but I had put my gun away, for I soon had enough of "scientific" destruction, even as I had had enough of killing in wartime. The search for tranquillity which had led me hopefully into science had failed, for now I could see only a brutal futility in the senseless amassing of little bird mummies which were to be preserved from the ravages of life in dark rows of steel cabinets behind stone walls. So I was simply living, without any particular aim, in a remote settlement of Cree Indian half-breeds; and there, among a people who had been brutalized and who had been degraded and led to decay by all that is evil in civilized life—there I found a man who unwittingly gave me a direction and a new goal.

From old Henry Moberly, a half-breed who had spent most of his years on the borders of the northernmost forests, I once again heard of the caribou that I had seen so many years before. Henry told me living tales of the "deer"—as the caribou are universally called in the land—so that I remembered *la Foule* with startling clarity; and it was then that the quiescent disease of the arctic sprang to new life within me, and began to possess me completely.

With the picture of the deer held firmly in my mind as a spiritual talisman, I returned to the cities for the winter, and my heart was closer to knowing peace than it had been in six years. I went back to the university and took a zoological course which would fit me to become a student of the deer, for in those days the habits and life of the caribou were a great mystery waiting to be solved and I had decided that the pursuit of this mystery was to be my endeavor. Perhaps not completely an honest endeavor, for even then I was dimly aware that the deer were to serve primarily as my excuse for a return to the North, which was calling to me. Nevertheless I worked hard during the winter, and in my spare time I read every book about the arctic that I could lay hands on, until I began to have some conception of what lies behind that unrevealing word.

As I read I came to understand that the arctic is not only a world of frozen rivers and ice-bound lakes but also of living rivers and of lakes whose very blue depths are flanked by summer flowers and by sweeping green meadows. The arctic not only knows the absolute cold of the pole but it also knows days of overpowering heat when a naked man sweats with the simple exertion of walking. And most important of all, I came to understand that the arctic is not only the ice-covered cap of the world but is also nearly two million square miles of rolling plains that, during the heat of midsummer, are thronged with life and brilliant with the colors of countless plants in full bloom. It was these immense plains which drew my special attention, and when I found them on a map of the continent, I saw that they formed a great triangle, with its narrow apex pointing west to the shore of the Arctic Ocean, not far from the mouth of the Mackenzie River and the Alaskan border. The triangle's base lies along the west shore of Hudson Bay, and its two arms extend westward, one along timber line and the other along the coast of the Arctic Sea. And the name of this vast, treeless land is the Barrenlands.

I saw it in my mind's eye as a mighty land and a strange one. As geological time is reckoned, it emerged only yesterday from under the weight of the glaciers, and today it remains almost as it was when the ponderous mountains of ice finished grinding their way over its face. It is a land of undulating plains that have no horizon, of low hills planed to a shapeless uniformity by the great power of the ice. It is a land of gravel, of sand, and of shattered gray rocks, but without soil as we know it. It is also a land that seems to be struggling to emerge from a fresh-water ocean, for it is almost half water, holding countless numbers of lakes and their rivers. And this was the land where I would have to seek out the caribou, for it is their land.

Toward the end of the winter I met an old army friend, who, in peacetime, was a mining engineer, and I told him something of my interest in the arctic. He was a little amused at the idea of anyone's heading out into those lands where he might be reaping the value of five years' war exile from the rich postwar fabric of the boom. But he did me a favor, a much greater one than he knew. He gave me a stack of old government mining reports his father had owned, and he said that he thought some of them might deal with the North I wanted to know. He was right, for in that musty old pile of books I found my lodestone to the land of the deer.

I looked through the pile of pamphlets and books which he had given me. One of the dingiest of the lot bore the prosaic title, *Report on the Dubawnt, Kazan, and Ferguson Rivers and the North West Coast of Hudson Bay*. It had been published in 1896 and on the surface it appeared to be a dry-as-dust compilation of outdated facts, written by some dull-eyed servant of government. But appearances were deceptive. I recognized the author's name—Joseph Burr Tyrrell —and I remembered that in some obscure paper I had read an old account of Tyrrell's fantastic explorations through the central Barrenlands of Keewatin. For Tyrrell had been the first—and the last—man ever to traverse the full breadth of the Barrens from south to north.

I opened his report eagerly. It was not quite like the usual run of official documents, for though Tyrrell had been devoted to his gods, mineralogy and geography, he had written about them with an undertone of enthusiasm and excitement which did not seem to belong between those staid covers and government seals. There was an ephemeral quality about his writings that made even his endless comments on the minerals he had examined seem interesting and fresh. And yet, in the Dubawnt Report there was only room for brief hints about the true nature of the land and about the trials and troubles which had beset Tyrrell.

Here and there I did come across scattered references to the deer and, in one place, Tyrrell spoke succinctly of seeing what may have been the greatest single herd ever to be seen by a white man—a herd so vast that for many miles the surface of the land was obscured beneath the blanket of living beasts! The mental image of this magnificent spectacle strengthened my desire to go to the Barrens, but I found one other thing hidden in Tyrrell's report that finally confirmed my resolve.

For Tyrrell spoke also of a "People of the Deer." Out in those endless spaces, along the river he called Kazan, Tyrrell found a race of men where it was thought that no men could live. And interwoven between his lists of rocks were fragmentary and tantalizing references to those men, who had remained completely cut off from the world's knowledge until the day of Tyrrell's coming. In the Dubawnt Report, a shadow of this forgotten race emerged for the first time before our eyes. And it was clear enough that they were a people who, in Tyrrell's day, had been living the same lives they had led before the Viking longboats first discovered the eastern shores of North America. Tyrrell could spare them only a few terse and niggardly paragraphs, yet he said enough to make the Barrens People seem as fascinating as dwellers in another world. Obviously they were men whose total strength had been devoted to a bitter struggle against the implacable natural forces of the Barrens, and the idea came to me that they might never have found the will or the desire to turn their strength against one another. If this was indeed true, then it was certain they were a people I wanted to know.

But half a century had intervened since Tyrrell discovered this inland race of Eskimos, and it seemed inevitable that during that time great changes must have come to the land and to its inhabitants. I renewed my search of the literature of the arctic in an effort to discover how much was known of the People, and of the land, which Tyrrell had seen, and to my secret satisfaction I found no further word about Tyrrell's people, though there were sufficient rumors and secondhand reports to convince me that those men of the deer still lived in their hidden world. I sent to Ottawa for the most recent maps of the central plains. When they arrived, I spread them out on the floor and studied them with mounting excitement—for they showed little more than the tenuous dotted outlines of those features which Tyrrell had drawn half a century before. For the most part the maps were unsullied white, defaced only by small printed legends, reading "Unmapped."

To the north of this clouded region, the coast of the continent was accurately shown, and it was studded with the settlements of Eskimos who had been in contact with our race for better than a hundred years. To the east, along the shoreline of Hudson Bay, the picture was the same. To the south lay the forests and the old river routes of the *Voyageurs* who had explored the timberlands centuries earlier. And to the distant west lay the rich and busy valley of the Mackenzie. But in the middle of all these lay only emptiness, not only on the maps but in the books as well.

There was a reason for this. When the first white men looked across the borders of this land, they named it "the Barrens" and shuddered at its terrible rawness. And so they turned from it, never knowing that it held rivers of life in its depths.

The existence of this barrier built upon an indefinable fear was made known to me when I sought definite information about ways and means to enter the land. I went to the books, but again they were not much of a help. I found that several men had indeed traveled in the boundary regions of the Barrens, and a few had even penetrated deeply into the narrow western neck of the plains, where they are squeezed between timber line and the seacoast. Yet all who had attempted to write of what they found had evidently been seized by an inarticulate paralysis when they tried to put their deepest impressions into their writings. They seemed to grope futilely for words with which they could express the emotions the Barrens had instilled in their hearts. And they were all baffled by that effort to speak clearly. Most of them gave up the attempt and sought refuge in minute descriptions of the component parts, which only if they are taken in their entirety can give the true measure of the great arctic plains.

It seemed to me to be a great mystery, this impenetrable obscurity that could not even be shattered by men who gave all their senses and their perceptions to the task.

But on a day in the spring of 1947, when I had almost completed my own plans to set out for the North, I received the first real clue to the nature of that mystery.

It was contained in a letter from a former Royal Canadian Mounted Police constable whom I had known during the war. I had written, asking if he had any personal experience with the arctic plains, and his answer told me of a time when he had gone into the western Barrens in pursuit of a suspected murderer. The fugitive escaped—from the police at least—and my friend turned back just in time to save his own life, for he was starved and half-frozen before he reached the shelter of a coastal trading post. Writing to me, he summed up all the Barrens had meant to him in these few, straightforward words:

I guess it was the emptiness that bothered me most. That damn and bloody space—it just goes on and on until it makes you want to cry, or scream —or cut your own damn throat!

Emptiness and the terrible space! These were the things which had haunted the imaginations of the few white men who had known the Barrens. And yet, somewhere in the hidden depths of that space there lived—if they still lived— not only the great herds of the deer, but also men ... the People of the Deer.

II

Into the Barrenlands

On a morning in May of 1947 I boarded the train and gave myself up to the demands of the fever that was in me. My preparations for the journey were simple in the extreme. A visit to a War Assets store had provided me with an assortment of old army clothing and a cheap sleeping bag. I already owned a camera of the snapshot variety and this, together with my binoculars and a dozen rolls of film, completed my scientific equipment. For weapons I took only the American carbine I had carried all through the war.

My actual plans were almost as shadowy as my equipment, for though I knew to within a few thousand square miles where I wanted to go, I still had only the vaguest ideas of how to get there. The canoe routes from the south that Tyrrell had used were closed to me because I intended to travel alone. The eastern and northern borders were impossible too, because the Barrens rivers flowing down to the sea will not permit men to ascend their violent waters to their sources, high on the inland plateau. And sheer distance ruled out any attempt on my part to enter the land from the west.

But with spring already sweeping into the southlands I had no time to ponder. So on a May morning I bought a ticket to Churchill, a familiar name and the only place in the arctic I knew. Churchill lay on the edge of the Barrens and so I hoped that when I reached the end of steel I would stumble on some means for completing my journey into the interior.

Again I passed through Winnipeg and The Pas and again I saw the white mile-boards standing sentinel over the narrow cut that traverses the forests to the north. Then the Muskeg

Special brought mile-board 512 into view and we swung into Churchill under a gray ice mist that came rolling over the still-frozen settlement. For a time I stood shivering in the chill wind while I examined this place that had been the shining memory of boyhood. But that memory dissolved quickly before the harsh impact of reality.

The port of Churchill was a miserable conglomeration of cowering shacks half-buried under great drifts. The stained snowbanks pushed tightly up against the slab-sided and scrofulous shanties. The freezing mist from Hudson Bay did its best to soften the ugliness and to hide the monolithic bulk of the huge concrete grain elevator that gives Churchill its sole reason for existence. For Churchill is nominally an ocean port, despite the fact that it is only for a few brief weeks each year that hardy freighters can dare the passage of Hudson Straits to enter the Bay and take on cargo. In May of 1947 that "ocean port" was the ultimate desolation of man's contriving.

Shouldering my kit bag, I trudged up the frozen ruts of Churchill's only road and found my way to the beer parlor. In a few minutes I was sitting comfortably close to the stove while a morose bartender brought me a bottle of sad ale—sans glass. As I drank the thin brew I looked out the dirty window at a clay-cold array of rusted boilers, abandoned donkey engines, and dead construction machinery. And I wondered just how the devil I was going to find my way out of this scrap heap of ruined ambitions and into the Barrens. I had several more beers but they seemed to grow weaker, if possible, and my spirits ebbed steadily.

Then the door swung open with a gusty crash and a massive Scandinavian rolled into the room. His eyes lit up with a quick gleam of recognition as he saw me and in an instant the gloom of Churchill was dispelled.

"So you come back!" he boomed. "*Ja!* I thought maybe you would!"

This was John Ingerbritson, and I had last seen him when, as a boy of fourteen, I had gone to look at his ship in the harbor at Churchill. Many years earlier, when he had been living at The Pas, the call of John's Norwegian blood became too strong to deny and so he built a sea-going vessel there in his backyard, five hundred miles from the sea. When all forty feet of the *Otto Sverdrup* was completed, she was loaded on a flatcar and taken north to salt water. Her full tale is a Norse saga that began when John announced that he intended to fish the treacherous bay waters. The scientists told him bluntly that there were no food fish to be had in Hudson Bay, but John set his nets anyway, and each week he shipped a fine cargo to the markets in distant Winnipeg. For John was a fisherman, though not much of a hand at science.

After hoisting a few for old times' sake, John took me to his home where Mrs. Ingerbritson welcomed me into her brilliantly clean little house and filled me with good food.

Then, over coffee, and surrounded by the ebullient offspring of John and his wife, I explained why I had come back to Churchill and where I wanted to go. When I finished, John suggested that I should charter a plane, but I was doubtful about the idea. For one thing, the cost of flying in the arctic can be prohibitive. For another thing, a pilot needs a clear-cut objective, and I had none in mind.

While we were talking, a lanky, dark-eyed young man had come quietly into the room and he was introduced as Johnny Bourasso, former Royal Air Force Pathfinder pilot, at present the captain and crew of an ancient twin-engined Anson aircraft that made a precarious living for her owner by flying improbable tramp-freighting runs over the top of the world. Bourasso was at once dragged into the discussion, and the three of us got out the maps.

There was much talk and telling of tales. Without attempting to discourage me, old John was evidently determined that I should be made fully aware of what I was proposing to do, and so he told us the yarn of the Englishman, John Hornby, who set out to winter in the Barrens in the late 1920's.

Hornby took with him two young Englishmen, fresh from the old country. The three men set out from Great Slave Lake, and then silence dropped down on their track. For a year no word was heard of their fate—and when it did come, it was a grim word.

A party of prospectors canoeing down the Thelon River the next summer found Hornby's shanty in a tiny wooded oasis hundreds of miles north of the timber line. The bodies of the three men who had challenged the Barrens were there. Their story was preserved in the diary of eighteen-year-old Edgar Christian, and it was as simple as it was tragic. The three had missed the great autumn migration of the deer, for the deer do not always follow the same path each year. Having missed the deer the intruders began the long winter without the supplies of meat that alone can ensure man's survival in the white plains. Winter came quickly and there could be no retreat, for the party had no dogs, and men do not walk out of the winter Barrens on foot. So it was only a matter of time—but of a very long time, eking out the thin thread of their lives and always aware that it was a hopeless struggle that they were making. In the end they died, very slowly, and under conditions of great horror.

There was a subdued silence when John finished this story. I was thinking about Hornby and trying to quell the doubts which were rising within me when old John began to mutter, under his breath.

"Dimints!" he said. "Dimints *and* gold cufflinks too!"

We asked him what he was talking about and he told us the rumor that when the bodies were found, the searchers also uncovered most of the essentials required for dinner at the Ritz. Dinner dress in a wolf den out on the Barrens! It was too macabre a thought to have any bearing on the reality which lay before me. Resolutely I put Hornby out of my mind, and went back to the maps.

A thought struck me, and I asked John what he knew about the mysterious Eskimos that Tyrrell had seen. Surprisingly, John knew quite a lot, though it was all hearsay, of course. He told me that in the boom days of the '20's a trading post had actually been established on the southern borders of the Keewatin Barrens, not far from the headwaters of the Kazan where Tyrrell had first met the inland dwellers. While fur prices were soaring this isolated outpost did well, despite the fact that seven hundred miles of canoe route separated it from the nearest point of supply at The Pas.

Then the fur market collapsed and the post no longer paid a big enough profit. So it was closed, and the brief contact with the inland Eskimos would have been lost again had it not been for a German immigrant, married to a Cree woman, who doggedly persisted in the attempt to keep an independent trading post going. Off and on, over the years, this man did keep contact with the Barrens Eskimos and, though he was no longer in the land himself, it was rumored that he had left a son on the edge of the Barrens, who was believed to make his living by trapping white fox and by occasional trading deals with the natives.

John pointed out the site of the abandoned trading post on the map, at a place called Windy River—a river that flows into a vast body of water named Nueltin Lake.

Nueltin itself was almost a legendary place, still unsurveyed and largely unknown in 1947. Yet from the rough dotted outline assigned to it on the map, it was obviously a truly great lake, at least one hundred and twenty miles long, with a third of its length inside the forests while the other two-thirds stretched northward into the open plains of the Barrens.

After hearing about the existence of the Windy River post I decided Nueltin should be my immediate goal. If I was lucky I might find that young half-Indian, half-German youth who was believed to be still living there. And with his aid, I might hope to realize my dreams; whereas alone I might only add another unpleasant paragraph to the grim tales that are told of the men who have challenged the Barrens and failed.

Nueltin, then, was the logical choice, but there remained the slight problem of how to cross the intervening 350 miles of frozen plains to reach it. I looked wistfully at Johnny Bourasso and wondered how much he would charge for such a flight. There didn't seem to be much point in asking, for he had just canceled a trip to Chesterfield Inlet on the advice of the weather men, who had warned of the imminent approach of the spring thaws. When the spring thaws come to the North, all flying ceases for at least a month and there are no exceptions. But I had nothing to lose by asking.

"Johnny," I asked, "would you take a chance on a trip to Nueltin tomorrow?"

He lifted his eyes from the map and took a long moment to think; then—"We'll give it a try," he said. He would charge me only $200 for the trip, which was phenomenally cheap for Barrens flying.

When it was full morning the next day we slogged through the already softening drifts to Landing Lake, where the Anson stood waiting. What had been a light-weight outfit designed for easy travel, when I left the South, had grown monstrously during my brief stay at Churchill. The Canadian Army authorities there, worried about my survival and about the possibility of having to come to my eventual rescue, had loaded me down with such items as a hundred-pound crate of smoke generators (presumably to use in communicating with distant Eskimos since few aircraft fly over the central Barrens), army winter clothing of unbelievable awkwardness and bulk, and a case of complicated meteorological instruments with which (it was hoped) I would make careful surveys of weather conditions at Nueltin Lake. Politeness forced me to accept all these things, though I had no use for them and was already grossly overequipped as a result of my purchases in the Hudson's Bay Company store at Churchill.

These purchases had been extensive since there was a definite possibility that I would never locate the young trapper at Nueltin and would have to subsist entirely on my own rations. Johnny had aided in saddling me with an unnecessary amount of freight by remarking that he might very well fail to pick me up before freeze-up in which case I would have to live on my fat until late December when ice conditions were again suitable for ski landings.

In consequence I had bought a quarter of a ton of assorted foods, the bulk of which consisted of flour, lard, sugar, tea, baking powder, bacon and salt pork. In addition there was a fair leavening of dehydrated fruits and vegetables plus—and how the old arctic hands stared when they heard about it!—a case of fruit juices.

My outfit was further increased by five hundred pounds of freight which had been consigned to the young fellow at Nueltin the previous fall and which had been moldering in a warehouse awaiting the day when some means of transportation might turn up. With the usual haphazard methods employed in arctic transport, this was all turned over to me on the chance I could deliver it.

The final item that I added to my load was easily the most important. It consisted of three gallons of grain alcohol labeled "for scientific purposes only" in order to conform to the law.

All of this gear was stacked aboard the Anson and after a startled look at the looming bulk of the load, Johnny turned quickly away and started up the engines. As the overburdened plane lumbered down the lake the homemade skis flung driving slush outward and upward, enveloping us in chill spray. Then we were airborne and we swung back over the forlorn desolation of Churchill so that the Ingerbritsons could wave a farewell. The Anson turned northward up the icebound coast. I looked out to sea, over the pack ice, and when I again turned to look inland the thinning trees had vanished and the aircraft was swinging westward, away from the sea, and into the Barrens.

The Anson grumbled forward on her quest. Johnny held a map before him on his knees, and over its expanse of vagueness he had drawn a straight compass course to where Windy River should be. But above his head the compass flickered and gyrated foolishly, for in such close proximity to the magnetic pole a compass is, at best, but a doubtful tool. Yet there were no other aids to navigation, for when we left the coast we also left the sun behind us—obscured by a thick overcast of snow-laden clouds. And as for finding our way by the land underneath us . . .

It was a soft white nightmare that we were flying over. An undulating monotony of white that covered all shapes and all colors. The land, with its low sweeping hills, its lakes and its rivers, simply did not exist for our eyes. The anonymity was quite unbroken even by living things, for the few beasts that winter here are also white, and so they are no more than shadows on the snow.

For a hundred miles there was no change and the monotony began to dull my senses. Johnny passed his map back to me and along the course line he had drawn a cross and added a penciled notation. "Halfway. Should be there shortly after noon."

I turned back to the window and tried to fix my gaze on something definite in the blankness that lay below. Then I glanced ahead and saw, with profound gratitude, the faint smear of a horizon. Slowly it took on strength, grew ragged, and at last emerged as a far-distant line of hills. It was the edge of the great plateau which cradles Nueltin, and the Kazan.

Now the white mantle below us began to grow threadbare. Black spines of massive ridges began to thrust upward through the snow. The undulations of the land grew steeper, as swells begin to lift before a rising storm at sea.

Again the map. This time the cross lay over Nueltin, but when I looked down I could see nothing recognizable to tie us to the map. I edged forward to the cockpit. Johnny's face was strained and anxious. In a few minutes he pointed to the flickering needles of the gasoline gauges which showed that half our gas was gone, and then I felt the aircraft begin to bank! I watched the compass card dance erratically until our course was south, then east—and back toward the sea.

The limit of our search had been reached, and we had found nothing in that faceless wilderness to show us either where we were, or where our target lay. We had overleaped the boundaries of the Barrens—and yet the land had not been caught unaware. It still seemed secure against our invasion.

The overcast had been steadily lowering and as we

turned eastward we were flying at less than 500 feet. At this slim height we suddenly saw the land gape wide beneath us to expose a great valley walled in by rocky cliffs and snow-free hills. And in that instant I caught a fleeting glimpse of something. . . . "Johnny!" I yelled. "Cabin . . . down there!"

He wasted no precious gas on a preliminary circuit. The sound of the engines dulled abruptly and we sank heavily between the valley walls. Before us stood a twisted, stunted little stand of spruce; a river mouth, still frozen; and the top foot or so of what was certainly a shanty roof, protruding slyly from the drifts.

We jumped stiffly down to the ice and shook hands, for there was no doubt about this being my destination. There was no other standing cabin within two hundred miles.

But only the wind met us. There was no sign of life about the cabin. We slipped and stumbled helplessly on the glare ice, and our exhilaration at having found our target against heavy odds was rapidly being diminished by an awareness of the ultimate desolation of this place. Our eyes clung hopefully to the handful of scrawny trees, none of them more than ten feet high, that thrust their tops out of the snow to give a ragged welcome. The leaden skies were closing in and the wind was still rising. There was no time to explore, only time to dump my gear onto the ice. Johnny stood for a long moment in the doorway of the plane, as if he was debating with himself whether to ask me if I had changed my mind. I'm glad that he didn't. I think I should have been tempted beyond my strength. But he only waved his hand and vanished into the fuselage. Then the Anson was bumping wickedly down the bay.

The plane vanished with appalling rapidity into the overcast. The gale from the Ghost Hills whipped little eddies of hard snow about me and I had arrived in the land that I had set my heart upon.

But now was no time to soliloquize! I needed shelter, and so I made for the half-hidden cabin. The doorway was snowed-in to a depth of several feet, and when I had dug my way through, I found only a log cavern in the drifts—dank and murky and foul-smelling. The damp was the stinking damp of long disuse, and I could trace the smell easily enough to the floor that was buried under the dirt of years and the accumulated refuse of a winter's meals.

Against one wall was a massive stove. But it did nothing

to cheer me up, for as far as I could see there was no fuel for its great maw. The wind outside, and the chill damp inside, made the thought of a fire like the dream of a lovely woman—irresistible, and quite unattainable.

The walls of the cabin were finished in fur. Wolf and arctic fox pelts, all as white as the snows of early winter, were spread over the log walls to dry, and by their simple presence showed that the place was not completely deserted after all. During the next week I came to regard them with affection, for they were the link with the unknown man who had brought them in and who, I sincerely hoped, would come himself before too long.

There was quite enough to do during the days of waiting. All my gear had to be hauled in from the ice of Windy Bay, and for the balance of the daylight hours I amused myself by wading hip-deep, and sometimes shoulder-deep, through the jealous drifts that guarded the puny treelets near the camp. Three hours' hard work would yield only enough green spruce and tamarack twigs to let me build one little cooking fire, but in the process of gathering fuel I grew as warm as if I had been able to luxuriate before a roaring blaze. So there were compensations in the fuel problem after all.

The storm that had heralded my arrival lasted for three full days, but on the fourth day the weather changed abruptly and the arctic spring exploded in a violent eruption. On June the first, the sun shone down upon me with a passion that it hardly knows even in the tropics. And it kept on shining for eighteen hours out of every twenty-four.

I climbed a ridge beside the cabin on the second day of spring and I was awed by what I saw. Thin sheets of water were sliding out from under all the mighty drifts along the shore, and there were already telltale mumblings from under the river ice. Above the ice a good-sized stream was bawling down upon the bay and spreading a lake above a lake, that was soon too deep to wade across.

In half a day the snow that lapped my observation ridge retreated a dozen feet, leaving the exposed gravel and dead moss to steam away like an overanxious kettle. It was a queer thing to see, and I felt as if I were sitting on the summit of a frozen world that inexplicably, and with an unbelievable swiftness, had decided to collapse and melt away.

Every hollow and low-lying spot harbored a freshet that

quickened and murmured without pause for rest, even during the brief twilight period that passed for night. The ice began to rot. The shining surfaces turned leaden, dulled and fractured into countless millions of tiny, separate rods that were held upright and together only by their mutual pressure on one another. It was no longer possible to crawl about the drifts in search of wood, for the wet snow refused my weight. After twice plunging over my head into the snow I gave up the search for fear of suffocating in that wet and cold embrace.

And the birds arrived. One morning I was wakened from an uneasy sleep by the mad laughter of many voices chuckling in zany mirth. I flung open the door and found myself staring into the brilliance, and meeting the eyes of half a hundred disembodied heads. The heads were chickenlike, but stained dull red as if by the lifeblood of the bodies they had been parted from.

With something approaching horror I stared at the weird visitors and they stared back from maniac little eyes, and laughed until the whole valley rang with sound. I flung a piece of ice at one, and the whole flock suddenly took flight. As they cleared the ground, their trim white bodies that had been invisible against the snow were projected into view, and I knew them then for ptarmigan, the partridge of the arctic.

And so my first week drew to its conclusion, and the nature of the land had changed so violently that I could not comprehend the magnitude of that change. I was overwhelmed by the rapidity with which it had come about, and since I had only just begun to get acquainted with the frozen land, I was too confused to make much sense out of the fluid wastes that I now found myself marooned upon.

Yet there was a familiar quality in the warm, humid air that is the quality of plowed fields in the spring, though magnified a thousandfold. The sterile, unbreathing land of winter breathed deeply now, and its breath was that of a strong woman in the grip of passion.

A restlessness and a great unease kept me from sleep even during the brief interval of dusk—the last remnant of the long winter dark. Loneliness was driven from me. I, like all things in the land, waited—for what we did not know. The awakening perhaps of that impalpable entity which is the Barrens.

On June 4, I climbed a long, rocky slope behind the cabin for a glimpse of the lands that lay beyond the camp. I was sitting in the lee of a great boulder, avoiding the hot glare of the sun, when I heard the cries of dogs from far up the half-frozen river. At once I was confused by an anticipatory excitement combined with a strange hesitancy to disclose myself until I had seen the approaching stranger first. I started down the hill at the double, but checked my rush and retreated nervously to the shelter of my boulder. I was still there when the dogs came into view—nine immense beasts hauling a sled that dwarfed them, for it was over twenty feet in length. Two massive runners with sparse crossbars supported a pile of deerskins, and on the skins was the figure of a man.

The team drove along the river's edge to avoid the thaw stream on the surface and the sodden drifts on shore. When it was opposite me and I could see that the driver was no Eskimo, the dogs swung inshore and halted in the cabin yard. Nevertheless I still clung to the shelter of my rock, for now that the moment had arrived, I felt very dubious about the nature of my reception at the hands of this isolated man who saw no strangers from one year's end until the next. So, weakly, I postponed the moment, and watched as the man got slowly from his sled and stood beside it, staring intently at the cabin door.

If his arrival had been a shock to me, it was at least an anticipated one. To him, the shock of arriving home and seeing that someone had been living in his camp must have been tremendous. He stood quite still for several minutes. Then he leaned over the sled and withdrew his rifle from its case. Rifle in hand he walked forward to where my ax was lying, and picked it up, staring at it as if it had been some celestial object fallen from the skies. Long afterwards he told me how it had been impossible for him to resolve the turmoil in his mind when he arrived home and found this mute evidence of a strange visitor.

You see, he had lived all his life in a land where strangers do not arrive as if by magic from another sphere. He had looked for tracks of dog teams and had seen none, yet he knew of no other way that a man could come to Windy River in wintertime. There are no strangers in that land— unless you count the unseen ones who dwell amongst the rocky hills and are not of human kind.

With his rifle in hand and fear in his heart, he opened the cabin door and stepped inside. The litter of my belongings and the strange supplies must have baffled him completely, but he stayed inside, and I chose that time to descend from my hill.

III

The Intruders

The dogs saw me at once and before I had reached the sled their hysterical outcry brought the man to the door with rifle crooked over his arm and his face blank and expressionless.

It was a tense and uneasy meeting. Franz—that was his name—like all men who live too long alone, had lost the hard shell that human contacts build for us. Such isolated ones become soft and defenseless on the outside, and so they come almost to dread even the casual meetings with their fellows that are routine to us.

That is but part of the resentment that men like Franz feel for the casual stranger. There are other things. I think that only in such tremendous isolation does one feel the fear of his own species that is a throwback to primeval days when any stranger was a potential enemy.

I set about explaining myself and my presence at the cabin as best I could, but the words sounded rather lame.

Franz gave me no help at all, though he showed visible relief when he discovered that I had come by air. After I had said my piece, he stood for a good five minutes staring stolidly at me without uttering a word, and I had ample time to study him.

He was still very young, but with an unkempt air about him that made him seem much older in my sight. He was not tall, but slender with a lithe, wild look. He wore an unidentifiable hodgepodge of native skins and white man's clothes, and on his head he wore a tattered aviator's helmet of the sort that children wear about our city streets. The helmet peak was down and half-obscured his face. Black eyes were in its shadow, and below them a prominent and uncompromisingly Teutonic nose set on the smooth, Asiatic background of an Indian face.

His unblinking scrutiny was rapidly unnerving me, and then I had an inspiration. Remembering what I had always heard about the North, I made a stumbling appeal for hospitality. Blankness faded from his face, he smiled a little and stepped into the cabin, beckoning me to enter.

I felt that I needed a stiff drink, so I burrowed in my kit and produced a bottle. Without asking Franz, I poured a drink for each of us. I suppose it was the first that he had ever had. He gulped it down and as he coughed and wiped tears from his eyes, his frozen taciturnity began to thaw, then melted with the same untrammeled rush that the snows had shown in the first spring sun. He began to talk—stiffly at first and in awkward monosyllables that slowly grew together and became coherent. Eskimo and Cree words were mixed with English, but as his conversation reached full flow, the native words dropped out and his facility with a language that he had little call to use returned to him.

Oddly enough he asked no questions and betrayed no curiosity about me after the initial explanations had been made. Instead he talked of the long trip that he had just completed, and from that point his talk worked backward through the winter, into the years before. Finally, when dawn was with us, he was back as far as childhood's memory would recall. It was an amazing experience that he and I went through that night. I listened as I have never listened to another man, and Franz talked as if his voice had been denied to him since childhood days. His story was the tale of the intruders in the land, and of their struggle to make the land their own. And his tale gave me a chilling insight into the manner in which the Barrenlands had kept themselves inviolate from us.

His father, Karl, whom he worshipped with a restrained simplicity, had come to Canada from Germany, three decades earlier. The immigrant brought with him some of the memories of a cultivated man, but for reasons of his own he shunned the semi-civilized South of Canada and wandered to the North. Here, in due time, he found a wife amongst the mission-trained Cree Indians who live on the south verges of the high Northern forests. Karl's wife was a good woman and she was a good mother to his children, bringing them the best of the Cree blood, which is not inferior to that of any race.

About 1930, the trading company at Nueltin Lake asked Karl to be their manager there. He accepted, and after a three weeks' canoe trip north from Brochet, the family arrived at Windy Bay. But it was a somber arrival, for the log building of a departed rival trader which Karl had hoped to use had been burned to the ground. And so, with autumn already bloodying the dwarf shrubs of the plains, Karl and the seven children had to build a winter home out of the meager trees that could be found.

When the one-room shack was finished and roofed with caribou skins, Karl was ready to do business. He anticipated no opposition in dealing with the Eskimos, for he was the only trader within two hundred miles. And his customers were the men that I had come to see, the People of the Barrens.

It must have been a strange childhood for Franz and for his brothers and sisters. They kept aloof even from the Eskimos. And the tiny outpost was visited only once each summer from "outside" when a canoe brigade arrived from Brochet to bring in the winter stock and carry out the season's fur. For the rest of the long months that stretched into years, only the deer kept Karl and his family company. The tremendous forces of the land beat down on the intruders without interference and drove them in upon each other. But the children, growing into youth in the protracted isolation of the place, slowly adapted to the land.

In the '30's the People of the Barrens were still numerous enough so that nearly forty hunters—all heads of families —could come to trade their fox pelts at the little post. But as the years passed, so passed the hunters. Their names upon the "Debt books" of the post were lined out one by one, and there were few new ones to take their places. The price of pelts on the world's markets fell and so the profits of the post fell off. At last the company decided to withdraw, and in due course that message came to Karl.

The message came and Karl received it gratefully, for during the winter of that year his wife had died, and this man who had never been able to put away his fears of the land was now desperately lonely.

And so it was that when the fall came, the tiny cabin by the shores of Windy Bay stood empty to the wind. When the Eskimo hunters came south with fur, they found the door open and snow piled within the room, but nothing else. The Eskimos returned without the food and shells that they had counted on—and by spring there were many of them who would live to hunt no more.

Yet though Karl had left the land with a vast relief, it was not so with his children. Down in the forests where there are many trading posts and many men, Franz and the other children found a way of life they did not like.

Unlike most mixed-bloods, Franz was, by reason of his long isolation, quite unprepared to meet the barriers of race. The inevitable rebuffs that he was forced to accept from the race-conscious white men of the trading posts, who make a practice of holding aloof from the "savages," as they are wont to call them, turned Franz in upon himself in a way that the Barrens had never done. He had not learned to think of himself as Indian, or as half-breed—but as a white man. He could not fit himself into the miserable borderline existence that is the best the "breeds" can ever hope to know. Instead he remembered the great open plains of the North, the

limitless lands where he was a man at his own evaluation. He remembered, too, the grave by the abandoned cabin, for Franz had loved his mother.

Though Franz was the eldest, and so felt it more deeply than the others, the rest of the children were also becoming aware of the social divisions of mankind, and they too recalled the Barrens with the regret of children who remember happiness.

In the late '30's Karl gave way to the desires of his children and undertook the long journey back to the shores of Windy Bay. But concern for the happiness of his children was not the only incentive. The price of white fox pelts had soared, and Karl was going back as a free trader who could gather the harvest of the Eskimos for a healthy profit, and at the same time make use of the trapping skill of his children. Nor was he disappointed in them, for Franz and his brother Hans became adept at the taking of the fox. Even the two older girls took part in the trapping, and they too came to be expert.

Yet the new life at Nueltin was not the same for Franz. He carried with him the bitter scars of his reception at the southern settlements, and as he ranged out into the plains, constantly expanding his trap line until he at last came into contact with the camps of the Eskimos, Franz was of two minds about them. They treated him as an honored guest and as an equal, and this treatment helped restore his self-esteem and relieve the bitterness. Yet he could not prevent himself from feeling the same superiority toward the Eskimos that the white traders had shown towards him.

I suppose it was this conflict, and the essential need of restoring his hurt ego, which made Franz blind to the slow fate that was relentlessly destroying his new-found friends. He became contemptuous of the apparent improvidence that seemed to bring the Eskimos only starvation. He echoed the sentiments of the white men who had belittled him—and perhaps he was also echoing his father's sentiments—when he called his friends "ignorant natives." He did not care to try to understand the nature of the evils destroying the People of the Barrens. In his own way, he even contributed to those evils, while with the part of him that was restored and revived by the Eskimos' friendship he was extending aid to them in their dire need.

The trading post of course was open once more and so the dozen surviving hunters of the People again gave up the pursuit of game for food, in favor of the pursuit of fur. They brought their furs to Karl and received only a token of their value, for Karl had neither friendship nor sympathy for them. Living in the Barrens again, he was beset by the memory of his wife and by the loneliness that his children did not share. He hated the land, and it was his desire to make enough money to be able to leave it behind forever. Since he was a free trader and had no overseer to watch his policy, he was able to harvest all the colossal profit margin which is considered legitimate throughout the North.

Then, in 1943 an event occurred that decided Karl on leaving the great plains. His eldest daughter, Stella, the one whom he most loved, was lost in the winter barrens for fifteen days.

The girl had been returning from a visit to a distant meat cache and she drove her own team, following the team of her brother Hans. Hans was then sixteen and Stella fifteen.

Some thirty miles from Windy Bay a blizzard enveloped them. Hans tied the lead dog of his sister's team to the back of his own sled and they drove on, trusting to the wind to remain steady so that they would not lose direction.

The blizzard rose to its full fury in one angry blast a few minutes after it had begun. Hans could not see his sister, nor could she see him. The wind was so violent and the ground drift so thick Hans did not notice that the traces of his sister's team had snapped between the lead dog and the next in line. Hans drove forward and a single dog followed him, dragging the broken traces.

Not knowing the trace had snapped, Stella rode on, sitting on her sled and keeping her face covered from the vicious gale. Her dogs were young, and without the leader they lost the trail at once, for it was blown over and obliterated moments after Hans's sled had passed.

Then the wind began to veer southward. Hans felt the change and was able to keep his team on course, but the dogs of Stella's team continued resolutely into the teeth of the veering wind. When Hans arrived at the post at last, he discovered—what he had not known till then—that he was alone.

There was no hope of going back and searching. It was suicidal even to think of going out into the mounting storm. So the family sat about the stove and waited for the wind to drop.

The blizzard lasted only a day, but it was fifteen days before Stella returned to Windy Camp. It is a true measure of how well the children had become part of the land that this girl managed to survive midwinter in the Barrens with almost no food, and with no bedding, for better than two weeks.

She realized that she was lost, and she did the only sensible thing—made camp. With her snow knife she cut a few blocks for a windbreak and burrowed into a drift behind the blocks. When the storm died she emerged and tried to decide where she was. But there are no landmarks in winter, not so much as a weedtop above the snow. The change in wind had gone unnoticed, and so Stella believed that she was a day's travel farther north than she really was. For the four hours of daylight she traveled south by the sun, but an overcast sky followed that first day, and for a week there was no sun. After three days her dogs were so famished that they could not pull, for she had long since abandoned the meat load she had carried on the sled. Now she cut all the traces, letting most of the dogs go in the hope that they would find their ways home alone. Three of the dogs she killed, for she needed their meat. Then she left the sled and walked on, carrying nothing but one thin robe and a pack of dog meat on her back.

She traveled in an immense curve, south and away from safety. She walked until fatigue threatened her with the sleep that ends in freezing death. When that danger came, she stopped and rested cautiously. Sometimes she scrabbled through the drifts on hilltops and found a few wizened bearberries or a handful of rock-tripe, a kind of moss. When she felt strong enough she picked up her robe and walked on to the south, knowing that she had missed the Bay of Nueltin, but knowing also that to stay still was to die. She was lost in an area of nearly fifty thousand square miles, and she might have been almost anywhere in that vast area for all she knew. Yet still she did not quit.

She walked the entire length of Nueltin Lake, more than a hundred miles, and at last she came out on the south bay of that lake. But Stella did not recognize it, did not even know that it was water she was walking over, for the snow and ice lay deep that year. She saw timber ahead then, timber on an island, as it happened, and with her last strength she reached the edge of the spruce bush and then she slept—and would have slept forever but for a miracle.

By the barest of chances the trapper who once a winter

came this far north drove his dogs around that wooded island on that day. He was the only living soul within a radius of better than a hundred miles and his team drove straight to the body of the girl. He found her within an hour of her arrival, and he carried her to his travel camp and there he cared for her.

But the incredible part of this tale is yet to come: after a single day Stella was fit, yes, and eager to travel home. On the sixteenth day of her disappearance she was heading north, warmly wrapped in the cariole of the half-breed trapper, and on the seventeenth day she was at home on Windy Bay. Old Karl shed tears to see her. The boys also shed tears, but they had been shedding them for days, and not only because of grief, for they were suffering the excruciating agony of snow blindness after two weeks of futile searching in the empty plains.

When spring came, Karl prepared to leave the land forever. He spoke to Franz and Hans, but they were unwilling to go south, and in the end he left them behind, for he was aware that they would continue to make a good catch of foxes every year. Karl took the freight canoe towards the south, carrying the younger children and the season's furs. Hans and Franz remained behind, Franz because he could not face the return south, and Hans for some inscrutable reason of his own.

In the distant world beyond, the war drove on to its appointed end, but in the silence of the Barrens even its muted echo did not intrude. The years passed, until in 1947 I unexpectedly descended on Windy Bay, and in those intervening years the pattern of life there had undergone no change. Once each year the boys loaded their canoe and traveled as far south as the nearest outpost of trade; and here, quickly, they disposed of their furs, bought what they needed for the year, and fled back through the forests to the arctic plains. For the rest of the year they roamed the Barrens, by dog team in winter, and on foot or with pack dogs in summer.

Oddly enough, each lived his life apart. Hans grew desperately quiet and often spoke no words for days on end. Each had his own trap line in a different area, and during the winter the brothers were often absent from the cabin in different directions for an unbroken month. They sometimes returned at the same time but more often they missed each other during their brief visits to the cabin. The pressure of loneliness weighed on them always, but Franz, with a legacy of strength from his Indian mother, and with his increasing intimacy with the Barrens People, managed to hold this loneliness partly at bay, and so escaped the madness that seeps into the spaces in the brains of lonely men. He built and ramified his own protective shield and it enabled him to hold his own against the impersonal animosity of the plains.

Among the Eskimos he came to be considered as one of the band, and yet not quite of it, for even when all other human contacts were denied to him, he still held the crumpled ramparts of his pride of race. Still, the People were his sole bulwark against the destroying loneliness, and so Franz compromised his pride. He was with but never of them, and as a result he was never quite beyond the reach of loneliness. It was a driving but controlled hunger which was in him, and it took the form of an endless restlessness that became anguish. He tried to solace it by expanding his hunting range so he could wander over new lands, farther and farther from the post in Windy Bay.

But Franz's restless thrusting into the distance brought him no comfort because he never understood his trouble. He did not know that though he had learned to live in the land and had established an uneasy armistice between himself and the hostility of rocks and elements, yet for all this, he remained—an intruder.

IV
The Children

After his first outpouring Franz became silent, speaking only in monosyllables and evading the questions that were constantly occurring to me. Perhaps he was ashamed of his outburst on the first night, as a sober man is ashamed of a drunken episode when he has revealed too much of himself to a stranger. Or perhaps he was engrossed only by the delayed arrival of his brother.

Each morning he left the cabin to climb the lookout hill near camp where he spent the hot hours of the spring days staring over the rotting surface of the ice-covered bay to the southeast. Hans was long overdue. Earlier in the spring he had made a trip to the south end of Nueltin Lake, a hundred miles away, to rescue a winter cache which had been left on a little islet. Now Hans had only a scant few days in which to make his return, before the ice passed completely from the bay and dog travel would be no longer possible.

On the third morning of our vigil together it began to

rain, and it rained as it did all things in this land—with overwhelming violence. Franz and I were driven into the leaking cabin. As we sat listening to the sodden drumming of water on the caribou skins of the roof, we both suddenly became aware of a new sound that had insinuated itself into the muffled thunder of the rain. I listened tensely until I recognized it as only the murmur of snow water flowing down above the ice of the river. It was a sound I knew, but there was a changed depth to its voice. The murmur seemed to swell, to become resonant, then in an instant's time it was transformed into a heavy-throated roar. The cabin shuddered and the tin plates on the table slid and rattled as if they danced to the erratic rhythm of an earthquake.

Heedless of the driving rains, Franz ran outside and as I followed him I caught a terrifying glimpse of an immense cake of ice, at least ten feet in thickness, rearing out of the river not more than twenty paces from our door. The great cake stood briefly on end like a gigantic tombstone, then it toppled forward and as it fell a gray geyser of tormented water flung itself high above the shifting ice. The river, so long contained, was surging up between the shattered floes, and in a few minutes had climbed the slopes below us and was lifting the debris about the cabin door.

I watched the cataclysm through the gray lens of the rain, while the rising waters lapped about my feet. The sound that had first given us warning of what was about to happen now moved up the river like the roll of a giant drum. As it passed, a thunderous and violent cacophony came into being as the great cakes shattered and moved ponderously down toward the frozen bay.

The momentum of that movement seemed irresistible. Yet where the river joined the bay there was resistance, and on a mighty scale. Along its forward edge the bay ice took the full onslaught of the river floes and shattered with such pressure that the air above the battleground was filled with a fine dust of ice crystals that defied even the down-driving rain. Floe cakes the size of buildings were ground out of existence in mere moments, to be instantly replaced by others which drove the stubborn barrier of the bay ice slowly backward from the river mouth.

At last, the bay ice would give no more, and the lumbering pans came down the river and were held. Behind them, the water rose so rapidly that it was soon knee-deep in the cabin, while the river was no longer fifteen but thirty feet in depth. Great cakes strayed in the eddies behind the ice dam, and one of them nuzzled the log walls of the cabin, as a bull elephant might try his strength against a standing tree. Franz and I had fled to the ridge and we were filled with a mounting excitement that gave us no time to worry about the possible loss of the cabin and all our belongings.

The dam across the narrow river mouth was steadily enlarging and it shuddered and rumbled wickedly as a constant succession of new blocks crashed into its upstream side and were thrown high to reinforce the crest. And then, when it seemed that nothing could save the cabin from the insane river, the dam began to give. Moving as an entity, it slid out over the yet unbroken ice of the bay. Ten thousand tons of obstacle slowly gave way before the power of that unleashed river.

The dam dissolved so easily that it gave the impression of a gentle and effortless decomposition. But the measure of its true ferocity appeared when a single cake of ice, the size of a small house, was suddenly flung clear and, like a curling stone, was shot for nearly half a mile across the creaking ice of Windy Bay. Spinning over that black, rotting surface, the great cake came to rest at last against the rocks of a small reef, and there it sat through the succeeding days until the sun at last destroyed it. While it remained, it was a fitting token of the forces which the land contains.

Both Franz and I were so engrossed in the sound and fury of the battle that we did not hear the approaching dogs as they climbed our ridge. Not until the wooden sled had rasped over the gravel and stood beside us did we see it.

The dogs sat back in their traces and I guessed that the slim boy who stood beside the leader was Hans. Before I had time to receive more than a brief impression of his shadowed face, two bundles erupted from the sled and one of those took form as a bounding mite of fur-clad child who rushed upon Franz and flung itself ecstatically into his arms. The second bundle detached itself from the nondescript baggage and came over to us with a little more restraint, stopping abruptly as it saw me standing there. This was a boy, thirteen years of age, clad in deerskins. He stood awkwardly beside Franz and his smile grew until his upper lip curled up over his flattened nose, almost obscuring it from view. His big even teeth glistened at me and I stared back at him in complete fascination, for I saw that these were children of the People I had come to find.

The little girl in Franz's arms was chattering and squirming, unable to contain her pleasure at seeing the man again. And as for Franz—there were tears in his black eyes. At length he put the child down, and I saw that she was no more than five, and small even for that age. She joined the boy and for the first time she noticed me. Her exuberance vanished at once, leaving her like a small graven image on the hill.

"Kunee," Franz said, pointing to her, "and Anoteelik" —pointing to the boy. It was a skimpy introduction, but I had to be content with it for the moment. As we all trouped down the hill to the cabin to assay the damage and clean up the mess, I wondered if Kunee could be Franz's child.

The sight of me had made the children shy enough, but on Hans my presence placed an intolerable restraint. He had long since withdrawn so far within himself that he could barely suffer even the rare contacts with his brother Franz. With me, white and an incomprehensible stranger, Hans's withdrawal was complete. He would speak no words to me at all, but sat alone in a dark corner of the cabin, staring at me as he might have stared at some dangerous denizen of his own bleak land. His skin was dark, much darker than his brother's, and it was stretched too tightly over the narrow, fragile bones of his thin face. His eyes were empty things—blank, still depths that shifted from my face no more than the eyes of a trapped fox shift from the face of its approaching nemesis.

But the shyness of the children was, after all, only the shyness of children. In a little while they were hustling about the cabin, evidently quite oblivious of me as they traded muted grins with one another. Anoteelik quickly got a fire going in the wet stove, while Kunee, that minuscule model of a woman, ran to the river's edge, got water, and in a few minutes had a brew of tea ready for all of us.

After it was poured into the tin mugs, she made herself comfortable on Franz's knee and proceeded to roll a competent cigarette. Franz gave her a light and she smoked happily while he crooned to her in the manner of a father talking to his child.

And now my curiosity could be contained no longer.

"Franz," I said, "is she—yours?"

Franz nodded slowly though he did not look up at me.

"Yes," he replied and his voice was almost hostile and

very different from the friendly voice that he had used to me before. "Yes, she's mine, I found her out there in the north, and she's all mine!"

There was a positiveness, almost a fierceness at the end, as if he was daring me to argue with his right to this incredible child. Then surprisingly, and with no further prompting, he began to tell me something of the finding of Kunee and of her brother Anoteelik. And later I was to hear more details from the Eskimos themselves.

Some sixty miles due north of Windy Bay, across the sodden plains and gravel ridges, there is a nest of Little Lakes huddled close up against the banks of the river we call Kazan but which is properly *Innuit Ku*—the River of Men. (*Innuit* is the People's own name for their race. Translated it means simply Mankind. The term "Eskimo" is not used by them but is a tag applied by the Indians, meaning Eaters of Raw Meat.) The waters of the Little Lakes flow into the Innuit Ku not far from its beginning at Lake Ennadai and for some centuries this little group of lakes and the surrounding Little Hills have been the center of the inland culture. The People spread up and down Innuit Ku until their camps stood on each lake and river in the rolling land. They called themselves *Ihalmiut*—which means The Other People—as distinct from those Eskimos who lived at the coasts and possessed a sea culture.

In all the time that the Ihalmiut have known the land and roamed its endless spaces, the Little Lakes that lie beside the wide Kazan exercised a special attraction. So it was natural enough, when the tide was turned against them by powers greater than even those the Barrens know, when plague and starvation struck their blows against the camps, that as the Ihalmiut retreated they should fall back upon this place.

By the year 1940, the last of the outlying camps had been broken. Those few of the People who survived the dissolution of the inland race returned to live once more, as their ancestors had before them, about Ootek, Halo and Kakumee Lakes under the Little Hills. That place became the last stronghold held by living men throughout the land, and it was under siege. It was a fortress without walls, with only the impalpable defenses that a fading will to live could raise against the overwhelming weight of the grim siege which had been laid upon it. The enemies were many, but foremost in their ranks were famine and diseases, and these were both strangers to the land and so were more frightful than the elemental antagonists that the Ihalmiut had long since learned to circumvent. By late autumn of 1946, the remnants of the People were clustered about the bleak shores of the Little Lakes, to stand off the never-ending sallies of these enemies as best they could.*

Among the People at that place there was the family of Angleyalak, and in his tent lived his mother, who was very old, his wife, called Iktuk, and his three children, Kunee, Anoteelik and Pama. Iktuk was a good mother to her children and a good wife to her husband, though her strength was often drained away by long coughing spells, which ended only when her bright blood dyed the white fox furs she held against her mouth. Angleyalak was a good hunter, yet his efforts were too often brought to nothing, for his old gun could not bring down its game when there was no charge of shot, no powder for its long brass cartridges. As for the old woman, she had outlived three hundred younger members of her race and now she waited, almost impatiently, for the erratic glance of death. Each winter she did not hope to see the spring, and yet each spring she lived to see another winter come.

Kunee and Anoteelik were but small children still, though Anoteelik was old enough to go with his father on the long hunting trips that so often ended with no more than tales of vanished game with which to fill the bellies of the family. Kunee, at four years of age, was already deeply serious about her duties as a woman of the camp. She helped her old grandmother to gather willow twigs for fuel, or else drew water from the lakes, or watched the cooking fires when her mother had bled too freely from the mouth and could no longer stand.

The igloo of Angleyalak stood on the north shore of *Ootek Kumanik*—meaning Ootek's Lake—and near it stood three other camps. On other lakes within a few miles of Angleyalak's there were eight more igloos, and these completed the short roster of the homes of the surviving People.

---

*During the summer of 1947, eighteen Ihalmiut men, women and children died of a disease which was probably diphtheria.

In the late winter of 1946, Angleyalak and his neighbor, Ootek, went out together on a hunting trip, for even then the food at the igloos under the Little Hills was growing scarce. The two men took only one sled, pulled by three dogs, for dog feed was also scarce; and they traveled southward to Franz's cabin. In all that broad sweep of land, they saw no deer, nor yet the tracks of any deer, and they were frightened men.

By chance Franz was at home when they arrived and the two visitors stayed overnight with him. In the morning they departed, carrying with them the few food supplies that Franz had been able to spare from his own scanty stocks. But after they had gone, Franz thought about the things they had told him, and in his mind there was a mixed foreboding. He knew that the camps of the Ihalmiut must be nearly empty of deer meat, for he knew that the fall kill had been a meager one. And on his own most recent trips through the Ihalmiut land, he had missed several deer carcasses which he had cached the previous autumn for dog feed; he was aware that this meat must have gone into human bellies. He was also aware that the People do not steal unless death has come close enough to make a mockery of morals.

On this midwinter visit, Ootek and Angleyalak had told Franz the deer had left the land, and that unless the spring came early, the People too would be gone before the warm suns brought the deer back again.

Franz had listened to this prophecy and in his heart anger almost outweighed pity. It was an anger that he should feel a duty and a responsibility toward these "savages," and an anger that they should be so foolishly improvident, failing to look to and prepare for the distant future as he, a white man, did. There was anger, too, that they had robbed his caches and so made it more difficult for him to travel around the trap lines on which his livelihood depended. And yet perhaps the thing which angered the young trapper most of all was the insistent feeling that his very presence in the place had helped to bring about the fatal misery of the People.

His father, and the other traders who had once brought furs from the Ihalmiut, had shown the People that pursuit of fox pelts was more desirable than pursuit of meat. And so, in a few decades, the People had learned to neglect the caches of good meat, which they had been used to making every fall. Instead they learned to trap the white fox and to trade the pelts for flour, shells and guns. As far as the Ihalmiut could discern, it was a satisfactory change, for they were able to meet their simple needs with much less labor, after the traders came.

But when trading ceased to pay the high profits always required of it, the great company withdrew its post and the new way of life that had been taught to the People in their innocence now became death. Men who were once great hunters of the deer had become instead great hunters of the fox, but men cannot eat fox pelts. The People could not change their ways again. "Surely," they thought, "if we trap fox this winter and take the pelts south, we shall find the trader has returned." But when the hunters traveled south, the trading post stood empty and decayed as it had stood for many hungry years.

The traders came, stayed briefly while their profits warranted, then left the land, abandoned it, and thought no more of the destruction they had wrought. Franz lived there still. And he could not drive out the hidden knowledge of the fault. Perhaps it was because of this that when Ootek and Angleyalak went almost empty-handed back to the Little Hills, Franz thought of them almost with anger in his heart.

The winter months dragged slowly by and there came no more cries for help. At last, early in March, Franz traveled northward to the Ihalmiut camps and stayed a day in the igloo of old Hekwaw. Here Franz ate his share of the communal food as he had always eaten it, but that share did not even take the edge off his healthy appetite and he quickly made his excuses and left the camp. He traveled north to his most distant trap line and once again found that many of his meat caches had been robbed by men.

It was mid-March and Angleyalak had returned from a futile hunt during which he carried no gun, but only a crude bow that served him little better than a toy serves a child; for the men of the Ihalmiut had forgotten how to make cunning bows of horn, during the long years when they had no need of bows, and the bright guns and shells were to be had in return for pelts. Angleyalak returned to the tent bringing with him two ptarmigan, and these winter-starved birds were to be all the food that five people and three dogs would have till the time came when many of them would have no further need of food.

For a month before that final hunt of Angleyalak's there

had been no more than a mouthful of food for each person on each day, and this hunt had been a last desperate effort to halt the slow attrition of the gut. The hunt had failed, as it was bound to fail, and now the course of things followed an inevitable pattern which the hunter could no longer break, no matter how he tried. Death was upon the camp and all that the people there could do was to channel the approach of death so that the least important of the living might go first.

There was no open mention of the problem, for none was needed. While Angleyalak still lived there was still hope. But should he, the hunter, die, then the family must perish even though the deer returned in numbers to the Little Hills.

Next to him stood the children, Kunee, Pama and Anoteelik, who were the visible expression of the Ihalmiut's waning will to live. Behind the children was Iktuk, wife, mother, and source of new life yet her work was nearly done, for the children were old enough to live without her aid.

Then came the dogs, the precious dogs, the three survivors of a once good team. These three scrawny things were treasures and irreplaceable. Mobility was their potential in the family, and without their power to move across the frozen land, not even a great hunter could survive for long.

That was the family then—except for the old woman, Epeetna. What was her place? Nothing more secure than the niche that love and filial affection could ensure for her, and these emotions die readily enough when hunger closes its inexorable jaws.

On the night after Angleyalak's return with the two birds, the old woman did not sleep. It was her time, and she had waited for it through too many starving years. She had looked forward with a hard relief to death and this night her seeking ended in a wall of snow. Yet now that it was time, fear rose within her—the fear that is so strong in the old, and which makes the terror of young men in danger look pallid and a sham.

It was not long before the members of her family took refuge from their bellies' agony in sleep. But the old woman sat on and stared unseeingly over their quiet forms. She heard the whimpers of little Kunee and the uneasy mutters of the man, her son. But most clearly did she hear the whisper of the sand-like snow as the never-ending winds drove it along the polished curve of the igloo's dome. The harsh rustle filled her hearing until she was no longer conscious of the little human sounds. The snow noise rose in gradual ascension and, as it grew, so grew her fear of death.

The long night was nearly over when the skeletal guardians of the passageway, the dogs, lifted gaunt heads and cowered against the snow blocks to leave the passage free for her. And the old woman passed out of the igloo into the darkness. The ground drift of driving snow enveloped her and the darkness grew about her. She stood naked but for her fur trousers, and now she loosened these and they slipped soundlessly into the drifts. The wind whined like a beast in pain, and the darkness drew about her frail and tortured form.

When morning came, no one in the family spoke of her. Not even the child Kunee made reference to the missing face. But later, when the brief half-light of day was upon them, Angleyalak went out alone into the snow, and he stood facing the wind with his amulet belt wound tightly about his waist. And then he spoke the words that he had learned as a child in the great and populous camps of the People, he spoke the phrases that he had been taught to say over the newly dead.

That was in mid-March. It was the time when the days grow slightly longer and when the eternal winter winds usually drop and die away for days on end. Yet on this year the winds forgot their place and mounted steadily, until the whole world that was the Barrens became a single roaring wind without cessation.

Had there been game to hunt, no man could have ventured out to hunt that game. In the igloo of Angleyalak, the family huddled under the skin robes upon the sleeping bench—and waited.

By day there was a faint pallid glow to lighten the still gloom of the snow house. By night there was nothing, for there was no deer fat to burn in the little lamp. The wind rang on the snow walls with such devilish persistence that its voice at last ceased to be heard and became one with a growing silence. The dogs no longer stirred, but lay in tightly curled, half-frozen balls, with noses under tails, sleeping the unconscious sleep of those who near the end of hunger.

The two birds were eaten. The children had the balance of their meat, but Angleyalak had a small share. The guts and feathers went to the dogs and only Iktuk ate nothing. Her husband tried to make her eat his own slim portion but she turned from him coughing blood, and would not eat.

A week after the old woman had left the place, Iktuk could no longer stir except to cough. It was at this time that Angleyalak went to the igloo of Ootek, which stood only a few hundred feet away, and he had trouble finding that igloo because the ground drift—the never-ending ground drift—obscured the way like a thick mist.

In Ootek's igloo there were the man, his young wife Howmik, and a child who was still nursing at her dried-up breasts. Ootek himself had eaten nothing for twelve days, and the scraps of old robes that had been boiled over the last

handful of willow twigs had gone to the two who could not live without each other. This was the third child of Ootek, and the first one that had lived a full year's span. Hunger had taken the others in their time, and now Ootek was prepared to disregard the law which says that first the hunter must be fed.

Angleyalak spoke to Ootek and they debated, quietly and with long intervals between their words, some course of action they might take. They knew Franz was away on his

distant trap lines and they knew that he might not return to
his camp for a month or more. And that would be too late.
But now Ootek remembered hearing of a white man who had
recently built a tiny trading post some ten days' journey to
the east, in order to trade with the coastal Eskimos who
sometimes wintered inland from the sea. It seemed to Ootek
that they should forsake the Little Hills and make their way
eastward, seeking to escape from death. Yet when Angleyalak
heard this suggestion he could not agree to it. He knew that
he could not join Ootek and the rest, for Iktuk could no
longer walk and Angleyalak had no dogs with strength to pull
the sled.

A week later there were still four igloos on the shores of
Ootek's Lake, but only one of these held human life. The
People from the other three had set out toward the east in a
forlorn and nearly hopeless struggle for survival, with the
inexorable presence of destruction close upon their wavering
trail.

In the remaining igloo, Iktuk wakened suddenly from a
long sleep, and she would have screamed in terror at what she
saw, but her thin blood ran backward down her throat and
choked the scream. The others slept beside her and did not
stir, for only Iktuk had glimpsed the devil who had come for
her.

Struggling terribly, she gained a brief control of her
choking lungs and in a wild paroxysm, she forced the life-
giving fluids from her chest. The hemorrhage flowed heavily
from her gasping mouth, dripped over the edge of the
sleeping ledge, fell, and froze instantly upon the floor.

In the middle of the day which followed, Angleyalak
awoke and found his wife's body frozen in a grotesque
contortion on the snow below the ledge. He tried desperately
to drag it out of the igloo before the children woke but he
could not bend the legs and arms that had been flung out
from the body in the last convulsive efforts of its life. He
could not move his wife and so, for the little time which
remained to him, he could look down upon the bloody face of
one whom he had loved so greatly that he had dared remain
on at this place, instead of following the faint hope that had
taken all the other People to the east.

A dog had also died that night, so it was eaten. The
children ate the dry and bitter meat of the dog that died of
hunger, and Angleyalak ate just enough to keep his strength

in hand for what remained. A week passed and the other dogs were killed before they grew so thin that they became completely useless to the living. March passed into April and at long last the winds retired and in the daytime the sun shone clearly, growing higher in the winter-faded sky.

The last of the dog meat was eaten and one morning Angleyalak took his old rifle and crawled out the door tunnel into the light of day. The hunter was going hunting once again. Dragging the rifle behind him, he crawled weakly over the ice-hard snow and he had gone perhaps a hundred yards, his eyes half-blinded by the glare, when he saw movement on a ridge ahead of him. Trembling with weakness and with hope, he raised his ancient gun, steadied it briefly and fired at the miraculous vision of the caribou that stood watchfully before him.

The children, huddled together in the igloo, heard no shot for none was fired. They ate no meat that day—for there had been no deer. And in the white brilliance of the day, the thing that was Angleyalak grew stiff, beside the old and useless gun which still pointed to the unblemished drifts where the hunter had seen the last of all his deer.

It was just after dawn of the following day when Franz reached Ootek's Lake. He made at once for Ootek's igloo, but when he found its tunnel drifted in with snow he knew the People had gone elsewhere, perhaps to Halo's Lake, and so he prepared to travel south again to his own distant camp. He swung his dogs along the shore, but when one of them raised its head and howled, Franz glanced off to the side and saw a brown, shapeless hummock on the snow. At first he thought it was a wolverine and he slipped his rifle free of its case. But the brown thing did not stir and when Franz reached it, he recognized the man.

Franz feared the dead, for his Indian blood runs strongly through the imagery of his white man's mind. He did not touch the frozen corpse, but turned his dogs back until he came to the igloo of Angleyalak. The passageway was open, though only a narrow cleft remained free of drifts. Fearful of what lay under the still dome, Franz called aloud, but got no answer. He would have turned and fled from the place then, but faintly he heard a sound, as of an animal that has been maimed and left for dead.

Franz tied his dogs. Then, summoning all his courage, he wormed his way down the long passage that was nearly filled with drifted snow. He came in time to save the younger children. They were both awake, and waiting for their father. Now dimly they saw that he returned, and the whimpers of the little girl grew louder.

Franz covered Pama's frozen corpse and the horrible body of Iktuk with some skins taken from the ledge, and then he stayed a full day in that igloo. He fed the two bony things he had found on soup, cooked on his primus stove—and he waited patiently while the two children retched it up again; then he once more fed them soup until their rebellious stomachs would accept the nourishment. He kept the tiny stove going at full heat until the igloo's dull walls brightened and filmed with ice, as the temperature rose rapidly. The little girl held out her hands to him, trembling little talons that were white with frost, and Franz massaged them gently till some warmth returned.

By the next day the children were already displaying the incredible resilience of the very young. Franz did not dare linger any longer for he had no dog feed on his sled, and little enough food for himself. Also there were the presences of Iktuk, Pama and Angleyalak. A hundred miles lay between Franz and Windy Camp and he was anxious to begin the trek.

He unloaded and cached the frozen corpses of a dozen white foxes from his sled, and in their place he spread out his own robes with the two children carefully wrapped amongst them. Then he drove south from Ootek's Lake, and in two days was lighting a wood fire in the stove by Windy Bay.

Hans came in from his trap line a short time afterwards, and if he was surprised to find the children at the cabin, he did not show it. In a few days he found himself left alone with the orphans, for Franz had forgotten his old anger against the People, and he had forgotten his impatience with their improvident ways. The finding of Kunee and Anoteelik had wrought a great change in him and as soon as he was satisfied that the children would be secure during his absence, he hitched up his dogs again and drove back to the Little Hills.

At Katelo's igloo, on the banks of Kakumee Lake, he found starvation had reached the ultimate limits before death intervenes. Franz distributed part of the flour and meat that he had brought with him, then drove on to all the occupied igloos he could find, giving to the family in each enough food to prevent immediate disaster. At Ootek Lake and at Halo Lake there was still no sign of life and Franz had no knowledge of what had happened to the families who had once been there.

When the food was distributed—and it was only a miserable handout, though it was all Franz had—he returned at once to Windy Bay and after one day's rest, drove southward on the three-hundred-mile journey to the nearest outpost of white men. This was a tiny trading post at Deer Lake, run by a young half-breed manager who was himself completely isolated from the world, in winter, except that he had an ancient short-wave radio over which it was sometimes possible to transmit his halting signals in Morse code.

Franz reached Deer Lake in seven days, and of those seven, he spent three fighting a spring blizzard. Once at the post, he and the manager labored over a message that would tell the outside world of the plight of the Ihalmiut. It was a message of great importance—for it was to be the first message ever to go out from the inland plains; the first cry for help in all the centuries that the People had lived their hidden lives within the land. Franz was the first of those—traders, trappers or missionaries who had heard of the People and their plight—to take it on himself to seek help for them. He was the first to care.

The message went out slowly, each word tapped out two or three times. At Churchill the big radio station picked it up and relayed it south. The days were passing and Franz waited at Deer Lake for the answer which was so long delayed. The days were passing.

As to what happened to the message—who can say? At first, no doubt, the authorities were skeptical of its validity, and in any case one must investigate before one spends the funds of government. Also it was the first time that the authorities had been called on to help the inland People—"Why should they need help now, after all these years?" But at last the wheels began to turn. A message was dispatched to The Pas. An aircraft was hired and a flight was made. That flight failed. A second flight was made and a plane landed at the extreme south end of Nueltin and unloaded its supplies.

Meanwhile Franz had been expecting an aircraft from Churchill, the direct and shortest route, and when he heard that someone had sent a plane from The Pas instead, he left Deer Lake to find the cache which had been made over two hundred miles short of its destination. Time was running out.

Franz traveled over a hundred miles to find the cache,

and when he found it he discovered that it consisted largely of things that would be of no aid to the dying men and women in the camps. There were white beans; sacks of white beans, for people who had no fuel for fires and whose world was still one of ice and snow.

Loading his tired dogs with the things that could be used, Franz started north again: two hundred miles of bitter driving, with the spring thaws already making progress very difficult.

Time had been running out.

Franz had traveled almost a thousand miles on behalf of the People. He came to the camps again in time to learn that Eepuk, Aljut, Uktilohik, Elaitutna, Epeetna, Okinuk, Oquinuk and Homoguluk—people he knew well—had not been able to await his coming. It was spring. These dead ones were buried under rock piles where the snow had left the ridges. There were others, too, who did not have the benefit of graves, but whose bodies were attended to by wolves and wolverines, so that their spirits may never know the rest that comes only to those who are buried properly. In the camps where these had died there had been none left to bury them.

Franz had done much for the Ihalmiut, and in so doing had done much for himself. The old bitterness and anger, the legacy of his own treatment at the hands of white men, was all gone. No, not quite gone, but turned against those who deserved it, and no longer against the People of the Little Hills.

As for the People—it was only another spring for them, no different from twoscore springs which had been theirs during the last half-century.

And there was something to balance the ledger this time, for now a message had gone out. Now the government could not ignore the People any longer, nor plead ignorance of the charges who had been placed in its care by the white man's law. The message had gone out. The response to it had been too slow, and badly bungled, but at least there *had* been a response; and at long last the government acknowledged that in the great plains there lived a people who were its wards.

Fifty years of darkness had intervened between the time of Tyrrell's visit and this belated recognition of the People he had found. Now half a century of casual forgetfulness was at an end, and for the second time in their long history as squatters in this land of ours, the existence of the Ihalmiut was admitted. And surely this was a bright victory for the conscience of our race, not dimmed or clouded because that victory came too late to do more than prolong the last dying spasms of the People of the Little Hills.

V

The Lifeblood of the Land

On the day following the arrival of Hans and the children, I was awakened by the sound of heavy firing. The crash of gunshots intruded itself into my dreams until I thought I was again back in the Italian hills, listening to an exchange of rifle fire between the German outposts and our own. When I came to full consciousness the firing remained, so I hurriedly pulled on my clothes and went out into the June morning.

Franz, Anoteelik and Hans were sitting on the ridge above the cabin and they were steadily firing their rifles across the river. On the sloping southern bank nearly a hundred deer, all does, were milling in stupid anxiety. I could see the gray bursts of dust as bullets sang off the rocks, and I could hear the flat thud of bullets going home in living flesh.

The nearest animals were waist-deep in the fast brown water and could not return to shore, for the press of deer behind cut off retreat. The does that were still on land were running in short, futile starts, first east then west again, and it was some time before they began to gallop with long awkward strides, along the riverbank. Their ponderous bellies big with fawn swung rhythmically as they fled upstream, for their time was nearly on them.

50

When the last of the straggling herd had passed out of range beyond the first bend of the river, the firing stopped and the three hunters ran down the bank and hurriedly began to clear the snow away from the green back of a canoe, which lay beside the cabin. I helped them and in a few moments the canoe was free and ready for the water. Franz and I pushed off into the still-flooded river, and we worked with all our power to gain the other bank before the current could sweep us out into the opening bay. It was hard and exciting work, but even in the fury of that struggle I had time to notice that the water was not all brown. Long, tenuous, crimson streamers were flowing down the river, fading and disappearing as they joined the full flow of the current. We grounded on the opposite shore and leaped into the water to beach the canoe, out of the river's grasp.

The excitement of the shooting, and of the river crossing, ebbed as suddenly as it had risen and I stood on the rough rocks along the slope and looked down on the dead and dying deer. There were a dozen of them lying in my sight along the shore. Their blood was still pumping thickly into the foam-flecked eddies at the river's edge, for only two of them were dead. The rest lay quivering on the rocks and lifted heavy heads to watch us blankly or, struggling to their feet, plunged forward only to fall again.

It was a sight of slaughter and of horror, and the knowledge that each of these dying beasts was swollen with young did not make the bloody spectacle easier to bear. I was seeing the blood of the land flow for the first time, but though my eyes were still those of a stranger and I was sickened by the sight, Franz was quite unperturbed. Rapidly, and with the agility of a deer himself, he leapt among the rocks to reach the cripples. He carried a short-bladed knife and as he reached each wounded doe he made one dexterous thrust into the back of her neck and neatly severed the spinal cord running inside the vertebrae. It was efficient and it was mercifully quick. Within ten minutes all the wounded animals lay still and Franz began the task of cutting up the meat.

One long stroke sufficed to open up the bellies. The sharp blade was used with such control that while it split the skin, it did not even mark the soft tissues of the swollen stomachs, distended with the fermenting leaves and lichens that the deer had fed upon. Then, reaching a bare arm into the hot cavities, Franz disemboweled each beast with one strong pull. Carefully he removed the livers and the kidneys and, using his knife as a chopper, he severed the hindquarters from the trunks. Leaving the forelimbs untouched, he sliced through the skin under the chins and cut out the heavy tongues.

I watched with fascination and repulsion, but so sure were all Franz's movements and so deft his touch, that the horror of the scene began to dull. I was filled with admiration for the man's skill. Though I did not know it then, I was watching a man of Tyrrell's deer people do his work, for Franz had learned his knacker's arts at the hands of the Ihalmiut, who are, in truth, a People of the Deer.

In less than twenty minutes all the carcasses were drawn and we were carrying the hindquarters to the shore. Where half an hour ago a herd of living deer had stood, now there were only shapeless, bloody heaps of meat that steamed gently upon the melting snow. The transition was too quick to have its full effect upon me then, and by the time I had lived in the land long enough to understand the truth behind a killing such as this, I too came to view it through Northern eyes, and to recognize the stark utility of death. But now it was my first spring in the Barrens, and the deer had returned. With their coming the long hiatus that life suffers during the interminable winter months was over. Outside the cabin the meat-hungry dogs raised their gaunt faces and howled exuberantly as each new change of breeze brought the strong smell of deer.

Kunee and Anoteelik were in an ecstasy. Anoteelik rushed knee-deep into the swollen river to help us land and eagerly snatched up a piece of still-warm meat and wolfed it down with feverish excitement. I remembered that this was the first fresh meat he had tasted in long months, and Anoteelik had not yet forgotten those starvation days by Ootek's Lake. Kunee was not far behind him, and I cannot describe the emotions that filled me as I watched this girl-child with a knife in one hand and a great chunk of dripping back meat in the other, stuffing her little face and burping like an old clubman after a Gargantuan meal.

For the first time Hans showed some animation. He smiled. I do not know whether it was from pleasure in the killing or from anticipation of fresh food. His smile was—well, expressionless.

Franz too was smiling as we unloaded the heavy cargo and he shouted at Kunee to get a fire going. A new spirit of enthusiasm and fresh life was in the place, as if new blood flowed through the veins of those about me. Even I was stung by an emotion I could not analyze, and I felt alive as I have never felt before.

The fire had just been lit and a pot of deer tongues just set to boil when a wild babble from the dogs brought me outside again. This time I looked directly to the crossing, and where the butchery had taken place there was a great new herd of does milling as it came up against the stream.

This time there was no shooting, though Hans could hardly restrain his urge to take up a rifle and empty it again. The deer seemed to ignore the cabin that stood in full view and in a minute they had all taken to the stream. Heavy as they were, they swam buoyantly and powerfully so that they made the crossing without losing ground and landed literally in our own front yard.

The dogs became insane and threatened to tear their tethering posts out of the frozen ground. The deer paid them, and us, but little heed. Splitting into two groups, they flowed past the cabin, enveloping it for a brief instant in their midst. The stink of barnyard was strong in our nostrils as they passed, then they were gone beyond the ridge.

In less than an hour I had seen so many deer that it seemed as if the world was full of them, but I had seen nothing yet. That afternoon Franz took me on his sled and we drove warily along the rotten shore ice of the bay, to the Ghost Hills. The heat was remarkably intense; at noon the thermometer had reached 100; and so we wore nothing but thin trousers and cotton shirts. Water lay deep upon the ice and the sled was really more of a boat than a land conveyance. An hour's travel took us to the north shore of the bay, and here we tied the dogs and climbed a long gentle ridge that faced the south. Below us lay Windy Bay, and beyond it the shattered slopes of the Ghost Hills. It was a scene to be recorded on gray paper, for the growing things had not been able to keep pace with the precipitate transition of the seasons, and the subtle overlay of color that would suffuse the summer plains had not yet begun to flow. The rotting surface of the ice was dark, but framed in ivory drifts, still lingering on the shores and in a thousand gulleys and ravines. The hills were dun-colored heights sheathed in rock and long-dead lichens, with startlingly black patches of dwarf spruce spotted along their lower slopes. To the north, the plains sank into white and snow-filled hollows, hiding the muskegs and ponds; then lifted to reveal a hueless and leaden waste that stretched to the horizon.

From our vantage point all of this achromatic world lay somberly below us as we waited for the coming of the deer. We had not long to wait. Franz caught my arm and pointed to the convoluted slopes of the distant southern hills, and I could just discern a line of motion. It seemed to me that the slopes were sliding gently downward to the bay, as if the innumerable boulders that protruded from the hills had suddenly been set adrift to roll, in slow motion, down upon the ice. I watched intently, not certain whether the sun's glare had begun to affect my eyes so that they played fool tricks on me. Then the slow avalanches reached the far shore and debouched over the bay. I tried to count the little dots. Ten, fifty, a hundred, three hundred—and I gave up. In broken twisted lines, in bunched and beaded ropes, the deer streamed out onto the ice until they were moving north across a front of several miles.

From that distance they barely seemed to move, and yet in a few minutes they had reached the center of the bay and had begun to take on shape. I had binoculars, but in my preoccupation with the spectacle below I had not thought to use them. Now I lifted the glasses to my eyes. The long skeins dissolved at once into endless rows of deer, each following upon the footsteps of the animals ahead. Here and there along the lines a yearling kept its place beside a mother who was swollen with the new fawn she carried. There were no bucks. All these animals were does, all pregnant, all driving inexorably towards the north and the flat plains where they would soon give birth.

The leaders reached our shore and began the ascent, but across the bay the avalanche continued and grew heavier. The surface of the bay, for six miles east and west, had become one undulating mass of animals, and still they came.

Without hurry, but without pause, unthinking, but directly driven, they filed down to the ice and, following the tracks of those who had crossed first, made for our shore. Highways began to grow. The black ice was pounded and shattered until it again became white with broken crystals. The broad roads stretched across the bay, multiplied, grew into one another until at length they disappeared and the whole sweep of ice was one great road.

The herds were swelling past our lookout now. Ten paces

from us, five, then we were forced to stand and wave our arms to avoid being trampled on. The does gazed briefly and incuriously at us, swung a few feet away and passed on to the north without altering their gait.

Hours passed like minutes. The flow continued at an unbroken level until the sun stood poised on the horizon's rim. And I became slowly conscious of a great apathy. Life, my life and that of Franz, of all living things I knew, seemed to have become meaningless. For here was life on such a scale that it was beyond all comprehension. It numbed my mind and left me feeling as if the inanimate world had been saturated with a reckless prodigality in that sacred and precious thing called life. I thought of the twelve deer slaughtered on the banks of Windy River and I no longer felt horror or disgust. I felt nothing for the dead who were drowned beyond memory in this living flow of blood that swept across the plains.

It was nearly dusk when we roused ourselves. We walked silently to the sled and I felt a little sick. I began to doubt the reality of the vision I had seen. The ice had begun to freeze as the sun went down and the sled bumped so wickedly over the endless hoofprints that I was forced to run along behind it. A dozen times we passed close to a late herd of deer and each time the dogs, in defiance of Franz, lunged in pursuit and could be halted only when we overturned the sled to hold them back. There was no doubt about it—the vision had been real.

That night I sat for a long time on the ridge behind the cabin, smoking and thinking of that vision. I knew little of the People of the Deer as yet and now that I had seen the herds, I was aware that I knew nothing of the deer themselves. The People and the deer fused in my mind, an entity. I found I could not think of one without the other, and so by accident I stumbled on the secret of the Ihalmiut before I had even met them. I believe it was this vague awareness of the indivisibility of the Barrens People and the caribou that made my later attempts to understand the Eskimos yield fruit.

Since the time of the first arctic explorations, *la Foule*—the Throng—has baffled the curiosity of men. Unlike the immense herds of the prairie buffalo whose habits were open to the eyes of human intruders, the caribou have always remained wrapped in an aura of mystery that has never quite been penetrated. It was known that at certain times of the year, and in certain places, the deer would suddenly appear in herds which blanketed the land. Then, in a few days, they would be gone again. Where had they gone? Well, to the north, the south, or to the east and west, but to what destinations and for what reasons, no one knew.

But as time passed a rough pattern began to emerge from all the conflicting tales told about the deer, and it became known that most of the great herds summered on the plains of the open Barrens and, for the most part, wintered southward inside the protecting timber of the high arctic forests. These two movements were known, but after I had been a year in the Barrens, yet another movement became obvious to me—a migration that I shall discuss in detail later on.

The does, moving up from the forests to cross the mouth of Windy Bay in the first weeks of spring, soon began to disappear and there came a week when only little bands of stragglers, the sterile does, were seen. These did not hurry, for they were not driven by the compulsion of their swollen bellies. Old does, and those that had not been bred, passed gently by but on their heels there came a new upsurge. The bucks arrived. For a few days the hard-packed crossing places were again so thickly carpeted by the brown backs of animals that the ice could not be seen. Then suddenly the bucks too had passed our camp, following the trails of their does who were even then giving birth on the flat lands five hundred miles to the north of us. The bucks passed, and that was the end of the spring migration, though stragglers continued to come our way for many weeks.

The beasts that passed under my eyes that spring were hardly things of beauty. Their rough coats were molting, and in places the passage through the thick forests had rubbed the winter hair away from great patches of black skin. The distended bellies of the does and the ugly bovine heads of all the animals, quite without antlers in the spring, bore no resemblance to the graceful shapes that our minds conjure up at the word "deer." Certainly these caribou were not graceful, swift-limbed animals; and yet their long and knobby legs, with huge splayed feet, carried them over the rough land with a deceptive speed and sureness.

Nor did their manners make them more attractive. Does, fawns and bucks, without exception, enlivened the long day's trek with a ceaseless succession of belly noises that made each herd seem like one noisy knot of rampant indigestion. The belly rumblings formed an undertone to the castanet-like clatter of their feet, for the "ankles" of caribou are fitted with a loose cartilage that, when they move, emits a clicking noise not unlike the muted sound of rocks being tapped against each other, under water.

By the end of June the last stragglers, the wounded and the sick, had passed by Windy Bay, leaving the land about our camp to countless flocks of ducks, gulls and sandpipers who kept up a constant cry and movement over the little ponds and the softening muskeg bogs. The snow was gone by then, yet the passage of the deer was still remembered, for the low bogs had been so cut and torn by the pounding hoofs that areas of moss, covering acres in extent, had been churned to chocolate-colored puddings of ancient peat, torn from its frozen sleep and left to melt under the heat of a forgotten sun. The heavy stench of barnyards hung over such spots as these for many weeks.

Even the surfaces of the great ridges, paved with frost-shattered rocks, clearly showed the eternal passage of the deer. Trails crossed and intersected everywhere, so that in all the country it was difficult to find a single square yard of land which did not bear the deep impress of a long-used trail. Even on solid rock the trails were clearly marked and some had been worn into the gray gneiss for a foot in depth.

But while the land at Windy Bay was given over to birds, the anxious does had borne their fawns on the chosen ground of the high flat plains that lie to the south of Baker Lake and Thelon River. The fawns were with the herds, grunting and coughing about their restless mothers. These precocious children can outrun a man within hours of their birth and can give even the great arctic wolf a difficult pursuit. It is well for them that they are so forward, for many of their mothers are singularly lacking in maternal instincts and it sometimes happens that the does desert their young in the face of danger. So it is not uncommon to meet young fawns roaming alone in the wide spaces of the plains. These lost youngsters will attach themselves to men and follow them for hours, for, like all caribou, the fawns are cursed with a great curiosity about things better left alone.

When the fawning is done with, the restless urge that brought the Throng northward still remains upon it. Now the great herds split into little groups which remain forever on the move. In eddies and milling crowds they circle aimlessly across hundreds of miles of tundra in each few days. The deer have no home. Winter and summer they must always be on the move, for when such numbers gather at any given spot, the lichens and dwarf willow leaves that form their chief foods are speedily exhausted and if the deer remain, they starve.

Thus throughout the hot July days the northern plains are filled with restless little groups of deer which shift about and pass like tumbleweed. But in late July a new compulsion seems to seize them, and this is the movement I referred to earlier as one that still remains quite unexplained. A few of the tiny groups suddenly decide to drift towards the south. As they move, they are like the beginnings of a growing avalanche, for they pick up and carry with them all the herds they meet, and the momentum of the march increases rapidly from day to day. By early August this movement is a flood. The blood of the Barrens flows back the way it came in spring, led by the does and fawns who congregate in immense herds. So the midsummer movement rushes southward at increasing speed until, reaching the forest edge, the wave of deer is halted and flung back in disorder and confusion, as waves are flung back under granite cliffs. The vast summer herds break up, and once again they eddy slowly about with complete aimlessness. Behind the wave of does, and sometimes mingling with them, the bucks, now carrying incredible spreads of velvet-covered antlers, follow along the trail of the stampede. Then, slowly, a recoil begins, and once again the deer drift to the North.

No man can tell the full reason behind this summer flight, for winter is still far away and before it comes, all the deer will have moved north again nearly to the limits reached in spring. Perhaps they make this summer migration because of the flies. Mosquitoes and black flies abound so richly in the Barrens that for weeks on end a wise man does not stir from his dark cabin by day unless driven by urgent need. Summer travel is a constant flight, an endeavor to escape the pursuing haze of winged tormentors. I have seen men remove their shirts after a day in the summer Barrens, and those shirts had to be peeled away from the body, for they were glued to the flesh with the blood of countless bites. The flies are not the least of the Barrens' defenses and they have greatly assisted in protecting the land so long from white men's violation.

If it is difficult for men to escape from the bloodsucking flies, then it is impossible for the deer to escape. At the height of the fly season the deer become emaciated shadows of themselves who hardly dare take time to eat and rest. They flee along the highest and most windswept ridges in a futile effort to escape a plague that has been known to destroy them from sheer loss of blood.

Yet the bloodsucking and the flesh-eating flies are not the most dreaded of the hosts. There are two other flies, both large, gaudy things which look like bumblebees. The arrival of a single one of these flamboyant raiders can inspire terror in a herd of deer that neither man nor wolves can equal. Once, while I was watching a small herd of bucks quietly feeding along a steep riverbank, I saw the animals suddenly go mad. The herd disintegrated and its members fled wildly in all directions, with tossing heads and with high reckless leaps that sometimes plunged them sickeningly on the sharp, shattered rocks. One buck turned to the river, and without a moment's hesitation flung himself over the steep bank and crashed into the shallow waters below, to lie dying with a broken neck.

I paddled over to the still-quivering corpse, and there met the murderer: a winged, yellow horror perched on the dead deer with its ovipositor throbbing and swelling as it sought a place to lay its microscopic eggs. These eggs hatch into minute larvae which burrow through the hide, enter the bloodstream and in time emerge from the flesh to lie in little pockets just underneath the skin on the back of the deer. By the next spring these pockets have reached full size, and each contains an aqueous grub as big as the end joint of a man's finger. I have counted two hundred of these white and repulsive parasites under the back hide of a single deer. In June the obese larvae burrow out through the skin, riddling it as if by machine-gun fire, and drop off to pupate on the ground.

The second of the two devil flies is of an even more evil nature, for its larvae live not under the skin, but in a tight and squirming mass the size of a small grapefruit which clogs the cavities of the deer's nose and throat until it seems impossible that the victim can escape death by asphyxiation. I once took a hundred and thirty of these giant maggots, each an inch long, from the nasal passages of a single doe.

Now perhaps—though I cannot prove the supposition—it is the threat of these many varieties of winged furies which drives the deer so far north in the early spring, for the farther north, the later is the coming of fly season. Then—again perhaps—as the flies die off from north to south with the progress of summer, the deer may follow that line of recession in search of undepleted pastures. I do not know if this is true, but I do know that the summer arrival of the deer in the central Barrens during my stay in the land coincided exactly with the final abrupt disappearance of the flies at that point.

While I am speaking of the flies I may as well exhaust the subject of the minute beasts who prey upon the deer. The big fly maggots are well known to all who know the caribou, but fortunately for their peace of mind few Northerners have any idea of the menageries of other unpleasant beasts that exist under the skin of the deer. Parasites are so numerous, I conclude from my own studies, that there comes a time in the life of every deer, if it survives the other perils, when it is so overloaded with parasites that it simply dies of outright starvation though it spends all day eating. All other things being equal, I doubt if a deer can expect to live more than a dozen years before it is so riddled with worms and cysts that death must inevitably ensue. For the record, and for the enlightenment of any reader who may someday be offered a prime roast of caribou, here is a list of the actual parasites I took from one old buck.

In the body muscles there was a concentration of tapeworm cysts that averaged two per cubic inch of meat. No part of the muscle tissues was free of these abhorrent things, and in addition to them, there was a liberal sprinkling of the cysts of nematode worms. The lungs also were very active even after death. I counted and removed 17 nematode worms, most of them over six inches in length. In the liver there were tapeworm cysts of two species, some of them the size of a tennis ball. The intestines yielded one adult tapeworm of great length and antiquity, and even in the heart muscles I found 6 tapeworm cysts. Of minor parasites, there were 190 warble-fly larvae under the hide and about 75 bott-fly larvae cozily ensconced within the throat and nasal passages.

Now this particular deer was no exception. It was simply old and therefore very heavily parasitized. But all deer which I have examined, except fawns and some yearlings, have yielded a corresponding count of parasites in degrees of intensity varying with the beast's age.

The interesting point here is that all the nematodes and tapeworms have at least two-stage life cycles. That is, they need another host, apart from the deer, to complete their lives. Encysted parasites reach maturity only when the flesh they are lurking in is eaten by another animal. That animal is often man.

I do not know what sort of internal shape the native eaters of deer—or I myself—may be in. Nor do I want to know. I'm sorry that I brought up the subject. I can only comfort myself with the reflection that if the parasites to be picked up from eating deer meat were pathogenic, then there would be no Eskimos at all. It is thin comfort when I recall the raw meat dinners I have eaten in the Barrens. . . .

About the end of August a new mood descends upon the deer. Slowly, and in small groups, they begin moving north again, for the time of rut is drawing near and a protracted atmosphere of tension grips the already restless beasts.

At this time the deer are fat. Freed of flies, they have time to graze on the thick lichens and on the leaves of the tiny bushes that carpet the dry lands. In late summer the bucks accumulate a layer of fat that may be three inches thick along their backs, for they will have no time to eat during the rut. Now the gleaming summer coats of the animals are a rich brown. The massive antlers of the bucks arch to the skies.

Even the does have recovered from the ordeal of bearing and nursing the young. They are sleek again and, if not eager, at least passively ready for the October days when the rut takes place. The does also are carrying antlers, and though these are only little spikes compared with those of the bucks, they are interesting because the doe caribou are the only female members of the whole North American deer tribe equipped with antlers.

The rut is a time of fantastic sights and sounds. The great angry bucks engage in constant battle, whether or not a prize awaits the victor. These battles go on incessantly through daylight and through darkness and at times the crash of horn on horn is so continuous and loud that sleep becomes impossible for a man camped near the rutting herds.

Yet the battles are mostly sound and fury. The tremendous sweep of antlers that dwarf their bearers are of little use as dueling weapons, and usually the only damage to the contestants is to the loser's pride. There is of course the constant and macabre danger of the two sets of antlers locking, and it is not rare to find the skeletons of such combatants still locked in mutual death.

For a few weeks the winning bucks take over, and defend the herds of does. But when the urgent drive of their loins is quite exhausted, the older bucks leave the harems and go back to their own segregated lives.

Until the first fall of winter snow the northward drift continues. But on a certain day, winter gives its brief warning before it roars down out of the darkening arctic and the coming of the first snow fills the deer with panic.

A frenzy seizes them and they turn as one animal, coalesce into immense frantic herds, and pound toward the south again. Herds run into herds until the concentration is so complete that all the animals throughout the land may be together in one single mighty wave which plunges wildly down upon the shelter of the southern forests.

In the fall of 1947, I met that panic-stricken wave of fleeing deer. One day the country stretched endlessly northward and was empty of all motion, save where a raven soared in lazy circles against a faded sky. But with the following dawn the land came alive. From a high hill beside the river I could see nothing but the backs of deer. The river seethed with the multitudes swimming its rapid width, and the clicking of the countless feet was more persistent than the cries of crickets on a warm summer evening in the South. But three days later that same land was dead again. A single wolf, following leisurely over the corroded muskeg, was all that moved upon the plains.

The winter Barrens seem empty of all living things, but there are still a few isolated little herds of deer, widely dispersed, sheltering in the islands of scrub spruce on the white plains. These deer are so few that their presence often remains unnoticed except by those white shadows which are the foxes and the wolves. Cut off from the forest herds by the arrival of full winter, the isolated ones find a precarious living in the Barrens by digging for lichens through the snow. It is no easy life, for the drifts are sometimes many feet in thickness and packed by the winds to the consistency of wood. Nevertheless, the dangers they face are as nothing to the dangers which beset the main herds sheltering inside the timber line.

I once met an old white man who had trapped for many years by the lakes in the wooded country of Northern Manitoba where many of the great herds winter. On an October day he took me to look at the narrow neck connecting his lake with an adjoining one. The ice was clear and free of snow and as I looked downward I could see that the floor of the narrows consisted of a chaotic tangle of bones that seemed to reach within inches of the surface. The antlers alone, in that vast boneyard, could have been counted only in the tens of thousands, and the deer that had contributed their bones to the charnel collection must have totaled many times that number.

After I had seen the narrows the old man told me the story of the days when he first built his cabin near the lake. In those days the deer, arriving from the North, were funneled by two parallel lines of hills into the narrow channel where the boneyard lies. He told me that the press of deer was sometimes so great that fawns were swept off their feet and crushed by the animals around them. He told me that this solid river of deer flowed for as much as two weeks without a slackening of the pressure. Perhaps he exaggerated, for an old man's memory is often greener than the event. And yet there were the bones under the ice.

I asked about the channel cemetery, and he went on to tell me how it came about. He spoke of how the *Idthen Eldeli* Indians—Eaters of Deer, their name means—came every fall to the narrows between the lakes, and each man brought with him at least a case of ammunition for his .30-30 rifle. The Indians remained until the ammunition failed or until the deer were past. Those that *did* pass. By the time the Indians were gone, the new ice of the narrows and the lakes was creaking with the weight of the dead deer that pressed it down.

In the spring the ice dropped its weight of bodies into the deep water, and most of those deer were untouched by man except for the bullet holes which scarred their carcasses and except that all had their tongues removed for a reason that I speak of later. In the course of six decades the deep channel became so clogged with bones that a canoe could not safely be paddled through it.

Now, in the fall, only a trickle of the great rivers of the deer flow past that place. The deer have not changed their routes—they have simply gone. And the rifles that destroyed the deer also destroyed the Indians who held the rifles, as surely as if men had turned the muzzles on themselves. For not even those immense herds could withstand the slaughter they were subjected to, and as the deer's ranks thinned, so were the ranks of the Idthen Eldeli thinned by the meat starvation which was the aftermath of the great slaughter.

It is almost the same tale throughout the entire wooded winter range of the deer. At Reindeer Lake, in the late thirties, the annual kill of deer was somewhere in the vicinity of fifty thousand animals. Now there are not that many living deer in all the Reindeer Lake district and in all the lands about the great lake that was named for them. In a little while the name will be an empty thing and men will forget why that name was given to the lake.

Still, no one but a fool will blame the Idthen people. Theirs was always a hard and dangerous life. Always the deer were their sole bulwark against starvation and oblivion. Through the long winters, the deer alone made existence in the thin forests possible for these Indians, even as the deer alone made life possible for the Eskimos in the Barrens. Both races were, in fact, Peoples of the Deer, and before the coming of white men, both races lived in balance with the animals who gave them life.

But when the trading posts began to spread into the Northern forests the rifle rapidly replaced the old weapons of the people. This was perhaps a good thing while those rifles were single-shot muzzle loaders. But profits from the sale of lead and powder were not high enough, and progress called the people through the voices of the traders. The magazine rifle usurped the scene. And a race of men who had devoted all the centuries of their history to the killing of deer with weapons that were efficient only when used with great skill, and when used unrelentingly, were now presented with a weapon that could destroy without restrictions and without the need of skill.

You have heard all this before. Possibly you heard it in connection with the buffalo and the Southern Plains Indians, but that was a century ago. That was in the time of your father's father. Listen to what I tell you anyway, for I am speaking of what happened in your time, and is still happening.

The trading firms grew wealthy and still grow wealthier. As recently as the 1920's, one outpost of a world-famous trading concern actually encouraged the sale of tremendous quantities of ammunition to the Northern Indians by offering to buy all the deer tongues that were brought in! Many thousands of dried deer tongues passed through that post, while many thousands of carcasses, stripped only of their tongues, remained to rot in the spring thaws. I hardly think it just to lay too great a blame upon the Indians.

The Idthen Eldeli went out to their winter hunting grounds, every hunter carrying a case of shells (a thousand rounds) and often enough they were back at the post before spring for more. The profits mounted pleasantly, so pleasantly that a recent suggestion that the sale of ammunition be limited for the good of the purchasers and of the game was denounced as interference with the liberty of men. It *was* interference, I suppose, interference with the free rights of men to destroy themselves through ignorance.

The slaughter of the deer and the destruction of the Deer People had gone on, is going on, and all that has been done to halt the twin massacres is this: agents of the government have been sent out to tell the survivors of the Idthen Eldeli that they must learn the arts of "conservation." The Idthen People listen to this strange, foreign talk, but in the privacy of their own tents they recall how the white trappers who have encroached upon their lands kill the migrating deer without compunction and without restraint. Then the Idthen People remember that the deer belong to them—to them alone—and have belonged to them for all eternity.

There is right on their side and more than a little truth. I have part of an actual diary kept by a young white trapper on the edge of the Barrens, and this diary was kept with great exactitude, no detail of his daily life being omitted. In the fall of 1939, when the deer came south through this man's territory, he went with his rifle to secure his winter supply of meat for himself, for his dogs, and for trap-bait. The deer that he killed for bait were shot all over his area and simply left lying in the open. No attempt was made to protect them from the many scavengers. Instead the man shot enough deer so that when the scavengers were through, he would still have enough carcasses left to set his traps upon. The part of the diary that I have runs only for five weeks, but it lists 267 deer killed in that period and this particular trapper considers his kill to be conservative. I think the Idthen Eldeli have reason to reject the pious "conservation" talk of the agents who are sent to succor them.

Words alone are sent to halt the slaughter, not only of the deer but also of the People. The few hundred survivors of the Idthen Eldeli, who in 1900 numbered nearly two thousand souls, are to be protected from the folly of white men by the good advice of those set in authority above them. But in a few more years they will need no more advice, and they will no longer be an embarrassment to those who must minister to their needs.

But I should not be fair if I did not speak of the single "constructive" thing the government has done to save the caribou. I have neglected to tell you of the "real culprit" in the destruction of the deer. He is the oldest scapegoat in man's history—the wolf. It is the almost unanimous opinion of white traders, trappers, and "sports" in the North, that the tremendous decrease in the numbers of the deer has come about solely because of the bloodthirsty ravages of that insatiable killer, the arctic wolf. There is no doubt about it. A white trapper who does not kill more than five hundred deer a year himself will go into a perfect paroxysm of fury as he tells you how the wolves are slaughtering the deer by the tens of thousands. He has no proof, of course; but then, who needs proof against the wolf?

The voices of these men make a loud and useful noise. Under cover of the cries set up against the wolf, the real faults lie deeply buried out of the public sight. Government joins the cry, accepts it joyfully, and pays a bounty of twenty-five dollars on the head of each wolf killed. Government is active and the public interest, should it unhappily be aroused to awareness of the situation, is laid to rest again.

Cry wolf, you men of little conscience! Ignore the fact that while there have been deer there have always been wolves, and that until your coming, wolves, men, and deer lived in mutual adjustment with each other for more centuries than we can count. Cry wolf! No one will give you the lie. The wolves cannot answer. The last survivors of the Peoples of the Deer cannot reply.

As for the deer themselves—in the spring, when the first thaws are still to come, the anxious does move northward and the great herds form. They are still great, and when they pass by, the talk of their destruction seems insane. Yet now they pass along one route where once they moved by many mighty roads.

Out on the frozen plains the Ihalmiut wait with famine in their low-domed homes. And they know fear, for they can no longer tell if the remaining herds will pass within reach of their camps or whether they will pass a hundred miles away

and bring no hope to those who starve and die. On the
narrows between the two lakes in the wooded country the
bones of the deer mount upward to the surface of the waters.
And along the frozen rivers of the Barrens, the new rock
graves of men mount upward through the drifts.

VI
Under the Little Hills

Summer, which follows spring so closely that the two are almost one, was upon us before it was possible to travel to the shores of Ootek's Lake and meet the People. I had arranged with Franz to take me there while Hans and the children were to remain at Windy Bay to feed the dogs we left behind, and to care for the camp.

As Franz and I prepared for the journey north, I was excited and at the same time depressed. Much as I wished to meet the Ihalmiut in their own land, the fragmentary glimpses of their lives that I had from Franz had left me with a strong feeling of unease at the prospect of meeting them face to face. I wondered if they would have any conception as to how much of their tragedy they owed to men of my color, and I wondered if, like the northern Indians, they would be a morose and sullen lot, resentful of my presence, suspicious and uncommunicative.

Even if they welcomed me into their homes, I was still afraid of my own reactions. The prospect of seeing and living with a people who knew starvation as intimately as I knew plenty, the idea of seeing with my own eyes this disintegrating remnant of a dying race, left me with a sensation closely akin to fear.

We could not make the journey northward by canoe, for the raging streams which had cut across the Barrens only a few weeks before were now reduced to tiny creeks whose courses were interrupted by jumbled barriers of rock. No major rivers flowed the way we wished to go, and so the water routes were useless to us. Since the only alternative was a trek overland, we prepared to go on foot, as the Ihalmiut do.

But there was a difference. The Ihalmiut travel light, and a man of the People crossing the open plains in summer carries little more than his knife, a pipe and perhaps a spare pair of skin boots called *kamik*. He eats when he finds something to eat. There are usually suckers in the shrunken streams, and these can sometimes be caught with the hands. Or if the suckers are too hard to find, the traveler can take a length of rawhide line and snare the orange-colored ground squirrels on the sandy esker slopes. In early summer there are always eggs, or flightless birds, and if the eggs are nearly at the hatching point, so much the better.

Franz and I, on the other hand, traveled in white man's style. We were accompanied by five dogs and to each dog we fastened a miniature Indian travois—two long thin poles that stretched behind to support a foot-square platform on which we could load nearly thirty pounds of gear that included bedrolls, ammunition, cooking tools and presents of flour and tobacco for the Eskimos. With this equipment we were also able to carry a little tent, and food for the dogs and ourselves: deer meat for them, and flour, tea and baking powder for us. We had more than the bare essentials, but we had to pay a stiff price for them.

Equipped with pack dogs, it took us better than a week to cover the same sixty miles that the Ihalmiut cross in two days and a night. I shall not soon forget the tortures of that march. While the sun shone, the heat was as intense as it is in the tropics, for the clarity of the arctic air does nothing to soften the sun's rays. Yet we were forced to wear sweaters and even caribou skin jackets. The flies did that to us. They rose from the lichens at our feet until they hung like a malevolent mist about us and took on the appearance of a low-lying cloud. *Milugia* (black flies) and *kiktoriak* (mosquitoes) came in such numbers that their presence actually gave me a feeling of physical terror. There was simply no evading them. The bleak Barrens stretched into emptiness on every side, and offered no escape and no surcease. To stop for food was torture and to continue the march in the overwhelming summer heat was worse. At times a kind of insanity would seize us and we would drop everything and run wildly in any direction until we were exhausted. But the pursuing hordes stayed with us and we got nothing from our frantic efforts except a wave of sweat that seemed to attract even more mosquitoes.

From behind our ears, from beneath our chins, a steady dribble of blood matted into our clothing and trapped the insatiable flies until we both wore black collars composed of their struggling bodies. The flies worked down under our shirts until our belts stopped them. Then they fed about our waists until the clothing stuck to us with drying blood.

The land we were passing over offered no easy routes to compensate for the agonies the flies inflicted upon us. It was rolling country, and across our path ran a succession of mounding hills whose sides and crests were strewn with angular rocks and with broken fragments filling the interstices between the bigger boulders. On these our boots were cut and split and our feet bruised until it was agony to walk at all. But at that the hills were better walking than the broad wet valleys which lay in between.

Each valley had its own stream flowing down its center. Though those streams were often less than five feet in width, they seemed to be never less than five feet in depth. The valley floors were one continuous mattress of wet moss into which we sank up to our knees until our feet found the perpetual ice that lay underneath. Wading and stumbling through the icy waters of the muskegs, floundering across streams or around the countless ponds (all of whose banks were undercut and offered no gradual descent), we would become numbed from the waist down, while our upper bodies were bathed in sweat. If, as happened for three solid days, it rained, then we lived a sodden nightmare as we crossed those endless bogs.

I am not detailing the conditions of summer travel in order to emphasize my own discomforts but to illustrate the perfectly amazing capacity of the Ihalmiut as travelers. Over sixty miles of such country, the People could move with ease, yes, and with comfort, bridging the distance in less than two days of actual walking. And they, mind you, wore only paper-thin boots of caribou skin on their feet. It is not that they are naturally impervious to discomfort, but simply that they have adjusted their physical reactions to meet the conditions they must face. They have bridged the barriers of their land not by leveling them, as we would try to do, but by comforming to them. It is like the difference between a sailing vessel and one under power, when you compare an Ihalmio and a white traveler, in the Barrens. The white man, driven by his machine instincts, always lives at odds with his environment; like a motor vessel he bucks the winds and the seas and he is successful only while the intricate apparatus built about him functions perfectly. But the Barrens People are an integral part of *their* environment. Like sailing ships, they learn to move with wind and water; to mold themselves to the rhythm of the elements and so accomplish gently and without strain the things that must be done.

By the time we were in sight of the Little Lakes I was aware of a desperation not too far from madness. I cursed the land and the ephemeral dreams which had brought me to it. I cursed Franz and the poor dogs whose eyes were swollen almost shut by the constant assault of the insatiable flies. I was so tired that I did not greatly care whether or not I survived—if only those bloodthirsty legions of winged horrors would let me die in peace.

On the last day Franz was in the lead, followed by three dogs, while I trailed a half mile behind trying to force my dogs to efforts beyond their powers. I heard Franz call and when I looked ahead I saw three human figures where before there had been only one. Franz stood on the crest of a ridge and beside him were two other men, all three gesticulating and shouting at me down the slope.

The sight of strangers seemed to offer some kind of hope and I abandoned the plodding dogs and ran heavily up the hill, slipping and falling among the boulders. When I reached the crest, Franz and the other two men were sitting cross-legged on the rocks and a little breeze was playing along the ridge to cool them off, and to hold back the flies.

One of the strangers was manipulating a little drill which looked rather like a bow and arrow, with the arrow pointed down into a piece of wood upon the ground, while the bow, with its string wound twice around the arrow's shank, was being pushed back and forth parallel to the ground. From the spinning tip of the drill rose a little curl of yellow smoke and I realized that the fur-clad man was making fire.

Our matches had long since been ruined when the top of the can in which they were carried came off during a river crossing. For three days we had had neither a smoke nor a mug of tea—two things that just barely make life endurable for white men in the Barrens. Now I stood panting on the hill and watched an Eskimo casually producing fire as our distant ancestors had produced it in their time. The man looked up at me and smiled, a transfiguring smile which spread like the light of fire itself over his face.

Franz motioned me to sit down while he got out the pail and the packet of sodden tea. Now the second Eskimo, a short and solid figure of a man, stepped forward, took the pail and with a broad grin ran down the slope to fetch us water from a tundra pool. Franz nodded his head after the water-getter.

"Ohoto," he said. "One of the best of them. And this one over here is Hekwaw, the biggest hunter of the bunch."

It was again a succinct introduction, typical of Franz. It was so brief because from his long contact with the People he had come to see them with straight eyes and could not understand how weird and curious they would appear to me, who saw them with the oblique gaze of a man of civilized experience.

However, if Franz would tell me no more than their names, I could at least appraise them for myself. Both were dressed in *holiktuk*—parkas—of autumn deerskin with the fur side turned out. The parka of Hekwaw, the firemaker, was decorated with insets of pure white fur about the shoulders and by a fringe of thin strips of hide around the bottom edge. Ohoto's was even more dressy, for it had a bead-embroidered neck and cuffs. But despite the beads and insets, the general appearance of both men was positively scruffy. Great patches of hair were worn off the garments and rents and tears had been imperfectly mended, evidently by an unpracticed hand. Food juices and fat drippings had matted the thick hair that remained, the dirt from unidentifiable sources had caked broad patches of the fur.

Below these heavy parkas, which the two men were wearing next to their skins, were short fur trousers called *kaillik*, and these were met, above the knee, by the yellow translucent tops of the skin boots.

My first reaction as I saw and smelled these men was one of revulsion. They seemed foul to me and I felt the instinctive surge of white man's ego as I wondered why the devil they couldn't find clean clothes to wear. That was, of course, the superficial thought of one who had no knowledge, but it typifies the conclusions drawn by most white men, particularly missionaries, when they view the "savage in his abhorrent state of nature."

But on that summer day in the Barrens I wasn't so interested in dress as it may seem. My curious glance at the men's clothing was perfunctory, for I was fascinated by the men themselves.

Hekwaw—the Bear, the others called him—was a mountain of a man, but a scaled-down mountain. His muscles bulged and flowed under the loose sleeves of his old parka and the rhythm of the spinning fire drill was reflected in the pulse of tendons in his short and massive neck. Sweat beaded up steadily under his lank black hair, then growing into drops it rolled down the oblique slant of his low forehead, ran along the deep seams of his skin until it found an outlet and, by-passing the broad planes about his half-hidden eyes, fell clear from the sprawling nostrils of his flattened nose. His broad and sensuous mouth with its wide, swollen lips worked in the same rhythm as the drill, and the half-dozen grizzled hairs that were his beard wagged to the same quick tempo.

It was a parody of a face, a contorted parody which was meant for comedy but which had a wild essential quality that restrained my desire to laugh. There was a deep intelligence where one might expect to see only brute instinct, and there was humor and good nature that belied the weathered hide crinkling, apelike, on the brow and on the flat-planed cheeks.

Hekwaw removed the drill and shook a little pinch of smoldering ash from the fire board onto a pile of dry and brittle moss. Then he knelt before it and his cheeks swelled while his eyes disappeared altogether under their taut folds of skin. He blew, and the fire caught, giving birth to a minute greenish flame.

Ohoto returned with the water and with a great armful of green willow twigs, none bigger in circumference than a lead pencil. Franz took our precious "tea-stick" from one of the dog's packs and jammed it into the moss so that the pail hung suspended from it over the tiny fire. And the day was so brilliant that the sun obscured the flames and only a twist of smoke from the green wood showed that the water was slowly being brought to the boil.

Now I had opportunity to see Ohoto. His was a young face, still rounded and without the crevassed wrinkling of old Hekwaw's. His hair had been roughly cut so that it hung like the uncouth tonsure of some pagan priest, and it was as coarse as the hair of the deer. The cut hair disclosed a high, broad forehead and the eyes below it had not yet retreated into caves to escape the glare of winter snows. They were black and very bright, with the alert curiosity of a muskrat. Ohoto had an empty stone pipe clenched between his immense and regular white teeth, and I was not too slow to take the hint. I pulled out a bit of plug, damp and covered with debris, and when Ohoto saw it, he beamed broadly.

Now I forgot the discomforts and despair of the long trek. At last I was amongst the People, in the heart of their own land. And it was evident that at least some of my forebodings had been groundless.

The tea pail boiled over and the tiny fire hissed feebly and died. Franz flung a handful of leaves into the pot and while they steeped I relaxed on the fragile reindeer mosses below the crest of the high ridge. For the moment I was free of the blindness which had been mine while we had been forced to struggle so hard against the unmerciful antagonism of the land. I was free to look out over the summer plains and for the first time to feel something of their beauty, and begin to understand the libel that is perpetrated by that name—the Barrenlands.

In winter perhaps the name has validity, and at all times of the year it has validity for those whose minds have hardened over visions of great forests or neatly cultivated fields. Even after two years in the land, I too have often found myself using the word, and meaning it.

Staring out over the limitless expanse I at first saw only a rolling world of faded brown, shot through with streaks and whorls of yellow greens, for when I tried to see it all, the individual colors merged into anonymity. It *was* a barren sight, and yet that desert face concealed a beauty that rose from a thousand sources, under the white sun. The deep chocolate bogs, laden with rich sepia dyes that stain the streams and pools, were bounded by wide swales of emerald sedges and tall grass. On the sweeping slopes that rose above these verdant meadows, the dark and glossy greens of dwarf birch scrub formed amorphous patches of somber vitality that were illuminated by broad spaces where the brilliance of ten million minute flowers drew to themselves small butterflies as gorgeous as any in the world. Even on the shattered ridges that are given over to the rocks, the creeping lichens suffused the gray stone with a wash of pastel tints ranging from scarlet through the spectrum into velvet rosettes of perfect black. There was no lack of color rising from living things—but it is only that the eye beholds too much in this land that has no roof and no containing walls. The colors flow together and are lost in distance that the eye cannot embrace. And so we only see the barrenness that follows when beauty flows too thinly into the sponge of an illimitable space.

These were the living colors that I saw upon the land, but there was much else to see as well. The lakes beneath us were quite uncountable, a meaningless jumble, looking like the shattered fragments of a great mirror. Between the shining shards of water were the Little Hills, low formless ridges whose slopes seen from the distance were gray-green with lichens, and whose crests were mottled with black rock. To the horizon on the north, the fading glint of lakelets caught the sun and glittered like dew upon brown grass. I knew that somewhere in that maze must lie the twisted course of Innuit Ku, River of Men, but for the life of me I could not distinguish it in the aquatic puzzle spread out below.

While I stared, Ohoto came over and squatted on his hams beside me, also looking out over the land—his land. I lowered the glasses. He grinned again, and, in the grand manner of a small townsman showing his city friend the sights, he began to point out the things of interest.

It did not matter that he could not speak my language, nor I his. Ohoto had the power of expression without words. There was a directness that made his gesticulations seem as clear as printed English. Now he stretched his arm toward a rather large lake that lay only a few miles to the north, and said, "Ootek Kumanik!"

Looking with my glasses, I could see three little grayish pimples by the shores of Ootek's Lake and as I strained my eyes I could also see a fine thread of smoke. The tents of the People!

Rapidly Ohoto swung his arm to the north and pointed out the other lakes: Halo Kumanik, Kakumee Kumanik and, lastly, Tingmea Ku, the little Goose River that leads the lakes into the great current of Innuit Ku itself. But I could still make nothing of Innuit Ku. It seemed to be only a string of lakes, set amongst countless other lakes, and lacking all the continuity of a great river. Later, when I traveled on it, I was to marvel at its clear-cut shape and its directness; but seen from the distance it simply blended into the watery chaos and disappeared. It became part of the chameleon shape the Barrens show to all outsiders.

We drank our tea on the crest of the hill, then packed up

and started down into the Ihalmiut land. The two Eskimos led the way, and their bounding agility over the rough rocks would have put a caribou to shame. We followed painfully a long way behind, and at last came to the low shores of Ootek's Lake.

Across the water we could clearly see the three tents, blending so well with the weathered gravel ridge behind that they might have grown from the hills. People and dogs were running aimlessly about amongst the tents and two new fires had been lighted, for the distant vision of the People had shown them that strangers were approaching, and it is mandatory that all strangers must be fed as soon as they arrive.

I was to learn later that the camps of the People were arranged in little groups of two or three tents on the shores of several lakes, for there is not enough willow scrub in the land to support the cooking fires of more than three families at any single spot. Here at Ootek Kumanik were the tents of Hekwaw, Ootek and Ohoto, and a few miles eastward on Halo Kumanik were the tree tents of Halo, Yaha and Miki. On Kakumee Kumanik there were three separate camps, Katelo and Alekahaw having their tents at one spot, Owliktuk and Onekwaw at a second, while the two tents of old Kakumee stood alone on the far side of the lake.

Thus, within a radius of three miles of each other, dwelt all the living People in a land which stretches for five hundred miles from south to north, and three hundred miles from east to west. It was the most ancient camp of the Ihalmiut, and it was also the last. And I was the first outlander to come upon it in all the centuries that tents had stood beside the Little Lakes. Yet if that thought filled me with excitement, the prospect of meeting a white man for the first time in their lives was filling the women and children from the tents ahead with equal excitement.

We rounded the lake and came up toward the camp. Here the foreshore sloping to the lake was not composed of rocks, but almost exclusively of bones. This was an ancient site and the piles of whitened caribou bones had mounted with the years until they had reached staggering proportions, for in the Barrens neither wood nor bone ever seems to rot or pass away. Dogs and the weather had broken up the larger pieces of bone and spread them evenly around until they formed a pavement all about the camp. But neither dogs nor weather had greatly affected the skulls, and these, with their huge anglers, formed a dead forest of white snags. Later on I counted over two hundred skulls within a hundred yards of an Ihalmiut tent, and these represented only a fraction of the total number of beasts whose remains lay in that place, for only the heads of kills made close at hand are ever brought to camp.

The three tents stood on a sloping ledge where they would catch whatever breeze might blow, for the breeze serves as the sole protection from the flies. Near each tent was a rough stone hearth and beside each fire a tremendous mound of willow twigs. These were, of course, quite green and the little fires were giving out great rolling coils of smoke. On the nearest fireplace was a huge iron pot looking ridiculously like the pots that cannibals seem to favor in our magazine cartoons.

As for the tents themselves, each was a cone about fifteen feet in diameter at its base and perhaps ten feet high. They were patchwork affairs composed of roughly scraped deer hides hung on a wooden frame. The hides had been stitched together while they were still green and, as they dried, the seams had pulled apart so that broad cracks outlined the position of each hide. Around the bottom of the tent a ring of boulders acted as an anchor. In that land you do not drive wooden pegs, even if you have them, for if the rocks did not prevent you, then the perpetual frost which often lies only a few inches below the surface of the ground would shatter the peg before it got a grip. The doorways faced the north, the direction from which the returning deer would come. The doors themselves were made of single hides, untanned, and dried to the hardness of wood.

In a way the Ihalmiut camp seemed only to accentuate the apparent desolation and emptiness of the arctic plains, and yet in the immediate vicinity of the tents was this little pocket of life in the center of the human vacuum that otherwise possessed the Barrens. We felt that we could breathe easily here, for we were no longer entirely alone, though I was still a little afraid of our reception.

It was a foolish fear. Hekwaw and Ohoto had run on ahead, shouting loudly as they went, but their warning was superfluous, for every man, woman, and child was out about the fires, driven to a kind of ecstatic fury by the approach of strangers. One old woman, bent and beaten as if by the rocks of the land, frenziedly blew at the coals of a fire and heaped fresh twigs upon it until she smothered it completely. Ootek's wife, Howmik, was wrestling with the hindquarters of a deer, still dripping wet, which she had hauled out of the cold storage of the frigid lake for supper. Between snatching furtive glances at us and trying to cut off chunks of meat with her curved *ulu*, or woman's knife, she was in imminent danger of slicing off her fingers too. Her wooden hair ornaments swung and jumped like live things as she hurried, and her child, Kalak, who lived in the back of her parka, screamed with pleasure as he batted at her flying braids.

Even the dogs caught the excitement. Three pups simultaneously began to chase their tails while a pair of older dogs joined noisy battle. Children hustled among the dogs, kicking them lightly in their exposed bellies either to drive them off, or just to have something to do as we approached.

Franz and I stopped about a hundred yards short of the nearest tent and the three men, Ootek, Hekwaw and Ohoto, came out to welcome us formally into their homes. Ohoto and Hekwaw acted as if they were meeting us for the first time. They were very correct and very solemn as they gravely touched our finger tips. Then, with the formal greeting over, Ootek produced a stone pipe, loaded with *atamojak*—the dried leaves of a low, bushy plant which make an inadequate substitute for tobacco—and offered me a smoke. Together we walked to Ootek's tent while the women and children ceased their frenetic labors and watched us with unconcealed anticipation. We had been welcomed formally, so that it was now good manners to give way to curiosity, a thing one must not do until a visitor is settled, lest you embarrass him thereby.

All the children, women and old people from the entire camp crowded closely into Ootek's tent behind us, and collectively they produced an overpowering odor—which, however, was canceled out by the obvious good nature and good feeling which also emanated from these People.

Ootek bade us sit down on the sleeping platform, and while his wife was organizing the other women in preparation for a feast, I had a good look at this home of the Ihalmiut. The tent was not even vaguely weather tight. Great streaks of sky showed along the joints between the skins. Under those portions of the tent which were more or less whole were the belongings of the family, and these possessions were simple almost to the point of nonexistence.

Along one half of the enclosed circle was the low sleeping bench of willow twigs and lichens, covered with a haphazard mattress of tanned deer hides. This was the communal bed where the entire family slept together under a robe or two of softened skins. The rest of the floor space was given over to an amazing litter of half-eaten, ready-to-be-eaten and never-to-be-eaten bits of caribou. I saw an entire boiled head that had been pretty well chewed over, and a pile of leg bones which had been cracked for marrow and then boiled to extract the last precious drop of oil. On one side of the tent was a more or less complete brisket, with skin attached, of a deer that obviously should have been eaten long ago. Later I discovered this was a sort of snack bar where hungry visitors could slice off a bit of raw, but well tenderized, meat while waiting for mealtime.

Around the inner surface of the tent, suspended from the dozen precious poles, were the odd bits of clothing not required for the moment. A few pairs of *kamik*, stiff and dry and half transparent, waited for their owners' feet. Nearby lay a couple of inner parkas, called *ateegie*, and some children's overalls that are one-piece garments of fawn hide. Pushed under one pole was a huge wad of dried sphagnum moss waiting the needs of the young child Kalak, for diapers are not used in the Barrens, where nature has provided a more efficient sponge.

And that about completed the furnishings of Ootek's tent, except for an ancient wooden chest which held the treasures of the family: the amulet belt of Ootek, the sewing kit of Howmik with its bone needles and hank of caribou sinew thread, half a dozen empty .44-40 brass cartridge cases which someday might ornament the bowls of stone pipes, a bow drill, a musk ox horn comb and some children's toys.

While I was getting my bearing, Franz produced a plug of trade tobacco, which is nearly as vile as the Ihalmiut product, and it went the rounds. I noticed with great interest that Ootek, after filling his pipe with the precious stuff, passed it to his wife so that she might have the first smoke. In fact, she smoked most of it before returning it to Ootek. A small gesture this, but one that I was to find was typical of the consideration and affection with which the Ihalmiut men treated their wives.

There was a tremendous amount of talk while we sat about the tent waiting for supper, most of it between Franz and the three Eskimo men, while the rest listened avidly and interjected comments and bursts of laughter. Franz translated a little of what was being said and the conversation was, as always, mostly about the deer. Where were they? Had we seen any fresh tracks? How long did we think it would be before

Tuktu—the deer—came from the north? It was an engrossing subject and I wanted to be in on it, but only by begging Franz to tell me what was going on could I get the gist at all. I began to get bored after a while, feeling left out, for Franz was soon too interested to waste time translating for me. To occupy myself I got out my notebook and began idly to sketch a caribou. The talk rose and fell about me and with no conscious thought I sketched a pipe in my caribou's mouth and gave the beast a self-satisfied and human leer.

I had not realized that I was being closely watched. Hekwaw, who sat a little behind me, had been peering intently over my shoulder. At first he was baffled, but suddenly the full humor of a caribou that smoked a pipe struck him with the force of a physical blow, and before I knew what was happening, he had rolled off the bench, quite literally, and was in the grip of a first-class attack of hysterics.

Startled, I thought he had gone mad or had had a seizure. Both Franz and I jumped to our feet in real consternation. The little notebook fell face upward on the floor where it was pounced on by Ohoto who took one quick look and burst into wild guffaws. The book was snatched from his hand and passed around the circle of eager faces, and with the rapidity of chain lightning the laughter spread and grew wilder until it engulfed the tent in one insane pandemonium.

Very slowly it dawned on me that this was neither a war dance nor a mass attack of zaniness, but a tribute to my wit. I grinned self-consciously at those about me who were shrieking and weeping with completely uninhibited mirth. Then I rescued my book which was about to disappear out the door in the hands of a howling small child. I looked at my drawing. Oddly enough it struck me, too, as being hilariously funny, and with no regard for propriety I began to bellow with laughter at my own feeble joke. The thing was now quite out of control. Hekwaw had a choking fit and someone hauled him outside for treatment. One old crone lost her balance and fell against the tent. The taut skin burst with a great boom and she sprawled, still shrieking like a demented thing, on the sharp rocks outside.

I began to worry. Really, I knew I couldn't have been as funny as all that. But mass hysteria had seized the People, and nothing seemed capable of stopping it. Nothing, that is, except food.

Howmik appeared in the doorway, looking properly curious and bearing a big wooden tray heaped high with steaming chunks of deer meat. The steam struck the roisterers and as if by magic the rich aroma quelled their mirth. Hekwaw, still a little shaky, came back into the tent, followed by the old woman, and everyone sat down and stared expectantly at the meat tray.

VII
Feast and Famine

I sat down, or rather squatted down, to eat my first meal with the People. Howmik placed the great tray on the floor of the tent and we five men grouped ourselves around it. That tray was a magnificent piece of work, nearly four feet long by two feet wide with upcurved ends and sides. It had been constructed, with what must have been heartbreaking labor, from little planks hand-hewn from the tiny dwarf spruce of the southern Barrens. At least thirty small sections of wood had been meticulously fitted together and bound in place with mortised joints and pegs of deer horn. The seams had then been tightly sewn with sinew so that the whole tray was waterproof.

The tray was magnificent, but its contents were even more impressive. Half a dozen parboiled legs of deer were spread out in a thick gravy which seemed to be composed of equal parts of fat and deer hairs. Bobbing about in the debris were a dozen tongues and, like a cage holding the lesser cuts of meat, there was an entire boiled rib basket of a deer.

There were side dishes too, for Howmik made a trip to a cache outside and returned with a skin sack, full of flakes of dry meat, which she unceremoniously dumped on the cluttered floor beside me. Nor was that all, for Hekwaw's wife fetched a smoking bundle of marrowbones as her contribution to the feast. These had been neatly cracked so that we would have no trouble extracting the succulent marrow.

I was very hungry, yet the sight of this vast array of meat left me a trifle weak. But it was evident that I was the only one to suffer any qualms of stomach. The others were waiting impatiently for me, as the major guest, to make the first move. The etiquette of the situation eluded me. I took my sheath knife and cautiously sawed off a good-sized chunk of leg meat, scraped the encrustation of hairs from it, and cuddled it in my lap since there was nothing else that could serve as a plate.

Now Franz and the three Ihalmiut men tusked in—I use that word advisedly—and Ohoto seized an entire leg. Sucking the gravy from it with appreciative lips, he sank his teeth into the tough muscle while with his left hand he held the joint away from his face, and with his right hand made a quick slash at the meat with his knife. I watched in horrified fascination. The sharp blade no more than cleared the tip of his broad nose, and he made his cut without even bothering to look where it was going. But the nose survived; the mouthful of meat was severed at the joint and was chewed a time or two and quickly swallowed.

Hekwaw seemed to prefer the soup. He dipped his cupped hands in it and then sucked up the greasy fluid with gusty relish, taking time out now and again to chew at a deer's tongue which he dropped back into the soup to keep warm between bites.

It struck me that I was being a little prissy. So I put my knife back in its sheath, took a deep breath and, seizing my meat in both hands, began to gnaw away on it. It was delicious.

Then Ootek, beaming with the pride of a good host, pressed me to try a marrowbone and showed me how to tap it with a little rock so that the long, jelly-like piece of marrow dropped out intact. I know I was in no position to be an epicurean judge, and you can doubt me if you wish when I tell you that I have never tasted anything quite as good as that hot marrow. Fat, but not oily, it did not compare at all with the insipid beef marrow we know. In fact it beggars all description, and it was wonderful!

By this time I had begun to understand why the Ihalmiut parkas were so badly matted, for they were pressed into service as table napkins and as bibs. A steady stream of juice and gravy trickled from Hekwaw's massive chin and was absorbed by the fur of his *holiktuk*. Try as I might, I couldn't entirely restrain a minor stream that was quickly saturating my flannel shirt. After a while I thought, "The devil with it!" and gave up any efforts to divert the flood.

Howmik, who seemed to be constantly on the run, now reappeared lugging the great iron cooking pot I had seen outside. Only it was no longer filled with meat. The dinner having been cooked, the pot was now doing duty as a tea "billy," without benefit of an intervening washing. We supplied the tea, of course, and the canny Ihalmiut had sought out the biggest vessel they owned to brew it in. Had there been a bathtub handy the tea would have been brewed in it, for if the People have one uncontrollable vice, it is tea drinking.

That tea was blacker and solider than any I have ever seen and it was also fortified with the inevitable scum of deer hair and with odd bits of meat. But it was popular enough. Ootek, who is a rather little man, filled and drank three pint mugs of it, stopping only for a burp or two between mugfuls. Then he ate a tongue and drank three more pint mugs of tea.

Everyone else was just as thirsty and the big pot only lasted about twenty minutes before it was sent back for a refill, with the old tea leaves left in it to help strengthen the new brew.

Naturally such a tremendous fluid intake had its inevitable results and the dinner guests were constantly leaping to their feet and dashing out behind the tent—all save Hekwaw, who was too old and dignified a man to dash on such a trivial errand. He solved the problem by making use of a large can standing near the bed. He simply reached for it when it was needed. As it grew full—and it did frequently—his elderly wife removed and emptied it.

It wasn't long before I was too full to tackle even one more marrowbone. Franz felt the same, but the other men continued their attack on the heaping mound of meat until it was all gone, to the last drop of gravy. Then while they sat back and burped with prolonged fervor, Howmik took the tray away, refilled it, and the women had their meal.

That was my first dinner with the Eskimos but not, as may have seemed inevitable, my last. Five times each day we sat down to a new meal, and in between we had light lunches. While there is food in the Ihalmiut camps, five meals a day is considered barely adequate, though on the trail a man must manage to subsist on three.

The cooking varied somewhat, but the food did not. The rule was meat at every meal and nothing else but meat, unless you could count a few well-rotted duck eggs which served as appetizers. To satisfy my curiosity I tried to estimate the quantity of meat Hekwaw put away each day. I discovered he could handle ten to fifteen pounds when he was really hungry—though otherwise he probably subsisted on somewhat less.

This tremendous intake of protein probably explains the Eskimo thirst for tea or, if no tea is available, for water. The toxic wastes from such quantities of meat would strain the best of human kidneys, and only by drinking several gallons of fluid every day can the Ihalmiut manage to adjust to their amazing diet. Their bodies seem to have undergone some physical modifications as well, for when you see an Ihalmiut naked—as a visitor sees them every night—you notice that their body thickness, back to front, looks as great as their body width, both measurements taken at the waist. This typical shape presumably results from the enlarged liver needed both to store glycogen against lean periods and to deal with the completely protein diet. It most certainly is not a sedentary "pot."

The words "food" and "deer" are practically synonymous throughout the Barrenlands, but though there is a certain monotony in the choice of food, there are many ways of preparing it. First there is the natural style, and I have eaten my meat this way and found no complaint with it, except perhaps that raw meat is singularly tasteless. If the Ihalmiut hunter shoots a deer for food when he is on a trip far from the camps, he seldom bothers to go to the trouble of building a fire. Usually his first act is to cut off the lower legs of the deer, strip away the meat, and crack the bones for marrow. Marrow is fat, and an eternal craving for fat is part of the price of living on an all-meat diet.

With the marrow disposed of, the hunter may slit the animal's throat and catch a cup of blood, for while the People do not know the use of salt, they do seem to crave it and to satisfy their craving with blood, where the saline concentration is very high.

Now having satisfied some of his specific cravings, the hungry hunter slices through the flank of the beast and carefully picks off the bits of suet clinging to the entrails. If he is still hungry—and he usually is—the hunter may also cut off part of the brisket if the animal is fat. Before leaving the carcass he takes out the tongue and sometimes the kidneys, and these he carries with him until he can find time and fuel to light a fire.

All the parts that I have so far mentioned can be eaten cooked, of course, and when it is possible they will be cooked, for the Ihalmiut do not eat raw meat from choice. When only an open fire is available, cooking methods are delightfully simple. The roast is simply shoved into the coals and left there until it is well charred on the outside. Pulled out and scraped, the inner core is found to be well cooked to a depth of an inch or so, and this part is eaten, then the roast is again pushed into the fire and the process repeated until the bone itself is reached and the hot marrow is ready for extraction.

When meat is cooked at camp it is usually boiled, if fuel permits, for the soup is greatly loved by everyone. Originally, and not so many years ago, the Ihalmiut used great square-cut stone pots made of a kind of soapstone. These were filled with water and chunks of meat, then hot pebbles were added to the water to bring it to a boil. It was a slow chore, and parboiling was usually chore enough, but now iron pots have been obtained in trade from the coastal Eskimos, and boiling meat is easier than it once was.

Amongst the special boiled delicacies I must mention fawn's head. Any deer head is good when boiled, but the heads of fawns are best of all. They are sometimes skinned before cooking, more often not, but the meat from them is the most delicious from the animal and the fat behind the eye is the best part of the head. Incidentally, when occasional fish are speared in summer, the boiled heads are again considered to be the choicest part.

Nearly all of the caribou is eaten, one way or another. But as you may have noticed, the steaks and roasts that we prefer don't often appear on the Ihalmiut menu. Usually the dogs get the rumps and thighs, for these parts of the caribou seem to be lacking in the specific nutriments that a meat-eating man requires. The Ihalmiut believe that only by eating all parts of the deer can they achieve a satisfactory diet. So the heart, kidneys, intestines, liver and other organs are greatly esteemed and often eaten.

There is a third way of using deer meat, and this is by preparing *nipku*, or dried meat. The Ihalmiut make this dish because it is a variation of an otherwise monotonous diet and because it can be easily stored to tide them over times when the deer are not about. Nipku is made by slicing muscle tissue paper-thin, then spreading it to dry on willow bushes near the camps. It looks, and tastes, like cardboard sparsely sprinkled with icing sugar, and it is as tough as blazes, but an excellent trail food since it equals five times its weight in fresh meat. I liked nipku, finding it as good as most Ihalmiut dishes, though I must admit to a certain indignation when Ohoto gave me a bag of it that was already in the possession of a lively collection of fly maggots.

Undoubtedly the most important item of Ihalmiut food is fat. Amongst the coastal Eskimos the supply of fat is limited only by the number of sea mammals that are killed, and blubber, that grossly overworked arctic word, is obtained in immense quantities from seals, walrus, narwhals and other aquatic mammals who build thick blankets of fat as an insulation against the cold of the arctic seas. The coastal people have so much fat and oil available that they can meet all their dietary needs and have enough left over to heat and light their igloos, and to cook upon. Well, they are lucky. The inland people of the plains must depend for fats on what they can obtain from the deer, and the caribou is no substitute for a seal as a source of oil.

In the fall of the year, just before the rutting season for the bucks and just after for the does, the deer are in their best physical condition and this is the only time of the entire year that fat can be obtained from them in any quantity. Buck deer, killed in the autumn, may carry thirty pounds of pure white suet under their hides, and though this sounds like a lot, when it is rendered down it gives a much smaller quantity. It takes a great many fat buck deer to equal one seal in the production of oils.

During the fall hunt the Ihalmiut must collect sufficient fat to meet the year's needs, but there is never enough to provide fuel, food, and heat together. As a result the winter igloos generally remain entirely unheated, and almost without artificial light during the interminable winter darkness. Yet the People manage to survive temperatures of fifty degrees below zero in their winter homes because fat *is* being burned —within their bodies. Each man is his own furnace, and as long as there are enough blocks of deer fat to last until spring, the People manage to stay alive under conditions which seem completely inimical to the maintenance of human life. Enough fat is the answer, and the sole answer, to winter survival in the Barrens.

The importance of fat as a fuel is, however, only part of the story. Even in summer, when the problem is to stay cool, fat remains absolutely essential to the well-being of the People. I had its importance demonstrated to me during one long canoe trip Franz and I took. We were short of supplies —in fact we were completely out of them except for a pound of tea, half a pound of lard, and some ammunition. So we lived by the rifle, and we lived on deer.

It was late summer then and the deer were extraordinarily thin as a result of long months of persecution by the flies, and so our diet consisted almost entirely of lean meat. For the first few days I made out very well on three meals of lean meat a day, but before the end of the week I was smitten with an illness which for want of a better name I called *mal de caribou*. It was an unpleasant illness to have during a canoe voyage. The river was fast and filled with rapids, but nevertheless I had to go ashore at frequent intervals, whether we were in "white water" or not. And I had to expose myself so often to the insatiable flies that it became painful for me to sit down.

But persistent diarrhea was only a part of the effect of *mal de caribou*. I was filled with a sick lassitude, an increasing loss of will to work that made me quite useless in the canoe. I began to get really worried. Memories of dysentery in Sicily came uneasily to mind and the thought that the nearest medical aid was three hundred miles away did not bring me much comfort.

Then Franz turned physician. One evening he took our half-pound of precious lard, melted it in a frying pan, and, when it was lukewarm and not yet congealed, he ordered me to drink it.

Strangely, I was greedy for it, though the thought of tepid lard nauseates me now. I drank a lot of it, then went to bed; and by morning I was completely recovered. This sounds like a shock cure, but in fact I was suffering from a deficiency of fat and did not realize it.

Exactly what the physiological effect of fat, apart from its straight nutrition value, is on the metabolism of a meat-eater is something I do not know. But I do know that man cannot function on lean meat alone. Perhaps there is an enzyme in fat which acts on lean meat in the digestive tract;

perhaps certain essential vitamins are present in the fat. Whatever the factor may be, it is clear that fat provides not only the large amount of calories essential to winter survival in the arctic, but also some essential substance without which a meat diet is impossible.

Of course the Ihalmiut have always been aware of this, and it is their custom, winter or summer, to eat not less than a mouthful of fat for every three of lean meat. This is the ideal proportion, but it is not always possible to maintain it, and when fat becomes scarce the Ihalmiut appear most susceptible to disease and show other symptoms of a greatly lowered resistance.

So the point I wish to make is that fat is not just a cold weather fuel to the Eskimos, but is a vitally essential part of their everyday diet. And this is a point which seems to have escaped the notice of those administrators who are entrusted with the well-being of the Northern natives. At any rate, the current trend in the arctic is to bring about the transition from native foods, and by that I mean animal or protein or fat foods, to the prepared foods of the white man which are largely composed of starch. I will have something to say about the appalling results of this policy later in this chapter.

Probably the thought has occurred to you that the Barrens ought to be able to provide some variety from the eternal diet of deer meat. Perhaps the total reliance of the Ihalmiut on the deer may seem foolish, particularly when death by starvation can result from this limited dependence.

Well, the Barrens are not given over to the deer alone. In the winter, great numbers of arctic hares move down from the northern fringes of the Barrens, and they make delicious and tender food. Then there are the ptarmigan, whose numbers are so great in spring and fall that the flocks may cover the hills like snow. The rivers and lakes are literally filled with whitefish, trout, grayling and suckers and these can be netted in quantity during the summer. Oddly enough the Ihalmiut have no nets, and have never used them, though they spear the occasional fish with the ingenious spear that is common to most Eskimo cultures.

With their usual acumen the authorities have seized upon this evidence of the remissness of the primitive mind. Obviously, they think, the ignorant natives must be unaware of the untouched reservoirs of food in the lakes and rivers, if they are so backward that they have not even learned to make and to use nets. So the authorities would supply nets, and thereby solve the starvation problem in the Barrens.

This plan was brilliantly reasoned out. On my return to the Barrens in 1948, I was given a large supply of nets to distribute to the Ihalmiut and I was told to instruct the People in their use so that they would never again be faced with a starvation winter.

I took the nets, for it is of no use to argue with men of government, and in due course I gave them to the People and showed them how to use them. The Ihalmiut thanked me, for they are a courteous lot, and they humored me further by borrowing my canoe and learning to set the nets. Certainly I fulfilled my orders and I have no doubt this was a source of satisfaction to the authorities in Ottawa.

However, there were some minor points which had been overlooked by the enthusiastic agents. In the first place the Ihalmiut have kayaks, but no other kind of boat such as the open *umiak* of the coast Eskimos, and it is exceedingly difficult—if not impossible—to set or service a net from a kayak. In the second place it is during the winter and early spring that starvation comes to the People, and the problems of setting nets under ten or twelve feet of fresh-water ice would baffle even the ingenious Ihalmiut.

Yet these physical problems are relatively unimportant. There *was* a reason why the Ihalmiut had never learned to make and to use nets; for they were perfectly well aware of the fish that could be had for the taking. But they also knew that the results of fishing on a large scale are simply not the kind of results that can support human life in the Barrens. It all comes back again to the problem of fat. No inland fish, and this applies equally to hares and ptarmigan, can supply even a fraction of the fat requirements of the People. Fish are fine in summer as a dietary supplement when there is plenty of food in any case. In winter, a prolonged diet of fish would be as disastrous as poison to the People, and starvation in the form of fatal deficiencies would smite those whose bellies are distended with fish as violently as it smites those whose bellies are empty. Later I will tell you of a race of Northern natives who *were* weaned over from deer meat to fish. It is evident that the tragedy which resulted did not make its mark upon the official minds of men in high quarters.

The deer must feed the People, and the deer alone can give the People life. In the years to come the Ihalmiut will eat deer meat as they have done for countless centuries and as their bodies demand that they continue to do. If, and when, the time comes that there are no more deer, then the last Ihalmiut will die in their igloos and the problems that they pose to use as their guardians will not be problems any longer. The fish nets will fray and whiten on the rocks by the shores of the Little Lakes, but there will be none to use them. They will remain for a while as symbols of the type of aid that we gave to the People in their extremity.

Now I am going to speak for a while of famine. I want to tell you something of the real but hidden cause of the destruction which has come upon all the Northern natives, Eskimos and Indians, wherever white men have come amongst them. It is not a pretty tale.

Perhaps you have heard of the decimation of the forest Indians, brought about by disease, by lack of adaptability, by inherent laziness and indolence or by other causes. You may have heard of these things but you have never heard the truth, for all of these apparent causes are but manifestations of the real destroyer, which is—starvation.

If you ask about the thousands of Indians and Eskimos who die each year of tuberculosis, if you ask about the measles and smallpox epidemics which in the last two decades have destroyed over one-tenth of the Northern natives, and if you ask whether these people too die of starvation, I will answer that they did.

Let me explain. To begin with, one of the most popular apologies for our failure to preserve the Northern races from destruction has been the theory of "acquired immunities." It is something the natives haven't got—and cannot get—if we believe the propagandists. And yet no medical authority has ever been foolish enough to say that certain races can develop specific immunities to disease while others cannot. The theory that Eskimos and Indians are, and always will be, lacking in the immunities we possess has been used to explain our inability to check the ravages of tuberculosis and the other diseases that yearly take a tremendous toll of the Northern natives. But this idea is as untenable as the theory that Aryans are superior to Semitic peoples. Immunities to disease are acquired. And the ability to acquire them belongs to all men. But if it *were* simply a question of immunities, then the Indians of the Mackenzie River region would long since have acquired all they needed, for disease has been a mighty killer in that land for a century and a half. And yet the children's children of survivors of ancient epidemics still die by the hundred when a plague comes down the river and into the huddled settlements. It looks then as if the "immunities" apologists may be correct—but it only looks that way.

I loathe statistics, but I must quote these to prove my point. The reported death rate from tuberculosis in the Canadian Northwest Territories between 1937 and 1941 was 761 per 100,000 as compared with 50 per 100,000 in the rest of Canada. This figure includes *only* those native deaths examined by a medical officer. There is good reason to believe the true figure should be well over 1000 deaths, since a high proportion of the Northern peoples die, and are buried, without the knowledge of white men. Now tuberculosis has been present in this area for 150 years and yet, oddly enough, the natives seem to have been quite unable to develop a resistance to it.

What has starvation to do with all this? I shall explain with men, instead of figures.

On Reindeer Lake in Northern Manitoba there is a settlement called Brochet. It is the center of the surviving members of the branch of the Chipewyan Indians who call themselves Idthen Eldeli—Eaters of Deer. In 1860 when Brochet was already a well-established trading post there were about 2000 members of the Idthen band and theirs was a peculiar and demanding life. In the winter they lived in tents within the borders of the high arctic forests where the deer also wintered. In spring, when the deer moved out into the great plains, the Idthen people followed after. So the Idthen band annually traveled over a thousand miles through the Barrens, the home of the Ihalmiut.

In the eighteenth century the famous explorer Samuel Hearne journeyed overland across the Barrens from Churchill to Coppermine River with a band of these Indians and he speaks, as do many others, of the almost superhuman endurance and physical capacity of the Idthen people.

In the winter of 1948 when I lived with the Idthen Eldeli at Brochet, they numbered a little over 150 men, women and children who spent the winters on their scanty trap lines, starving through the cold months until they could fish for life along the opening rivers. They no longer followed the deer on the long trek into the Barrens. Instead they followed the deer on the long trek to extinction. They are a passive, beaten, hopeless people who wait miserably for death. They are unclean, weak-bodied, sick caricatures of men, who spend their days in an apathy broken only when utter necessity drives them to make an effort to live a little longer. Also— and despite almost a century of contact with white men— they have acquired no immunities.

It has been nearly one hundred years now since the Idthen Eldeli began to starve. Starvation first came to them when they began to exist on a winter diet which now consists of 80 per cent white flour, with a very little lard and baking powder, and in summer almost nothing but straight fish. The Idthen people now get little of the red meat and white fat of the deer, once their sole food. Three generations have been born and lived—or died—upon a diet of flour bannocks and fish eaten three times a day and washed down with tea. Each of these generations has been weaker and had less "immunity" to disease than the last. Some of the people died from outright hunger, with their bodies shrunken into hard bundles of dry skin, and with bones which showed startlingly clear through the parchment tissues. But most of them died coughing blood, or with festering membranes clogging their throats, or with huge sores upon the surfaces of their thin bodies. They also were the victims of that long starvation.

Before the opening of the trading posts, the People lived, as the Ihalmiut do, upon the deer. After Brochet was established by the Hudson Bay Company as a "meat post" that is, as a point of supply where deer meat could be made into pemmican and sent out onto the prairies where the buffalo had already been destroyed and meat was scarce—the Idthen people began to change their diet.

They were encouraged by the traders to forgo the summer trips out into the Barrens to live with, and on, the deer, and they learned to live instead on fish and on the handouts of flour given them on credit so that they would remain tied in the infamous "debt system" which was, and is, the white man's way of trading with the natives. They were encouraged to slaughter the deer not for their own use but for the meat trade, and on such a scale that the deer inevitably began to follow the buffalo. The Idthen Eldeli were discouraged from eating the meat they killed, for there was no profit in that for the traders. There *was* profit in flour at seventy-five dollars a sack. There was profit in sugar, baking powder, and in an array of useless knickknacks, but there was no profit in the deer as food for the people.

And so today disease, the fatal apathy which prevents men from looking into the uncertain future, and weakness of body which prevents a man from defending himself against the approach of death—these three are present in the land, and they have one name, and the name is starvation.

The Idthen people who have been tricked and bribed into abandoning the gift of the deer are passing quickly from the high forests. Each year the energy of men grows less and the hunters catch less fur. Each year more women cough their life's blood onto the filthy dirt floors of the wooden hogpens which their ancestors would have scorned. In the winter tents, with the subzero cold passing at will through the shoddy cloth of trade clothes instead of being kept out by warm caribou skin garments, the women mix flour and baking powder to feed the children who may live till spring. In the summer the men lift the nets they have been taught to use and the people eat fish each day, and when fall comes they are impotent beings against the night of winter. It is true—such people as these cannot acquire our immunities, for starving bodies have no strength to repulse the onslaughts of disease.

The Idthen people, who are but one of the many tribes in similar condition across the Territories, are dying of starvation.

Nor is it far from the silent campsites of the Idthen Indians to the tent of Ootek, where I sat down to feast upon the meal he set before me, amidst the laughter and strength of people who have not yet reached the poverty of spirit and of mind which is now the birthright of the Idthen Eldeli. The Ihalmiut still have a little way to go, for as yet the starvation they have known is only the direct death of famine and though it has thinned their ranks, the hidden starvation that has come to the Indians has not yet destroyed the hearts of the Ihalmiut. Now that we have made our decision to aid the few surviving inland Eskimos, no doubt it will not be very long before they are brought to the same pass as those other Eaters of the Deer, for then there will be no eaters of the deer, and in a little while, no People of the Deer.

Remember that I am talking in terms of the present, and not of the past. When I was in the forests amongst Indians, I met a doctor who is sent in twice yearly by the authorities, and I spoke to him of the number of Indians who were dying of tuberculosis in that area. He replied by telling me he could do little for them. The hospitals were full and, anyway, the Indians did not seem to respond to treatment. But he pointed out with righteous pride that the government was spending hundreds of thousands of dollars building hospitals to cure the natives of their ailments across the North.

Surely there is but one way to cure a man of the diseases which are the products of three generations of starvation, and that is to feed him. It is so simple an idea that I suppose it cannot possibly have real validity—or else it would have been tried long before this. But it does not greatly matter any more, for soon there will be no mouths to feed. These disintegrating men, contemporary Indians, are not God's creations as the missionaries would insist, but were created at our hands. They will not need great hospitals, for it is quite true after all, they are incapable of building up immunity— against starvation.

VIII
Of Houses and Tongues

During the summer of 1947 I remained at the Little Lakes only long enough to develop my overmastering curiosity about them. Franz had shown increasing impatience as our stay by the Little Lakes lengthened out. Superficially he appeared to be worried about the dogs he had left at Windy Camp, under the care of Hans and the two Eskimo children. But the real reason why he was impatient to leave the Ihalmiut tents was to be found in his poorly concealed anxiety for Kunee, the child he had adopted, and who was all that Franz knew of love.

So I went back with him, over the muskegs and the hills, all the time wishing I had the strength of character to throw in my lot with the People. But the baffling limitation imposed by the barrier of tongues was one I did not think I could surmount alone. As it was, even with Franz's aid as interpreter, it had been hard enough to establish any spoken contact.

We returned to Windy Bay, where Franz received the ecstatic welcome of Kunee and Anoteelik and the stolid welcome of his brother Hans. Things were in a bad state at the cabin. The nets, which should have provided the dogs with plenty of fish, were rotted and torn and had become nearly useless. The dogs were almost starving, and for ten days Franz and I were so occupied in replenishing the supply of dog feed that I had no time to dwell upon my regrets at leaving the camps of the People. Before I could begin to deplore my lost opportunities they were partially restored to me by the arrival of several Eskimos who had come to repay my visit. They built travel camps on the hills near our cabin and succeeding groups of *Innuit* visitors made these camps their home until well into the fall. But again I was denied full opportunity to increase my intimacy with the People, for the last month of summer had to be devoted to accompanying Franz on a six-hundred-mile canoe trip south to Brochet and then back to Windy Bay. This was a matter of urgent necessity since not only was the camp nearly out of food, but Franz still had to dispose of his previous year's fur catch, and bring back his winter stock of supplies.

That long and arduous voyage in an ancient freight canoe is not part of this book, except that at Brochet—the trading settlement on Reindeer Lake—I met a very old white man who had traded on the north edge of the forests where the Ihalmiut were still a great and numerous people. From him I heard stories about those almost forgotten days, and much later I was to hear many of these stories again from the lips of the People themselves. When I first heard them at Brochet they served to inflame further my desire to return to the Barrens, but I already knew I could not realize these desires in 1947. At Brochet I had been given a radio message that came from the distant southlands I had almost forgotten. The message momentarily shattered my dream, for it demanded an early return to distant Toronto. At the same time I was informed that Johnny Bourasso was missing in the Western Barrens. This meant I would have to get out of the plains by my own efforts.

Because Franz could not undertake his homeward journey alone, I returned with him to Windy Cabin, but with the understanding that he would help me to leave the Barrens after our freighting trip was completed.

In late September I reluctantly said good-by to the land and we two traveled east by canoe. Six long weeks later we reached Churchill, where I took the Muskeg Special, southward through the forests. After a few days at Churchill Franz returned by aircraft to Windy Bay, but he was not destined to remain there for long. He had met his father at Churchill and the old man had lifted the exile of his sons. Franz was instructed to close up Windy Cabin as soon as he could and to make his way back, by dog team, to Churchill, where more lucrative work awaited him as a laborer on a construction gang. Franz's father had decided that the rewarding days of trappers and traders in the Barrens were at an end. It was a reasonable conclusion, for he knew the Ihalmiut were doomed, and had perhaps known it for some time. There was no more wealth to be made from the handful of surviving Eskimos, particularly since the market for white fox pelts had slumped to a new low.

By the beginning of the new year the Barrenlands were empty of all intruders, and once again the door of Windy Cabin swung in the wind, and there was no welcome—and no succor—for the Ihalmiut hunters who made their way south to the place of the white men. Franz and his brother had rejoined the family at Churchill, taking with them the two Eskimo children. None of these would ever again return to Nueltin Lake. The white men were done with the land of the River of Men and had fled from it forever. But behind them, in the still depths of the land, there remained the People who could not flee, for there was no haven for them except under rock graves by the shores of the river.

Those whose interests in the land were measured in dollars and cents had abandoned both it and its People. My interest was nothing so tangible, and when the winter of 1947–1948 was near its end I again traveled north, but this time I had a companion. Andrew Lawrie, a student of zoology who shared my restless curiosity, and who had also fallen under the ephemeral spell of the North during an arctic tour with the Canadian Navy, had chosen to accompany me back to the Barrens. It was our ambition to spend a year in the study of Tuktu so that we might be able to provide the data on which an effective conservation plan could be based.

In 1948 there was no sturdy Anson aircraft waiting to help us bridge the space between Churchill and Nueltin Lake. Johnny Bourasso had flown his old plane through the uncertain skies of the North for the last time, and her burned-out fuselage now lay forgotten in the muskegs far to the west. But again John Ingerbritson came to our rescue. Gunnar, one of his sons, had used his airforce training to establish an independent "Airline," operating out of Churchill with one small aircraft. It was in this cramped little plane that Andy and I crossed the void to the west, and I came once again to the half-hidden outline of Windy Cabin, lying under its mantle of drifts.

We arrived much earlier in the season than on my first visit, and winter had not yet begun to show signs of releasing the land to spring. After the plane had left us, Andy and I began to make our way over the ice to the shanty, and it was so cold the frost from my breath prevented me from seeing that this time we were to be met and welcomed at Windy Cabin. Andy caught my arm suddenly and pointed to the snow-shrouded shore, and I saw the dark shape of a man running swiftly toward us.

We waited, and on the glare ice of the bay, with the wind moaning its dirge from the Ghost Hills, we were confronted by the man Ootek. He stood before us and on his gaunt face a smile spread and grew until it could not contain the wild laughter, born of relief, that sprang from his throat. It was indeed a most happy meeting for Ootek. When the three of us had reached the cabin and burrowed through the drifts to its dubious shelter, Ootek explained with signs and gestures that he had come from the Little Hills in the forlorn belief that white men might have returned to Windy Bay. Starvation had driven him to this place, though he knew it was deserted and had been so for much of the winter. A hope, kept alive by old memories, brought him south, and it did not die even when he saw the unmarked snow in front of the cabin. Stubbornly he stayed on for two days without food, and with only the blind hope that help might come from the skies to sustain him. On the third day he had begun his dark journey homeward when he heard the miraculous roar of *Konotaiv* the wings of the white men.

Ootek remained with us only long enough for a meal and to receive some ammunition for his rifle. The forerunners of the deer herds were already in the plains and so, now with shells for his gun, the spring famine was at an end for Ootek. Yet had we not come, or had we come a month later, the evil spring when Kunee and Anoteelik were orphaned would have been repeated. It appeared that the recognition so tardily extended to the Ihalmiut by the government had been only temporary, and had been withdrawn again.

During the next month Andy and I spent most of our time near Windy Bay studying the returning herds of the deer. We were not lonely, since only four days after Ootek left us he returned accompanied by all the men of the Ihalmiut. Those were cheerful and pleasant days, for the Innuit were as delighted to welcome us as if we had been benevolent Gods. Ootek and his fellows could not do enough to show their joy at our arrival. When there was wood or water to get, the Ihalmiut jumped at the opportunity to serve us. They made special hunting trips over the hills to find for us the few rare deer that were fat, and to bring us deer tongues. At night they crowded into the cabin and stayed until we were so exhausted we had politely to pack them off to bed. Hekwaw and Owliktuk had arrived with white fox pelts, and these they gave to us as tokens of friendship, accepting our return gifts with deep gratitude.

Unfortunately all this popularity had its drawbacks. Andy and I were not traders and we had brought with us only sufficient supplies for our own needs. By the time we had also met the urgent needs of the Ihalmiut we were running short of many things including the most precious item of all, ammunition for our .30-30 rifles. We had to become parsimonious with our gifts, and this seemed inexplicable to the Ihalmiut, who were willing and anxious to give us anything and everything they possessed. They believed, not without reason, that white men could call on unlimited sources of supply. I made strenuous efforts to explain that we were not traders and were in effect only poor men endowed with nothing of greater value than big curiosities. But it didn't go over.

The barrier of language which had bothered me the preceding year now seemed even more formidable and frustrating, for it was impossible to convey our explanations in sign language alone. I missed Franz, though his interpreting had always been sketchy and he had never been very willing to act as my tongue with the People. Yet without him I found myself in a growing web of confusion, and it was clear that, as things stood, I could never hope to delve into the memories and minds of the Ihalmiut. Unless I could learn the Ihalmiut tongue I would leave the Barrens in as great ignorance of its People as when I came. But I had been led to believe by "old Northern hands" that learning an Eskimo language entailed many years of hard labor, and I was loath to begin a task that could not come to anything in time to be of service to me. So for a month Andy and I blundered about like deaf men whose eyes could not tell us the things our ears needed to know. Then one day, in complete exasperation at some impasse that had arisen between Ootek and myself, I took the bull by the horns and made it clear to the man that I was damn well going to learn the language of his People.

I don't know quite what I expected his reaction to be. Disinterest, perhaps, or reluctance. Or even worse, the attitude of one who is presented with an infantile demand and who treats it carelessly and without thought.

But I got none of these responses from the Ihalmiut. The

unadorned fact that I, a white man and a stranger, should voluntarily wish to step across the barriers of blood that lay between us, and ask the People to teach me their tongue, instead of expecting them to learn mine—this was the key to their hearts. When they saw that I was anxious to exert myself in trying to understand their way of life, their response was instant, enthusiastic, and almost overwhelming. Both Ootek and Ohoto, who was called in to assist in the task, abruptly ceased to treat me with the usual deference they extend to white strangers. They devoted themselves to the problem I had set them with the strength of fanatics. To begin with, Ootek taught me the meaning of the word *Ihalmiut*. When I had mastered its meaning by the aid of devious drawings executed in sand, Ootek stood Ohoto in one place, then placed me a few feet away to the south. Now he pointed to Ohoto, and repeated "Ihalmiut" over and over again with a remarkable excess of emotion in his voice as he spoke. At last he came over, took me by the arm, and led me to the side of Ohoto. Both men now beamed at me with the anxious expressions of people who hope their acts have been understood, and fortunately I did not disappoint them. I understood. I was no longer a stranger; I was now a man of the Ihalmiut, of the People who dwell under the slopes of the Little Hills.

It was an initiation so informal, so lacking in the dramatic gestures, that for a little while its deep significance was not clear to me. It was some time before I discovered that this simple ceremony of Ootek and Ohoto had not only made me an adopted man of the land, but had also given me a relationship with both men. I became their song-cousin, a difficult relationship to define, but one that is only extended on the most complete and comprehensive basis of friendship. If I wished, I might have shared all things that Ootek and Ohoto possessed, even to their wives, though this honor was not thrust upon me. As a song-cousin I was a counterpart of each man who had adopted me. I was his reflected image, yet cloaked in the full flesh of reality.

Of course, under the law, it was assumed that I would reciprocate to the fullest, and had I been born an *Ihalmio* I would have given that reciprocity without any thought. Yet as a white man I unconsciously refused it to both Ohoto and Ootek times without number, but never did they feel the need to retaliate by withdrawing any of the privileges of the relationship they had so freely extended to me.

As a man of the People it now became a matter of urgent need that I should learn the language. Ootek and Ohoto put their heads together and for the space of two days they discussed the problem from all angles. At last I grew impatient and seized the initiative by asking the names of objects about me, and by acting out verbs. This, though I did not know it, was what they had planned, though they preferred to let me believe I was setting the pace. One or the other and usually both of my two mentors would attend my efforts with such serious concentration that sometimes we all tried too hard, and finished up the pursuit of a simple word by becoming so completely confused that nothing short of an outburst of laughter could destroy the impasse. Nevertheless I learned quickly, so quickly that I thought the tales I had heard of the difficulties of the Eskimo language were, like so many popular misconceptions about the Innuit, absolute nonsense.

In a month's time I was able to make myself understood and I could understand most of what was said to me. I became pretty cocky, and started to consider myself something of a linguist. It was not until nearly a year had gone by that I discovered the true reason for my quick progress.

The secret lay, of course, with Ootek and Ohoto, who, with the co-operation of the rest of the People, had devised a special method of teaching me a language that is, in reality, a most difficult one. They had approached the problem with great acumen, first reasoning that a white man probably possesses a rather inferior brain which cannot be expected to cope with the full-blown intricacies of the language. They made a plan and, apparently letting me lead the way, they actually led me by a shortcut invented solely for my personal use.

When I asked the name of an object, they would give me a straightforward answer not burdened with detailed explanations. Deer, for instance, was simply *Tuktu*, an easy word to remember and one I could include in fairly complex sentences without much trouble. But I did not know that, properly, it has an exceedingly limited usage. It means only deer as an entity, in the largest sense. For specific reference to a deer, as to a two-year-old buck, there is one special word which accurately defines it. Thus it happens that there are dozens of words in the tongue of the Ihalmiut which mean "deer" in some specialized sense. Ootek wisely refrained from overloading my inadequate memory with such a superabundance of shades of one meaning, and he not only allowed me to use the one generic term in all possible cases where I needed to speak of the deer, but the People, in their turn, refrained from using any of the other specific words in their conversations with me.

It was the same with most nouns. The People taught me a root word, shorn of the multitudinous suffixes and prefixes which give their language a flexibility and a delicate shading of meaning that is probably unsurpassed by any tongue spoken today. In effect, they developed a specialized "basic" Eskimo entirely for my use, and they themselves learned to use it, not only when talking to me, but when talking to each other within my hearing. The development of a pidgin tongue is not new, of course. But with most races these bastard languages come into being over many decades of gradual growth, and no conscious effort is involved. But the Ihalmiut deliberately set out to develop such a tongue. It was planned, carefully taught, and spoken solely for the benefit of one man, and he a stranger to the land.

So I learned an Innuit vocabulary, and I was tirelessly drilled by Ohoto and Ootek until I mastered all the subtle sounds of their words. I found I was able to speak about quite abstract subjects, and incidentally give the lie to those who say that these "natives" are unable to think, or express themselves, in abstract terms. I was pretty proud of my prowess, until the truth came out.

A year after I became an Ihalmio, I had an opportunity to talk with a coastal Eskimo near Churchill. Nonchalantly and with perfect confidence I addressed a long-winded remark to him for the primary purpose of impressing some white friends who were present. And the blank stupefaction that swirled over the Eskimo's face was reflected in mine as it dawned on me that he hadn't the faintest idea of what I was saying. It was not just that the words were strange (many of the Ihalmiut words are not known at the coast) but simply that the construction and idiom I used with such perfect assurance were mere gibberish to him.

It was a sad disillusionment, but it shed a revealing light on the character of the Ihalmiut. I wonder what other men in this world would have gone to the trouble of devising what amounted to a new language, simply for the convenience of a stranger who happened into their midst. I know of none.

In time I was gradually weaned away from the special jargon to a more exact knowledge of the language. But I must

frankly admit that I never came to speak the real tongue of
the People. Despite this, I did come to know the Ihalmiut,
their life, some of their folk tales, and some of their history,
and I believe I came to know these things with truth. That
was my gift from the Ihalmiut—the most precious thing they
could have given, for it was made under no compulsion other
than the sympathy of men for another.

After I had begun to master the problem of communica-
tion, one of the first questions I put to Ootek was to ask why
the Little Hills area had been singled out from an apparently
similar, but almost limitless, expanse of plains to be the home
of the Ihalmiut. It was a question that had been on my mind
since my first visit to the Little Hills, for I suspected that the
location of the camp might have an historical significance
which would provide a starting point for future attempts to
probe into the past of the People. But when Ootek began to
talk about the Little Hills camps, it was to give me an
initiation into the hidden complexity of cause and effect
which makes the apparent simplicity of the Innuit way of life
a matter of deep complications. It was a lesson for me, and I
learned then that it is errant stupidity to look for simplicity in
so-called simple cultures. I learned that, if I was ever to
understand the Ihalmiut, I must be prepared to grapple with a
complex of interrelated factors which are essentially as involved as any I might find in civilized lands.

To begin with, Ootek gave me to understand that the
selection of any permanent campsite is based primarily on
three major considerations. The first is: "Will the deer, who
are our life, approve?" Or, in direct terms, will the site
provide the supply of meat which is essential to human life?
There is no easy answer to this condition, as you may guess
after reading what I have already said about the deer.

The next major consideration is that of a fuel supply. In
this part of the arctic where animals cannot supply fat-fuel
for cooking and for heat, the camps must be placed within
reach of a good supply of the dwarf shrubs of the Barrens.

The third and most complex factor in the choice of a
camp is concerned with the proximity of the dead, for it is
not wise to build igloos or tents in a place where there are
many graves. The ramifications of this condition are extensive, so I will deal with them at length in a later chapter.

The choice of the lakes under the Little Hills was an old
one, for it was by these lakes that the greatest of all deer
herds used to pass in the days that are gone and it was

believed that here a man might always be certain of making a good kill. As for fuel, there was sufficient willow scrub about, and it grew quickly enough, so that the People never exhausted the supply by the lakes, although often they might have to journey for fifteen or twenty miles from the camps to find a satisfactory stand. As to the dead, this alone of all the once mighty camps of the Ihalmiut had been spared the terrible presence of plague. Death had struck lightly under the shade of the Little Hills, in comparision with the bludgeoning blows he had dealt to the other camps throughout the land. The dead had room by the shores of the lakes, and still left enough space for the tents of the living.

The location of the Ihalmiut homes had roused my curiosity, but it became even more acute as I examined the houses the Ihalmiut built for themselves. As I grew to know the People, so my respect for their intelligence and ingenuity increased. Yet it was a long time before I could reconcile my feelings of respect with the poor, shoddy dwelling places that they constructed. As with most Eskimos, the winter homes of the Ihalmiut are the snow-built domes we call igloos. (Igloo in Eskimo means simply "house" and thus an igloo can be built of wood or stone, as well as of snow.) But unlike most other Innuit, the Ihalmiut make snow houses which are cramped, miserable shelters. I think the People acquired the art of igloo construction quite recently in their history and from the coast Eskimos. Certainly they have no love for their igloos, and prefer the skin tents. This preference is related to the problem of fuel.

Any home in the arctic, in winter, requires some fuel if only for cooking. The coast peoples make use of fat lamps, for they have an abundance of fat from the sea mammals they kill, and so they are able to cook in the igloo, and to heat it as well. But the Ihalmiut can ill afford to squander the precious fat of the deer, and they dare to burn only one tiny lamp for light. Willow must serve as fuel, and while willow burns well enough in a tent open at the peak to allow the smoke to escape, when it is burned in a snow igloo, the choking smoke leaves no place for human occupants.

So snow houses replace the skin tents of the Ihalmiut only when winter has already grown old and the cold has reached the seemingly unbearable extremes of sixty or even seventy degrees below zero. Then the tents are grudgingly abandoned and snow huts built. From that time until spring no fires may burn inside the homes of the People, and such cooking as is attempted must be done outside, in the face of the blizzards and gales.

Yet though tents are preferred to igloos, it is still rather hard to understand why. I have mentioned the great, gaping slits which outline each hide on the frame of a tent. Such a home offers hardly more shelter than a thicket of trees, for on the unbroken sweep of the plains the winds blow with such violence that they drive the hard snow through the tents as if the skin walls did not really exist. But the People spend many days and dark nights in these feeble excuses for houses, while the wind rises like a demon of hatred and the cold comes as if it meant to destroy all life in the land.

In these tents there may be a fire; but consider this fire, this smoldering handful of green twigs, dug with infinite labor from under the drifts. It gives heat only for a few inches out from its sullen coals so that it barely suffices to boil a pot of water in an hour or two. The eternal winds pour into the tent and dissipate what little heat the fire can spare from the cook-pots. The fire gives comfort to the Ihalmiut only through its appeal to the eyes.

However, the tent with its wan little fire is a more desirable place than the snow house with no fire at all. At least the man in the tent can have a hot bowl of soup once in a while, but after life in the igloos begins, almost all food must be eaten while it is frozen to the hardness of rocks. Men sometimes take skin bags full of ice into the beds so that they have have water to drink, melted by the heat of their bodies. It is true that some of the People build cook shelters outside the igloos but these snow hearths burn very badly, and then only when it is calm. For the most part the winds prevent any outside cooking at all, and anyway by late winter the willow supply is so deeply buried under the drifts, it is almost impossible for men to procure it.

So you see that the homes of the Ihalmiut in winter are hardly models of comfort. Even when spring comes to the land the improvement in housing conditions is not great. After the tents go up in the spring, the rains begin. During daylight it rains with gray fury and the tents soak up the chill water until the hides hang slackly on their poles while rivulets pour through the tent to drench everything inside. At night, very likely, there will be frost and by dawn everything not under the robes with the sleepers will be frozen stiff.

With the end of the spring rains, the hot sun dries and shrinks the hides until they are drum-taut, but the ordeal is not yet over. Out of the steaming muskegs come the hordes of bloodsucking and flesh-eating flies and these find that the Ihalmiut tents offer no barrier to their invasion. The tents belong equally to the People and to the flies, until midsummer brings an end to the plague, and the hordes vanish.

My high opinion of the People was often clouded when I looked at their homes. I sometimes wondered if the Ihalmiut were as clever and as resourceful as I thought them to be. I had been too long conditioned to think of home as four walls and a roof, and so the obvious solution of the Ihalmiut housing problem escaped me for nearly a year. It took me that long to realize that the People not only have good homes, but that they have devised the one perfect house.

The tent and the igloo are really only auxiliary shelters. The real home of the Ihalmio is much like that of the turtle, for it is what he carries about on his back. In truth it is the only house that can enable men to survive on the merciless plains of the Barrens. It has central heating from the fat furnace of the body, its walls are insulated to a degree of perfection that we white men have not been able to surpass, or even emulate. It is complete, light in weight, easy to make and easy to keep in repair. It costs nothing, for it is a gift of the land, through the deer. When I consider that house, my opinion of the astuteness of the Ihalmiut is no longer clouded.

Primarily the house consists of two suits of fur, worn one over the other, and each carefully tailored to the owner's dimensions. The inner suit is worn with the hair of the hides facing inward and touching the skin while the outer suit has its hair turned out to the weather. Each suit consists of a pullover parka with a hood, a pair of fur trousers, fur gloves and fur boots. The double motif is extended to the tips of the fingers, to the top of the head, and to the soles of the feet where soft slippers of harehide are worn next to the skin.

The high winter boots may be tied just above the knee so that they leave no entry for the cold blasts of the wind. But full ventilation is provided by the design of the parka. Both inner and outer parkas hang slackly to at least the knees of the wearer, and they are not belted in winter. Cold air does not rise, so that no drafts can move up under the parkas to reach the bare flesh, but the heavy, moisture-laden air from close to the body sinks through the gap between parka and trousers and is carried away. Even in times of great physical exertion, when the Ihalmio sweats freely, he is never in any danger of soaking his clothing and so inviting quick death from frost afterwards. The hides are not in contact with the body at all but are held away from the flesh by the soft resiliency of the deer hairs that line them, and in the space between the tips of the hair and the hide of the parka there is a constantly moving layer of warm air which absorbs all the sweat and carries it off.

Dressed for a day in the winter, the Ihalmio has this protection over all parts of his body, except for a narrow oval in front of his face—and even this is well protected by a long silken fringe of wolverine fur, the one fur to which the moisture of breathing will not adhere and freeze.

In the summer rain, the hide may grow wet, but the layer of air between deerhide and skin does not conduct the water, and so it runs off and is lost while the body stays dry. Then there is the question of weight. Most white men trying to live in the winter arctic load their bodies with at least twenty-five pounds of clothing, while the complete deerskin home of the Innuit weighs about seven pounds. This, of course, makes a great difference in the mobility of the wearers. A man wearing tightfitting and too bulky clothes is almost as helpless as a man in a diver's suit. But besides their light weight, the Ihalmiut clothes are tailored so that they are slack wherever muscles must work freely beneath them. There is ample space in this house for the occupant to move and to breathe, for there are no partitions and walls to limit his motions, and the man is almost as free in his movements as if he were naked. If he must sleep out, without shelter, and it is fifty below, he has but to draw his arms into his parka, and he sleeps nearly as well as he would in a double-weight eiderdown bag.

This is in winter, but what about summer? I have explained how the porous hide nevertheless acts as a raincoat. Well, it does much more than that. In summer the outer suit is discarded and all clothing pared down to one layer. The house then offers effective insulation against heat entry. It remains surprisingly cool, for it is efficiently ventilated. Also, and not least of its many advantages, it offers the nearest thing to perfect protection against the flies. The hood is pulled up so that it covers the neck and the ears, and the flies find it nearly impossible to get at the skin underneath. But of course the Ihalmiut have long since learned to live with the flies, and they feel none of the hysterical and frustrating rage against them so common with us.

In the case of women's clothing, home has two rooms.

The back of the parka has an enlargement, as if it were made to fit a hunchback, and in this space, called the *amaut,* lives the unweaned child of the family. A bundle of remarkably absorbent sphagnum moss goes under his backside and the child sits stark naked, in unrestricted delight, where he can look out on the world and very early in life become familiar with the sights and the moods of his land. He needs no clothing of his own, and as for the moss—in that land there is an unlimited supply of soft sphagnum and it can be replaced in an instant.

When the child is at length forced to vacate this pleasant apartment, probably by the arrival of competition, he is equipped with a one-piece suit of hides which looks not unlike the snow suits our children wear in the winter. Only it is much lighter, more efficient, and much less restricting. This first home of his own is a fine home for the Ihalmio child, and one that his white relatives would envy if they could appreciate its real worth.

This then is the home of the People. It is the gift of the land, but mainly it is the gift of Tuktu.

IX

Eskimo Spring

As I became more competent with the language I discovered that the talk of the People was largely devoted to times past. It almost seemed as if the Ihalmiut were making a deliberate effort to relive those dead days, as if they wished me to see them, not as they are, but as they had once been. Slowly and carefully they used words to rebuild the old shattered pattern of life as it had been lived in the Barrens, so I might also live with them in those happier times. And it was not long before their efforts began to have the desired effect, and I could see, in my mind's eye, something of the richness and vigor of the life the People had led in those vanished years when a man might stand on a hill and though he looked to the east, to the west, to the north or to the south, he would not know where the land was, for all he could see was Tuktu the deer. All he could hear was the sound of their feet. All he could smell was the sweet scent of the deer.

In the days that are gone, the deer came out of the forests in spring and the doe's bellies hung heavy with fawn, and the strident demands of new life rang through the land. Then the People would come from the tents which stood by the abandoned igloos of winter, and old men and old women stood by and smiled a toothless welcome for Tuktu. The hunters came from the tents and saw to it that the kayaks

110

were ready. If the kayak coverings were torn, then the women hurriedly soaked hides in the melting streams and stretched the new skin over the slim ribs of the hunting craft.

When the deer began to cross the thawing rivers that ran near the camps, the men went out to hunt. They carried their deer spears and they pushed their kayaks into the ice-filled waters of rivers and lakes. The women walked down the shores to the places where converging rows of stone pillars had been built many generations before to funnel the migrating herds to where the hunters waited. These fences were put right by the women, for the winter gales might have toppled the stones and torn off the headpieces of moss which help make the pillars look like men to the deer.

As soon as these deer fences were ready, the women and the young children would go out into the plains which were still covered with yielding spring snow. There they lay hidden in depressions amongst the rocks or in the moss until a deer herd came by. As the deer passed, the watchers shouted and jumped to their feet and closed in behind the fear-stricken beasts, driving them into the embrace of the stone fences. The deer ran down between the narrowing arms of the fence until they came to the bank of the river and to the place appointed to the hunters. As the fleeing animals entered the water, the kayaks were unleashed against them and the spring killing began. Spears flashed in the sun and dead deer floated down with the current into the bays below.

The spring was a time of great killing and yet the People took only enough in those days to meet their needs until fall. For the hides of the spring deer are useless for clothing and the meat is lean and lacking in fat.

There was much gorging on fresh meat in the spring, for when the sun again stands high in the sky, the bellies of men revolt from the dry meat and the frozen meat that is their diet all winter. Down in the backwaters of the bays on the river, the old men pulled the floating bodies ashore and the women came with their sharp curved knives and flensed the deer where they lay. Then, bent double under the weight of fresh meat and of great bundles of marrowbones, they went back to the camps. But not all of the carcasses of the deer were butchered and skinned; a great many were only gutted and anchored with rocks deep under the fast, cold flow of the waters where the meat would stay fresh well into the last days of summer.

After the herds had passed by to the north, the People

moved their camps up to the slopes of the hills so that the long winds could battle the flies which were coming. Here the People lived till midsummer, awaiting the return of the deer.

Summer was the time of eggs and young birds. Even the children went daily out over the plains with their toy slings and bows to search for the eggs and the young of the ptarmigan, of the curlew, the ducks, and even of the tiny song birds of the Barrens. The men too did not let their hunting skills grow rusty, for they searched out the dens of the great arctic wolves and took enough pelts for mats and for the trimming of parkas. But during most of the summer the men worked at building new kayaks, repairing their sleds, and preparing for the return of the herds. In the evenings they went to the hilltops and stared into the flaming sky of the north, waiting and watching for sight of the deer.

By midsummer the first herds of does were again passing down into the land of the People, and for a month the hunting was done out on the plains. At this time of the year, and until the deer had again swung to the north, the skins were still of little value, except for those of the fawns, and there was no need for a large kill. So the hunters went out with the bows made of the springy horn of the musk ox, and they stalked the deer over the hills and killed only a few, picking the fattest beasts with great care.

At last, in late summer, the herds again swung to the north and passed out of the Ihalmiut land. This was the time of the greatest activity during the year, for it was known that when the deer came back again it would be only for the brief few days as they fled south before the approach of winter; and after that the herds would not be seen again in the land until spring. It was known that when the deer came for this last time to the Little Hills, they would not linger but would come like a flood and pass quickly. All things had to be ready to greet their arrival, for the lives of the People depended on the success of the fall hunt.

The last rotten ice was all gone from the rivers and from most of the lakes before fall and so the deer followed new routes, swinging along the curved shores of the great lakes, and crossing the rivers just below or above open bodies of water. In the land of the Ihalmiut there were many such crossing places, all of ageless antiquity, where the deer were funneled by the lakes and hills into narrow defiles. To those places the People now moved their tents, setting up hunting camps a few miles away from each crossing so the presence of the tents would not interfere with the movements of the deer.

In the old days the Ihalmiut told me about, there would be thirty or forty tents near each of the seven most famous crossings, and there would be many scores of tents at other minor crossing places scattered over the land. In these camps the men worked lovingly on their kayaks and sharpened the copper points of their spears till they were as keen as fine razors. The women roamed the land all about, and heaped up piles of willow twigs against the days when they would build the biggest fires of all the year to render down the sweet deer fat. The youths paddled for two or three days to the north and camped on the hilltops from which they could see the approach of the deer and carry the warning back to the camps.

The men who were too old to hunt watched for signs. They watched for a sudden upswing in the numbers of foxes and wolves and for the forming of the great flocks of scavenger gulls that accompany the herds; but most of all they watched for flights of ravens coming out of the north, for these are the sure heralds of the approach of the deer.

Excitement and tension built up in the camps as the fall days slowly passed. There were alarms, occasioned by small wandering herds that happened into the land ahead of the migration. And as always some of the People wondered if this time, by some terrible malice of fate, the deer might fail to move south by the particular crossing where the skin tents stood waiting. There was no sleep and little rest. At night the drums sounded and the voices of the hunters sang the songs of the killing of Tuktu, or the People told tales of the deer they had seen and killed in their time, until the late dawn crept into the sky.

Then on a day in October there would be snow in the air. A kayak would sweep up the river out of the north, and the man in it held his spear aloft as a signal. "They come!" was the cry in the camps, and the hunters ran to their places and the women and children ran to the tops of ridges north of the crossing.

This was the time of the great slaughter. Swimming the rivers, the deer met the repeated onslaught of the kayaks. At the valleys and gulleys the deer met the hunters. Blood flowed at the crossings and the hunt went on far into each night.

In the camps huge fires burned all day and all night and blocks of white deer fat began to mount up in the tents. On the bushes which spread their dead leaves in the hollows, thin slices of meat were laid out to dry until the valleys and hills about the camps by the crossings glowed a dull red under the waning sun. All over the land, but most thickly about the deer crossings, little cairns of rocks sprang up like blisters on the gray face of the plains. Under these cairns were the quartered bodies of deer. On the sandy shores by the tents, many thousands of fine hides lay staked out with the naked sides upward, and women and children worked over these hides, cleaning and scraping them thin.

The excitement mounted to a frenzy of action until, in less than a week from the day the man in the kayak had first signaled the approach of the deer, the great herds were gone. The crossings were empty of living deer and only the dead remained there.

The snows came, and all things—save man and the ravens—turned as white as the snow. The ptarmigan found their white feathers, the fox turned white, and the weasel. The snowy owls drifted out of the most distant north and they too were white, as white as the great arctic wolves.

Then it was winter and the great herds were gone, but there still remained game to hunt out on the bleak winter plains. In the valleys protected by hills, so that the snow did not drift thickly over their floors, and in the high places where the wind kept the land scoured free of snow, and the lichens were not too deeply buried, there were still a few deer who had been caught, and cut off, by the advent of winter.

If it happened that by accident or bad luck a family of the People became short of meat in the winter, then food could still be procured by a good hunter. It was harder to hunt Tuktu in winter, for then the deer were in small groups, widely spaced, and they were wary. Only when the ground drift was thick or during a blizzard could they be approached by the hunters.

But if the deer were hard to hunt, they could be easily trapped. When a hunter set out, not from need, but from a desire to eat of freshly killed meat, he might choose to dig a pit in the side of a drift. The pit had high walls, sometimes built up with snow, and there was a ramp up one side also built of hard snow blocks. On the top a thin layer of brush covered with snow concealed the trap, and for bait there was a handful of moss, or better yet, a piece of frozen urine of a man or of a dog. It is a strange fact that the deer smell urine from a great distance in winter, and because it is salty they will abandon all caution to reach it. Even the wolf knows this, and often a wolf will lie hidden near a snow hummock where he has urinated, knowing that if there are deer near at hand, they will come to the bait.

Sometimes, if the snow was not deep enough for a pit, the hunter dug a sloping trench, only as wide as a deer, into a snowbank. At its end he would place the bait, and when a deer descended the sloping incline, it could neither back out nor turn around, and so it was caught.

Briefly that was the way of things in the old days the Ihalmiut remembered so well and talked of so freely. But the way of things now is so bitter that it was hard for me to persuade the People to speak of the present. For a while I knew no more about it than I could see for myself, or had picked up from Franz. Then little by little I began to gather odd fragments of tales from the time that is now, and at last I was able to reconstruct the present pattern of life as it is shown by the happenings which took place under the Little Hills in the spring of 1947.

I have already written of what came to pass by Ootek Kumanik in that fateful spring when Franz found the two orphans, Kunee and Anoteelik. I also mentioned three other families who had fled eastward in search of help. Now I will take up their story and complete it, so you will see the new way of life in the plains as I came to see it, and so you will understand why the Ihalmiut dwell so much on the days when the deer were many, and life was good to the People.

The story was told to me—mainly by Ohoto—in a series of short incidents spread over a year in time. Some of the details and much corroboration came from others of the Ihalmiut, particularly Ootek and Owliktuk. But in some places I had to supply the continuity of events from what I know of the men and women concerned, and from what I know of their land. This tale therefore is not given to you as being completely factual in all its details. Nevertheless it *is* a true history of one spring in the present years of the Ihalmiut.

Because it is primarily Ohoto's story I have chosen to let him be the spokesman for all:

In the time of my father we of the People exchanged our spears and our bows for the rifles of white men and in the early years of my youth the rifles gave us meat when we had need, and though the old ways had changed a little, life in this land was still a pleasant thing.

But now, often enough we do not have any shells for the rifles we own, and that seems strange to me. When the white men first came to the edge of our land and told us of the virtues of guns, we believed them. When they told us to put by the ancient deer hunts of our People and turn to the killing of foxes instead, we did what they wished and for a time all was well, and we prospered. Like most of the People I became a fine hunter of foxes from the days of my youth, and I knew all the ways they might be caught. But I did not know much of the hunting of Tuktu as it was done in the days of my father, for I never needed to know while there were shells for my rifle.

Now, often enough, there are no shells for the rifles, and I cannot tell why, for I still trap many foxes as the white men wished me to do, yet when I take my catch to the wooden igloo in the South, there is no one to greet me but Hikik the squirrel. It was that way first on a winter many years before you came into the land, and I remember the winter well, for the traders told us they must have many foxes that year. They were so anxious that we gave up the great fall hunt of the deer and used all of our skill and our strength to trap foxes, believing we could trade them for food at the place of the white man and so we would have little need of deer meat. But when, in midwinter, we took our pelts south, the door of the wooden igloo stood open and the white man had gone, leaving only the smell which lingered for many long years. Only dead things lay in his camp. The boxes were empty and there was no food in the place and no shells for our guns, so we could not even hunt meat for ourselves.

Indeed I remember that winter, though I wish it would go from my memory. Epeetna, who was my first wife, died during that time and my two children died with her. Nor was I alone in hunger and sorrow for in the camps of the People only one out of five lived to see spring.

Some of those who survived tried to return to the old way of living given us by Tuktu the deer, but it was found that we did not have the old skills we needed. Some hoped and believed the white man would return and so, stubbornly, clung to their fox traps. These are gone. Only those remained who tried to return to the deer, and few of these are still alive.

Then five winters after the first white man went away, another came in his place. Once again we threw away the pursuit of the deer, for we felt that this time the white man would surely remain. Once more we had shells for our guns, and all things seemed well, yet last winter the white man again left the land, and again we had nothing to eat but the skins of the foxes we had trapped for the trade.

Why is it you white men should come for a time, stay for a time, and then suddenly vanish when we are most in need of your help? Why is it? Why can we not take our fox pelts to the trader and have shells for our guns in return, for this is what the trader taught us to do? This mystery I cannot understand....

Well, because we did not have shells, we did not have enough meat in the camps during the winter. You have already heard of the winter I speak of, and of the death of the parents of Kunee and Anoteelik by the shores of Ootek's Lake. But you have not yet heard how it went with those of us who fled toward the East where we had heard a rumor of the presence of a new trader.

There were four hunters living on the shores of Ootek's Lake and their families were as I shall tell you. There was Angleyalak, his wife, his old mother, and his children Pama, Kunee and Anoteelik. There was Ootek, and Howmik his wife, and a child in her womb and another in her amaut. There was Owliktuk, his wife and his mother and his children. There was myself, and Nanuk my wife, my old father called Elaitutna, and the children Aljut and Elaitutna who were the sons of my wife by a man who is dead.

In the late months of the winter I speak of, Ootek and Angleyalak took all the dogs we four families still had and traveled south to the camp of Franz to tell him of our need, which was great. While they were gone I went out alone over the snow-covered land to seek out the caches of deer meat Franz had made as bait for his fox traps in the fall. I found only one cache, for the snow had hidden the rest. And the one I found had also been found by Kakwik the wolverine, who had left only bones and chewed skin for me.

When I came in empty-handed from my trip over the Barrens, I found Ootek and Angleyalak had returned from the South. They told us Franz had little food to give to the People, for his own caches were empty. Then I knew a very great fear, for the deer could not come again to our land until long weeks had passed.

Although we did not have hope, still while we had dogs to pull our long sleds, we went out to hunt on the sterile slopes of the snow. But when the dogs began to die from their hunger, we could go no more to the plains. That did not matter, for there was nothing to hunt and had there been, we had no shells for our guns.

One night we heard that the old woman, the mother of Angleyalak, had gone from her igloo and had not returned in the morning. It was our duty to mourn. My wife went to the igloo of Angleyalak and when she returned she told me the wife of that man was sick nearly to death, with the evil which lies in the lungs.

The sickness of death was not far from us all. In our igloo, the boy Elaitutna sat as still as his grandfather, and neither spoke when I came in, nor went from the igloo. Young Aljut still had life enough to help me dig under the snow for old bones that might have some strength left upon them.

Nanuk had grown desperate for the lives of

her children and on a day she whispered to me that we must kill the old man, my father, and so have food for the starving bellies of ourselves and the children. I could not bring myself to agree to her plan, for Elaïtutna had been a good hunter all the days of his life and he had given freely of his strength and his years to me and my family in the days that were gone. But Nunuk was desperate as only a woman can be, and so she spoke directly into the ears of the old man who sat on a far part of the high sleeping ledge, his wrinkled eyes closed. Elaitutna did not open his eyes as she spoke, and for a long time it seemed he had not heard the urgent voice of my wife. Then at last he slowly nodded his head and we knew he was willing that we should take what little of life remained in his heart.

I would not help, and when Nanuk got the rawhide and tried to tie the noose in its end, her fingers shook so that she could not tie the knot. At last she flung the cord from her and threw herself, weeping, on the ledge between her two children. So Elaitutna lived a while longer.

It was more than three weeks since we had eaten meat, and we lived only on scraps of old bones and on the dog and human excreta found near the camps. At last Ootek and Owliktuk came to my igloo and Ootek told us that in the summer he had heard of a white man who was said to have built a log igloo on a lake many days to the east of our camp. He and Owliktuk had decided to abandon their igloos, and journey east out of the land of the Little Hills, to seek the white man. I agreed to go with them for it was certain death to remain. But when we asked Angleyalak to come with us, he refused, saying his woman was dying and he would not leave her to die by herself.

There were three living dogs in our igloos and these we killed and ate, even to their guts and their skin; and so we had enough strength to start out on our journey.

The bright sun brought the first warmth of spring on the day we set out. We walked slowly and the men, being strongest, carried a few skins to make shelters, and they also carried the children. The women and old ones carried only themselves—and that was enough.

When we came to Halo Lake we found only the families of Halo, Miki and Yaha. Hekwaw and Katelo had gone with their surviving families, leaving behind in their igloos the bodies of their wives Eepuk and Oquinuk. Hekwaw and Katelo had fled out into the plains, hoping to reach a far valley where they believed some deer might have wintered. But no one at Halo Lake ever expected to see any of these people again in his life—though before spring they returned, having found and killed a few deer.

In this place we heard news of the camps on Kakumee Lake, and we heard that Kakumee and all of his people were living and had enough meat to eat. Yet we knew there was no use traveling there to ask him for food, for being an evil man he would have turned us away and set devils against us.

We spoke to the three families who remained by Halo Kumanik of our plans to go eastward for help, and these people decided to join us, for they too lived with the dead and with the presence of death and they had but little hope for their lives.

It was a good thing for us that they came, for Miki owned a spit-rifle [a .22] whose bullets are as small as a bee and can kill ptarmigan or hares, though they can seldom kill deer. Miki also had some of the little bullets, a present from Franz in the early days of the winter.

We traveled for two days before we were out of sight of the hills of our land, a distance a strong man could have walked in half a day. But we had no strength, and we had to stop every few feet while the women and old people rested their thin bodies on hummocks of snow, and tried not to complain of the dull pain in their bellies.

On the fourth day we came to the edge of the forests and here by good luck we found the corpse of a deer the wolves had killed and half eaten. Enough still remained for us, who were more hungry than wolves. We cracked all the bones and in a tin pot that Yaha had brought we made a good soup, for now we were in a land where the little-trees are and there was wood to burn.

We stayed for two days in that place, until the deer that Amow the wolf had given to us was gone to the last shred of sinew which had clung to the skull. Our strength was a little renewed and we pushed on into the thin forests for another three days before we knew that we could not go any further. There was no food where we halted, not even a ptarmigan to be seen, but nevertheless we put up our shelters, for at least we had wood and we could keep warm by the fires. We melted snow and drank great quantities of warm water to still the agony of the teeth that gnawed at our bellies.

On the second day at that camp, we had luck once again. Ootek had borrowed the spit-rifle of Miki and gone hunting alone, for Miki did not have the strength to walk in the deep snow of the forests. Ootek came suddenly on a hare, and by falling on his knees in the snow he managed to aim, and to kill the hare as it watched him from the edge of the woods.

Now when he brought the hare into camp, I thought the women would be frantic to eat it, for the women had much reason to eat. Ootek's wife carried only dry breasts to feed her young child and she also carried a new child who starved in her womb. My own wife should have snatched at the hare to give life to Elaitutna and Aljut, and the others of the women should have fought for the meat.

But this did not happen. The women decided that the three men whose bodies had suffered the least damage from famine alone should eat of the hare, in order that its flesh would enable these men to travel on to the trader and bring his help back to all the others of our party who could push on no further.

So we took the hare into the bush, Ootek, Owliktuk and I, where the smell of the cooking could not reach the noses of those who had given up their share of the food. Though it was a terrible torture to wait while it cooked, we had to cook the meat, for our bellies would have retched it up had we eaten it raw. I wolfed down my portion and did not let myself think of the children who lay in the shelter at the camp. Then with the sharp pangs of food in our stomachs, we three set out down the course of a small frozen river to find the place of the trader.

It was a two-day march, though we traveled fast, before we came to the shores of a lake, and across it we saw the walls of a log igloo which could only belong to a white man. It was the trader. Surely it was a great thing that we had found him in all of the land there was to search. We hurried over the lake, and the white man's dogs heard us and howled as we came near.

We knew then that the famine was done—done with and gone. Already I found myself beginning to forget what had happened in the camps of the People under the Little Hills. There was no longer any need for the strength which does not come from the muscles but from the spirit. My legs gave way beneath me and I fell in the snow, yet I did not care for I knew we were safe.

The trader, a short little man, came out of his igloo and looked at us as we sat and lay in the snow. We laughed with embarrassment when he saw us, for we were ashamed of our weakness, and we were ashamed that we could not speak his language.

We got to our feet and stood there not sure what we should do. At last Ootek pointed to the hollows that lay on his cheeks, and showed how his ribs stuck out from his belly. I lay down again in the snow and closed my eyes like a dead man so that the *Kabluna*—the white man—would know how it was at the camps.

And the trader—did not understand!

He went to his cabin and brought back a fox pelt, holding it up with one hand, and stretching the other hand out to us. Then a great sickness filled me, for we had no fox pelts to trade. Starving men cannot trap fox pelts and I saw that if pelts were demanded there could be no help for the People.

When we showed him we had no foxes, the white man suddenly grew very angry and I thought that perhaps he had not understood why we came. Again and again we tried to show what our need was, and again and again we lifted our parkas so he could see the bones of our bodies. But something was wrong, and he did not understand.

As I think back on it now I know the trader could not have understood what we tried so hard to tell him, for no man who has food will turn away one who is hungry. We knew this man had food, for his dogs were fat and well fed, and we would have been glad for some of that dog food, if he had only not misunderstood what we said.

Perhaps he was afraid of us three, for Ootek still carried the rifle of Miki, and perhaps this strange white man was afraid. I know he went back to his cabin and when he came to the door he had a deer rifle in his right hand, and in his left hand a sack of flour, but so small a sack that it could have been carried by a child. He flung us the flour and slammed the door shut—and we never saw him again.

I had a wild thought that I should take Miki's rifle and shoot this man, so we could take what we needed out of his little log store. But the thought was born only in the memory of the boy Elaitutna who was dead now, whether he still breathed or not. The thought flickered and passed. And we three turned away and went back to the west to the camps of those whose lives were in our hands.

There were no words between us—all words were dead. We ate none of the flour, and so in our weakness it took us four days to return, and I crawled the last little way to the fire.

Elaitutna, my father, was finished. He was still sitting by the door of the shelter, but frozen and stiff with his eyes closed as they had been at the end of his life. I was afraid Nanuk would speak and demand that we eat the flesh of the dead, but she was too weak to speak and the body of my father sat there where it was.

The flour we brought from the white man was enough for a single small meal for each one who lived in the camp. Many could not retain the raw flour, but it did not matter for it could only hold off the devils of death for a day.

In the tent of Owliktuk, his wife held a dead child to her breasts, and this child was Oktilohok. Owliktuk could not make her release it, so it too stayed in the tent.

So also in the tent of Ootek and Howmik. One child lay dead on a scrap of deerhide, the other near death in her womb.

Then it was my turn to mourn for the death of a child. Elaitutna did not wake to my calling, and his small hands were frozen by the frost which is colder than ice. After him Aljut, the son of my wife, died and was gone. Death meant nothing to us in that place. There was no weeping, and no woman cried out the laments of the dead. Death meant nothing to us in that place. . . .

But those were terrible days, days I do not wish to remember. Let them be forgotten in your ears and your heart. I will say nothing more of that time.

Two days after our return from the place of the white man, Tuktu came at last and so the rest of us lived. It was the deer in the end, the deer who alone in all of the world know the needs of the People, who took pity on us in our camp by the edge of the forest when there was no pity in all of our land. Tuktoriak—the Spirit who lives in the deer—sent a great buck into our camp and made him stand so close, and so foolishly by the fire of Ootek, that Ootek was able to kill the deer with the tiny bullets of Miki's rifle.

That was in the spring of the year. Late in the spring we returned to Ootek Kumanik, there to find the wolverine-scattered bones of Angleyalak, his wife and his daughter. These bones we buried, as we had buried our dead in the foreign lands of the forest. But for a long time we thought the devils had taken Kunee and Anoteelik, and we were very glad in our hearts when we heard they were safe.

So ends Ohoto's memory of the spring of the year 1947—a year that belongs to the present—a year that took twelve lives from the twoscore people who were the last survivors of the thousands of men who roamed the plains country only a few decades ago.

X

These Are Their Days

The present still holds varying moods for the Ihalmiut, and many are pleasant. These are the moods the people exploit and enjoy, and as for the others—they are put out of mind in the times when their presence is not felt in the flesh.

One day in the fall there was a frost at Windy Cabin, and I began to look over my supplies of winter clothing. I had checked them over rather carefully before Andy and I left Churchill, but that had been several months earlier, and since that time I had looked at many things, and my eyes were beginning to see with the vision of my foster folk. Now I looked again at my long woolly underwear, three or four thick woolen sweaters, and my heavy blanket capote. These things no longer seemed to offer the warmth and protection for which they were intended.

After a while I put them all back in a box and hunted up Ootek, my song-cousin.

126

"Nipello aqako!" Ootek remarked as I came up to him. Snow tomorrow! Yes, I believe him, and it was that forth-coming snow which had brought me to him. It was a delicate problem. I did not like to ask Ootek outright for skin clothes for he would probably have disrobed on the spot and, while we *were* song-cousins, my intimacy with the man had not extended to the point where I wanted to wear the clothes he had been living in all summer. I tried to be subtle.

"Ootek," I said, "I am told your mother is the finest maker of clothes in all the camps. Is that so?"

Ootek did not take the bait. His natural modesty evidently extended to the work of his mother as well. He looked at me sadly.

"The old woman makes clothes that would fit well on a musk ox! Who told you this monstrous lie?"

I tried a different tack. "The snow will be here tomorrow, just as you say," I told him. "And that may be all right for you—but we poor white men who do not know how to dress in this land will probably freeze." I shivered with appropriate emphasis, and glanced at Ootek to see how he was taking it all.

He was beaming. The text of his reply cannot be quoted, but the gist of it was that I had no need to fear from the cold, for Howmik, his wife, would be delighted to take care of the problem, and that care did not entail the making of clothes.

This time I nearly gave up; but I decided on a last try. I pulled out a plug of tobacco and said bluntly:

"How many plugs for a suit of new winter furs?"

I expected Ootek to look hurt, but he beamed even more and told me the clothes would be ready in two weeks if the snow came that night. (Work on winter clothes may not be begun until after the first snow has fallen.) Two plugs of tobacco would be about right, and they would go to his mother, the one who made clothes which might fit a musk ox but hardly a man. Ootek measured me on the spot, taking a length of rawhide line and, with it, measuring waist, height and arms. For each measurement he tied a knot in the cord, and when he was through, we set off for his camp to put in the order.

Fall days in the camp under the Little Hills were short, for the sun was losing its place in the sky as winter approached. At Ootek's camp the white pavement of ancient deer bones was carpeted with the fall-killed hides of buck deer. Perhaps fifty of these were staked out or held stretched with stones at their edges, and the bluish tint of fresh skins was fading into the gray-white of dried hides. The scars of warble flies dotted the skins like smallpox eruptions, but the little pockets of larvae which began to swell in the fall had been carefully scraped away along with the remnants of fat and tissue. Howmik came from her tent and selected one of the hides which was nearly dry. She examined it with great care, testing the hair to make sure it was firm in the skin. Then she took it back to the tent and squatting by the smoke of the fire made ready to tan it. The tanning of hide for clothes is simple. All that Howmik had to do with the stiff, untreated skin was to work it between her hard hands until it grew soft. Then it could be cut to the pattern by Ootek's mother and made part of a new winter outfit.

All tanning is not quite so simple. The boots of the People must be made of caribou hide, and for boots, the hide from the neck of the buck deer is the thickest and best. This hide must be soaked in water for a long time until the hair rots from the skin and the skin itself can be scraped with the curved woman's knife until it is as thin as good parchment. For the sole of the boot the skin from the forehead of the deer is the toughest, though it is not nearly so tough as the sealskin soles the coast people use.

Boots and clothes are still sewn with the fine sinews which lie in a broad band along the back of the deer, and Howmik still does her sewing with delicate needles carved and filed from the shoulder blades of the deer. Her stitching is a miracle to behold. In order that the summer boots shall be waterproof, she must make the seams perfectly tight solely by virtue of her sewing. The stitches are often so fine they cannot be counted at all with the naked eye, and how Howmik makes them is something that no man can say.

Not all boots are made in the same manner as these summer ones I have mentioned. For winter use there are boots made with fur soles turned down so that a man will find a good grip on the ice. There are others fur-lined throughout, and there are the fine and delicate slippers of fawn or of hare to wear next to the skin.

All this cleaning and preparing of hides, this making of boots and of clothes, is the work of the women; and in its season is the work of their days. I have spoken only of a few of the things they must make. The full list is almost endless. Bags, buckets, ornaments, clothing, tents, kayak covers and robes are but a few of the many things the woman must make from Tuktu the deer. There is no lack of work to make the days full when the deer hides are prime.

It was old Kala, Ootek's mother, who made my suit of furs, my "winter house." And she made them without seeing me from the time she began until she was done. Yet when Ootek brought them to me, they fitted well. At two plugs of tobacco, she did not overcharge, for to show me her skill, she had inserted pure white inserts of belly skin over the whole of the outside parka, in a pattern which combined grace and beauty with the most remarkable blending of fur.

The days in the camp of Ootek held room for a great many skills as fine as those displayed by old Kala. The family was a well-regulated one and work did not seem a burden even to those who had the most to do. For one thing, it was the particular task of Kala, as the eldest one of the family, to keep the cook fire in fuel. Daily the old woman walked out from the camps, and sometimes her search took her ten miles over the land before she found a willow thicket which met with her needs. Then she would cut, and tie up, a tremendous bundle of twigs and carry this bundle home on her back. Yet what was a twenty-mile walk for old Kala? There was plenty to enjoy on the way. There—a herd of fat does grazing high on the slope of a hill, fine beasts, with sleek velvet coats... Or Uh-ala, the long-tailed duck, calling its woman's gossip loudly from the edge of a pond ... Perhaps Kala might flush a ptarmigan from its well-hidden nest, and the half-developed eggs made her a welcome snack during the walk.

Often, if there was no fuel close at hand, the camp's children went with her. Atnalik, the orphaned son of Ootek's sister, would carry his little toy sling, and stubbornly chase the alert birds of the ridges, the snow buntings and longspurs, and sometimes he would come proudly back to old Kala, with his tiny catch held high in his hand.

If she went alone to her search, there were memories enough to keep Kala happy. Rich memories, those of old Kala—she who had known three husbands and a dozen children in her time, had seen Tyrrell, the first white man, come to the river, and knew all the tales of three generations of men.

Kala gathered the fuel, sewed clothes for her son, kept the fires burning and, not least of her tasks, made acid comments on the way her son and his wife ran their lives. That is an old woman's privilege, one the Ihalmiut do not refuse to the old. Perhaps one day Ootek fails to bring in fresh meat when it is needed and so he must accept the tongue-lashing of this old crone. Nor will he grow angry at her, but he will laugh a little bit sheepishly, shake his head, and reply, "Mother, I shall do better tomorrow—and you shall have a fine fresh marrowbone to worry away at with your old teeth."

In the camps of the People the days of an old woman are full—in the summer. And though she works she is not driven as old people may often be in other lands. She has her time to gossip and to visit the nearby camps and she has both the right and the freedom to speak out against the ways of her children, and of their children too, while she lives.

Well, her days are as they should be. For with the coming of winter the old woman's life is a pawn without value. If the winter be hard, and famine comes to the family, then the old one must die. It is something that all people know, but that is never spoken aloud. In summer the old ones live their lives free of much of the restraint which lies on the younger ones of the People. In winter youth may turn to age and call on it to walk into the night and never return.

For Howmik too, life can be pleasant enough. In the summer of 1947 she bore a child—Kalak—and it was a great happiness to her that this child was born. Three other children, small heaps of rocks over their bones, had not seen the end of their first year in the land. But surely Kalak would live and do well. A fine healthy child, she would eat and grow fat, for Howmik was certain that in the winter ahead there would be much good meat laid by in the caches about the camps.

There was enough for Howmik to do in the summer, and yet she had ample time for the pleasures of living. Although there was no clothing to make until fall, there were many pounds of *nipku*, dry meat, to attend to out on the hills. When the sun shone, the meat had to be turned before the flies quite possessed it, and when rain threatened, the widespread slices of meat had to be quickly gathered and stored safely away.

There were five meals a day to prepare for those of her tent and perhaps two or three visitors from the tents of Ohoto or Hekwaw—all these had to be fed. Soup three or four times a day, with plenty of fat and bone marrow melted in it, and cold roasts or boiled meat for the other two meals—this was enough to keep everyone happy.

The dogs were also in Howmik's charge during the summer. But they were light work, for there were only three of the beasts, and these had been obtained by Ootek only that spring, for none of his own dogs had survived the starvation of the previous year. These three were young dogs not yet broken to work with the sled, and so they still had the freedom of camp. Despite the trouble they made for Howmik, being great thieves, nevertheless they were never tied. The Ihalmiut look upon dogs much as they look upon people. The time of hardship and of bitter labor comes soon enough both to men and to man's beasts. The Ihalmiut say, "While they are young, while life here is easy, let them find what joys they may. Let them be as free as all young things should be." So the dogs have no labors except when Atnalik hitches a model sled behind one or the other of them and makes the dog drag the sled in imitation of the real work it must soon learn to do.

The dogs were well fed, fat animals of infinite goodnature. It was not unusual to see one of them lying on its back while the naked child, Kalak, sprawled on the dog's belly, pummeling it with small hands, or pouring fistfuls of sand and grit into the gaping red mouth. Things would soon change for these dogs, but now they lived free lives, subject only to the sibilant hiss with which Ootek warned them when they trespassed too far over the bounds.

Howmik's main labor was for the child she had borne. Each day she devoted long hours to Kalak, amusing the child, feeding her from her breasts at the first sign of hunger, bathing her with wet lumps of moss, or simply talking to her as all women talk to their young.

In the camps of the People the child is king, for childhood is short and tragedy often comes after. As it is with the dogs, so the early years of a child are made free of compulsion and of hard labors, for these years must always remain in the child's memory to alleviate the agonies which come with mature years.

It has been said by people who should know better that Eskimos treat their children well only so the children will in turn treat their parents well when old age is upon them and their time of usefulness is at an end. In point of fact, the People treat their children with great sympathy and forbearance because they know so much of humanity.

I remember once when Ootek, who had agreed to stay with us for a couple of weeks, left Windy Camp to walk sixty miles over the tundra simply to assure himself that Kalak was well and happy. Then he turned and retraced the sixty miles, arriving back at our camp five days after he left it. When he arrived back, he was contrite that he had been forced to leave Andy and me, and he apologized because he had been so weak in his concern for his child. Again, I remember one day when I was talking to him about children and I expressed surprise that no Ihalmiut child knows corporal punishment even when the provocation is great. I spoke casually, but Ootek replied with vehemence, for it seemed he was honestly puzzled that I should not know why a child is never beaten.

"Who but a madman would raise his hand against blood of his blood?" he asked me. "Who but a madman would, in his man's strength, stoop to strike against the weakness of a child? Be sure that I am not mad, nor yet is Howmik afflicted with madness!"

There was something that might have been contempt in his voice as he spoke, and I never again raised that question.

So the children live their lives free of all restraint except that which they themselves impose; and they are at least as well behaved as any child anywhere. For three years after birth a child is suckled and by the time it has been weaned it is already aware of the general pattern of its life. I told you of Kunee who, at the age of five, was already an accomplished woman of the People, yet Kunee had never been taught what she must do. She was simply observant and imitative, as most children are, and she saw what others did and longed to do as well by herself.

The children's work is also their play. At night, when the adults are asleep or resting on the ledge, no voice is raised to chide the girl children, who remain active until the dawn, keeping the fire alive under the cooking pot and concocting broths and stews, not with toy things, but with the real equipment which will be theirs in maturity. No regimen or hard routine is laid upon them. When they are sleepy, they sleep. When they are hungry, they may always eat, if there is food. If they wish to play, no one will halt them and give them petty tasks to do, for in their play they learn more of life than can be taught by tongues and by training.

Suppose a youth, a ten-year-old boy, decides he will become a great hunter overnight. He is not scolded and sent sulkily to bed for his foolish presumption, nor do his parents condescend to his childish fantasy. Instead his father gravely spends the evening preparing a miniature bow which is not a toy, but an efficient weapon on a reduced scale. The bow is made with love and then it is given to the boy and he sets out for his distant hunting ground—a ridge, perhaps a hundred yards away—with the time-honored words of luck ringing in his ears, which are the same words spoken by the People to their mightiest hunter when he sets out on the two-month trip northward for musk ox. There is no distinction, and this lack of distinction is not a pretense, it is perfectly real. The boy will be a hunter? Very well then, he *shall* be a hunter—not a boy with a toy bow.

If the child is brave enough he may search the ridges and valleys through the hours of summer twilight which span the interval from dusk till dawn. When he returns at last with hunger gnawing at his stomach, he is greeted as gravely as if he were his father. The whole camp wishes to hear of his hunt, and he can expect the same ridicule at failure, or the same praise if he managed to kill a little bird, which would come upon a full-grown man. So he plays, and learns, under no shadow of parental disapproval, and under no restraint of fear.

The evenings are the best times in the summer camps. The men return from hunting over the plains, from building a new kayak, or perhaps from spearing lake trout at the rapids on the river. Hunger is satisfied. The old ones sit in the place of honor about the fires with the willow sleeping mats beneath their bony hams. Husbands and wives speak of the day's events. The children drift in from the outlying shadows hoping to hear the tales that may be told of other times.

Here is Atnalik who has learned a new "string-figure"—"cat's cradle," we should call it—during the day, and now he must show it to his family. He fumbles it, knots the string by accident, and joins in the general good-natured laughter at his clumsiness. But everyone has caught the infection now and lengths of sinew appear in everyone's hands. The space about the fire becomes a flashing spiderweb of thin gut strings as young and old hands play at the ancient game. Now Howmik makes the figure of the Two Fighting Wolverines. All the rest of the company stops to watch the battle of the two wolverines in the figure and Ootek provides a realistic two-way sound effect to make the fight all the more vivid. At last a loop collapses, one of the figures vanishes, and the victorious wolverine slides down the string and also disappears.

Ootek goes on to relate the story of the Ground Squirrel That Slept as it is recorded in the stylistic figures of the shapes he weaves from string. Even old Kala bends her stiff fingers painfully to create the figure of Kumanik Angkuni, the Great Lake. The figures go on endlessly, and there is shouting when a new one appears, and laughter when an old one is fumbled.

Suddenly the three dogs that have been watching the proceedings with puzzled interest break into high-pitched and puppyish howls, announcing the coming of old Hekwaw. Howmik stirs up the fire so the soup will heat, for a visitor, even if he comes only from the next tent, must always be fed at once.

It is a rare night when someone does not come to visit. Often the entire population crowds around one fire and at such a time perhaps Hekwaw will heed the patient pleading in the black eyes of silent children and will begin a tale:

This is Kiviok I will tell you about, and Kiviok was a wandering man. He was the grandson of Tuktoriak, the Spirit of the deer, and that is why he was a wandering man.

It is told that Kiviok once lived far to the west of here, somewhere by a great lake that even I have never seen. Kiviok was a young man then, and he lived with his parents, but one day when Kiviok was away hunting musk ox, Ejaka, the half-men from the Northwest, came on the camp and cut the life from his mother and father and left him alone in the land.

So Kiviok took his kayak and paddled south down the shores of the lake until he came to a channel between two great mountains. When he drew close, he saw that these were not mountains but the two jaws of a gigantic bear, and the jaws opened and shut without ceasing, and the crash of the enormous white teeth was as loud as the thunder of Kaila. But Kiviok was not afraid, and he waited until the jaws just started to open, then he dashed his kayak through the channel. The big jaws of the bear closed at once and they chopped off the stern part of the kayak, but Kiviok escaped.

Now Kiviok came to a new land in the South and there he found a tent with a woman and her daughter Ularik. Kiviok slept with the daughter and she was his wife and for a time all went well. But it came about that the old woman grew jealous and wished Kiviok was *her* husband. She waited until Kiviok had gone off on a hunt. Then she offered to braid her daughter's hair. She pretended to fix the *tuglee*, the wooden ornaments, in the hair of her daughter, but instead she wound the hair around the girl's throat and choked her to death. Then she took her sharp *ulu* and skinned the girl's face, and pulled the skin right over her own ancient head.

When Kiviok came home from his hunt he went to bed with the old woman, thinking she was his wife, but as it happened he had got wet during the day, and the moisture shrunk the false skin on the old woman's face so that it all split and came off. When Kiviok saw how he had been tricked, he jumped into his kayak and fled.

He came to a place where there was a musk ox who talked like a man, and the musk ox offered Kiviok his daughter, if the man would stay with him and defend the musk ox from the wolves. But Kiviok said, "Your daughter is too hairy to come into my bed!" And he fled away in his kayak again.

Kiviok traveled on and many strange things happened to him and he saw many strange things, but all at once he found himself back on the great lake where his parents had lived, and he saw that a party of Ejaka stood on the shore waiting for him to land so they could kill him.

Kiviok stayed in the kayak and he called out, "Hey there! You half-men! Come into the water and fight!"

The Ejaka were so angry that they swam out into the lake, but Kiviok dived into the water and swam underneath them, stabbing them all in the bellies so that they died.

That is the story of Kiviok the wandering man, and of his fight with the Ejaka. I don't know any more about him.

After Hekwaw has finished, there will be other tales by other people. Old Kala may tell her favorite story, of the man who had five wives who turned into lemmings one winter night. . . . And so it goes, for there are hundreds of these tales in the minds of the People and, though they have been told many times, the listeners never grow weary of hearing them yet again.

If several visitors come of an evening, then Ootek will take his great hoop-drum down from the poles of the tent, and after holding it over the fire so that the gut will be stretched taut by the heat, he will offer it to one of the visiting men. The men are modest and the drum will be passed from one to the other until at last one of them, Ohoto perhaps, will take it. He gets up from the squatting circle of People and walks to the center of the group, hard by the fire.

For a while he stands there, embarrassed, and the

audience shouts and argues about what song he should sing. At last Ohoto says, "Very well then, all you with big noisy voices, I will sing my own song, the one I composed in honor of myself as a hunter."

He holds the drum by a handle and twirls it around and around, striking it lightly along the edge of the hoop with a stick. The tempo begins as a slow rhythmic beat, and Ohoto begins to shuffle about looking like a trained bear at a circus. He bends sharply forward from the waist and suddenly he begins singing his song. It goes something like this:

> *Oh indeed I am a mighty hunter of deer!*
> *Out on the plains where the rocks are.*
> *But with my little eyes, like the lemming's,*
> *I can hardly tell the deer from the rocks.*
> *And with my weak arms, like a snowbird's,*
> *I cannot shoot an arrow straight from my bow,*
> *Out on the plains where the rocks are.*
>
> *Nevertheless I go out on the plains,*
> *Out on the plains where the rocks are.*
> *And I shoot my arrows into the rocks,*
> *For someday one of the rocks may be a deer.*
> *Then indeed will I be a great hunter,*
> *Out on the plains where the rocks are.*

At the end of each verse the audience takes up the time-honored chorus, and the listeners sway in their places with their eyes tightly shut as they cry out the chant:

> *Ai-yai-ya-ya ai-ya-ya ai-ya-ya-ya . . .*

Ohoto shuffles about more and more quickly. The sweat pours from his face as the dim glow of the little fire sends his distorted shadow slithering in and out among the rocks by the fireplace. The tempo increases and when all the verses of the song have been sung, Ohoto collapses limply in his place and the drum is taken up by another.

The songs go on for hours. Most are songs of self-derision or perhaps sarcastic songs directed at a notorious coward or a lazy hunter. No man praises himself, and when he sings of himself, he always appears in the song as a fool, or as a man who is inadequate in the ways and skills of a hunter, or of a lover. Even ten-year-old Atnalik has invented his own song and he is encouraged to sing it, while his elders chant the chorus with particular gusto, and loudly applaud him when he is done.

Only the women do not sing their songs, for this is tabu while there are men present, but they carry the burden of the chorus and their high-pitched voices chant in the darkness like the unearthly voices of spirits.

The night passes quickly. Games, songs and stories fill the hours until the sun is again on the upsweep of its course in the round white belly of the dawn sky. The People eat a little and then go to sleep, all together up on the willow mats of the ledge.

In winter, the great length of the nights passes in the same pleasant manner. This is the time when the almost continuous darkness and cold could well drive men mad, but it is also the time of the greatest song feasts. Then song-cousins visit each other's camps and they give valuable presents and receive presents as valuable in return. Song-cousins contest with good-natured rivalry in the singing of songs to the accompaniment of the drum. Many new songs are composed and sung in the igloos in winter.

But songs alone do not fill the nights. There is a wide variety of games and of these the gambling games are the most interesting. The favorite gambling sport of the Ihalmiut is, like so many things in their culture, almost indistinguishable from an Indian counterpart. To play it, two men or two teams of men face each other over the expanse of a robe. The "dealer" has a stone or some other small object concealed in his hand and very rapidly he places that hand under the robe, then under his backside as he squats on the ground, then behind his back, and finally he holds the clenched fist up in full view of his opponent. Instantly the second man must indicate where he thinks the object is—in the hand, under the buttock, behind the back or under the robe. When, and if, he guesses correctly by putting his own hand in the corresponding spot, he becomes the dealer. The odds against him are three to one, and he may lose just about everything he owns before he gets a chance to carry the ball, but then he usually wins everything back again, with interest. The game is played with such speed that it is almost impossible to follow the motions of the players and, if nothing else, it makes for a remarkable quickness of eye.

In other days the Chipewyans used to hold gambling contests with their blood enemies, the Ihalmiut, on the narrow strip of land which divides their territories. I have heard the tale of one such game which lasted for two days and two nights without a break. The particular tournament I speak of ended with the Eskimos holding the entire wealth of the Indians, and they had to level their rifles and spears at the losers to prevent what threatened to become a sanguinary battle.

Among themselves, the Ihalmiut gamble with an eye to reality. They are well aware that a man who loses his rifle or his team of dogs will probably die of starvation. So it is the custom for the winner to return most of what he has won at the conclusion of the game. Thus the loser suffers no hardship. He may even have the dubious pleasure of losing the same rifle five times over, in the course of one evening of gaming.

These are but a few of the pleasures which belong to the days of the People. Their most lasting pleasures come from the labors of creation. Old Hekwaw at work on a new kayak is a man who is lost in his task. He knows the exquisite pleasure of creating a thing he can love. He knows all of the subtle joys of a fine craftsman as he delicately shapes the slender ribs of his craft. And it is only because he is in love with his labors that he can bring to completion this vessel, so light and graceful. He has only tools that he makes for himself. Using a bow drill constructed of a small bow, a wooden rod and a fine point of metal, he drills tiny holes in the willow ribs of the kayak and laces them firmly to the frame with delicate lashings of rawhide. He prolongs the easy sweep of the little craft into a long fragile beak supported by longitudinal stringers composed of dozens of short sections of spruce which have been intricately mortised and fitted together to make a piece of the requisite length. When the kayak frame has been finished, it looks like the exquisitely delicate skeleton of a great fish. It is a true work of art. Later, when it is covered with hides, Hekwaw paints a brilliant design on its decks with colors he grinds from stone and mixes with the fat of the deer. At length the kayak will take to the water, it will live under the hand of old Hekwaw and give him joy.

The Ihalmiut do not fill canvasses with their paintings, or inscribe figures on rocks, or carve figurines in clay or in stone, because in the lives of the People there is no room for the creation of objects of no practical value. What purpose is there in creating beautiful things if these must be abandoned when the family treks out over the Barrens? But the artistic sense is present and strongly developed. It is strongly alive in their stories and songs, and in the string-figures, but they also use it in the construction of things which assist in their living and in these cases it is no less an art. The pleasure of abstract creation is largely denied to them by the nature of the land, but still they know how to make beauty.

They know how to make beauty, and they also know how to enjoy it—for it is no uncommon thing to see an Ihalmio man squatting silently on a hill crest and watching, for hours at a time, the swift interplay of colors that sweep the sky at sunset and dawn. It is not unusual to see an Ihalmio pause for long minutes to watch the sleek beauty of a weasel or to stare into the brilliant heart of some minuscule flower. And these things are done quite unconsciously, too. There is no word for "beauty"—as such—in their language; it needs no words in their hearts.

XI

The Boy and the Black One

From several of the people, and through many evenings of talk and of storytelling, I have gathered together the parts of this story. I tell them now not as history, but as living memories which are woven, impartially, from threads of legend and from threads of reality. Here are three such memories, and these recall three days from a year which is past—days that are linked together by the passage of time, by the spirit of the Black One and by the recollection of men. To our eyes the stories the Ihalmiut love to recount of the past must appear as creations of fantasy, but in the eyes of the People these stories are the stuff of which life is made. It matters little whether things happened as they are said to have happened. It only matters that the three days I speak of were good to the People who treasure their memories.

The first day was a cloudless one in September. A steady south wind kept the glowing leaves of the dwarf willows in motion above the close-cropped lichens. A raven circled lazily over the river called Innuit Ku, alone in the sweep of the sky, playing and rolling in the wind like a leaf caught in an updraft of warm air. The raven could see more than the man, yet Hekwaw knew without seeing that the tundra to the north had come alive and was moving.

Hekwaw climbed carefully into his nervous kayak from an overhanging ledge of rock at the river's edge. With a few quick strokes of the long, double-bladed paddle he sent the kayak clear of the slack water and into the swift and steady flow of the river. The south wind carried the smell of cattle and the rough banks of the river were scarred by deeply worn ruts like the trails thirsty cows leave on the muddy banks of placid woodland streams in the far South.

The kayak drifted on toward the mouth of the river, where it emptied into Kakut Kumanik, and the stink of fresh manure grew heavier on the air. A strange waterline ran along the shores, a wide band of pure white, set between rock and water in sharp contrast to the brown stream and the black rocks. This was a belt of hair, a solid mat of hair shed in the river during the passage of the deer which had come that way in the space of a week.

A hundred yards short of the river mouth the steep banks abruptly subsided and the low rolling plains lay open to Hekwaw's gaze. Now he thrust against the paddle and the kayak fled into a backwater and hung there, rubbing its thin flanks on the edge of the rocks.

Hekwaw loosened the lashings of his deer spear and lifted the short-handled weapon until the arrow point just grazed his lips. Then he laid the spear across the thwart in front of him, satisfied that it was ready. He waited.

Three minutes, four . . . then the deer came!

They seemed to emerge from the rocky banks of the river as if by some strange geological genesis. They came quickly to the edge of the water in single file, a fawn leading and agilely threading its way between the sullen shapes of the boulders.

Hekwaw moved no more than the rocks about him. He held the kayak in check against the overhang and watched steadily as the fawn reached the water and, behind it, a hundred deer crowded forward on the slope.

The fawn stopped by the edge of the river and grazed idly amongst the harsh sedges while the rest of the herd reached the bank and began to shoulder each other forward. Turning a startled look on the throng which pressed upon it, the fawn left the sedges and waded carefully out until the current caught it and swept it off its feet. Then, with head high and its minute tail erect, it struck off bravely for the opposite shore.

Still Hekwaw did not move. He waited without motion until half of the deer had crossed, and the great bucks who were in the rear had entered the water. Then the kayak leaped into the swift current like a dog unleashed and in an instant it was among the swimming deer. With his left hand on the trailing paddle, Hekwaw steadied the fragile craft, and with his right hand he gripped the spear at its balance point—lifted it high—and made his first thrust.

His appearance had been so sudden that for a few moments the deer flow continued unbroken, but as the spear went home the river of deer dissolved into clots and fragments. There were perhaps fifty beasts in the river when Hekwaw appeared among them and these gave way to panic. Some swam for shore, and when their feet were almost on the rocks, turned about and thrashed back into the dangerous center of the river. A doe plunged in eccentric circles while her fawn, borne under by the surging hoofs of a group of bucks, was carried lifeless downstream. With their massive antlers raking the air, the bucks turned and followed the drowned fawn towards the bay.

Hekwaw sent the kayak after the fleeing bucks. He closed with them in half a dozen strokes, but for the moment he made no effort to come into spear distance. Instead he held the herd as a good cowboy holds a herd of beeves, and the bucks swam ahead of him with all the strength they could muster, holding their heads half sidewise to catch recurring glimpses out of white, staring eyes of the pursuing thing.

The hunter held them until a good mile of open bay separated them from safety on all sides and they were thrusting their weary bodies far beyond the river mouth. Then things were as Hekwaw wished. Without effort he drew abreast of the last buck in the line. It shook its head, swerved violently, but could not avoid the flickering thrust of the spear. The spear barely seemed to touch the beast before it was withdrawn, and the kayak was gone leaving the doomed buck to die.

Hekwaw killed with the ease and dexterity of a trained butcher, but with far less effort. Soon the herd of fat bucks swam no more and the surface of the bay was free of all motion except where the wind ruffled the clear waters.

Meanwhile a raven had dropped steeply down out of the

white sky until he was flying heavily above the dying deer
back at the crossing place. But his hunger was held in check
by the sight of three tiny figures approaching along the south
bank of the river. Angrily he circled over a doe, unwilling to
acknowledge the approach of the woman, the boy and the
dog. Then they were close. The raven suddenly forgot his
anger and towered steeply up from the rocks, and the boy's
sling whirred like a grouse in flight. The smooth stone caught
the raven on the bend of his outstretched wing and sent him
spiraling wildly into the current of the River of Men.

Finished with the bucks, Hekwaw turned back toward
the river mouth. As he passed each of the floating deer he
stopped to hook the foreleg cunningly behind the antlers in
such a way that the deer's nostrils were held above the water
and the animal could not become waterlogged and sink. The
breeze was rising and it was brisk enough to make the kayak
bound like a live thing. Hekwaw bent forward over his flying
paddle. Under the worn parka his muscles ebbed and flowed
until the kayak slipped above the river's grip, rising lightly
above the touch of the fast water, and skimmed upstream to
the crossing place.

He was half way there when he met the struggling body
of the drowning raven. Hekwaw grasped it swiftly and stuffed
it into the cockpit beside him, then drove on and beached the
kayak on the shore, where his wife waited.

Later that day, Bellikari, the son of Hekwaw, walked for
many miles around the shores of Kakut's Lake. Whenever he
found the grounded carcass of a deer, he waded into the
water, gutted the dead beast and dragged it up on the land. If
the hides were prime, he skinned them off with the skill of
one who knows his work well. Then the naked carcass was
quartered and placed in a hollow on a nearby ridge. Above
the meat, and around it, Bellikari erected a bastion of great
stones to hold the wolverines away. Atop the pile he placed
the antlered skull with the antlers still stretched against the
pale sky, so that when the snows came, the dead deer would
still signal its whereabouts to the man who had killed it.

When Bellikari returned to the night camp near the
crossing place, the work there was nearly done. His mother,
Eput, was squatting before the fire, carefully tending the iron
pot she had carried on her back the whole thirty miles from
Ootek's Lake. The pot was black with the thick soot of oily
bones and scraps of fat meat, for inside the pot the fat was

being rendered from the deer. The liquid fat bubbled silkily up to the rim as Eput threw in new strips of fine white suet which she was stripping from a pile of meat beside her.

Hekwaw sat on the ridge by the river, surrounded by a towering, bloody mound. Brilliant red meat it was, caught in the driving crimson rays of the setting sun which made the meat glow like the coals of a great fire. Hekwaw saw Bellikari and hailed him.

"Come here, little belly!" he called. "There is still much meat to slice while you spend the day walking pleasantly looking for duck eggs on the shore. Take these piles and spread them carefully upon the willow bushes and keep them clear of the ground."

Grinning broadly at the jibe, Bellikari went to help his father make the dry meat for the winter's food. At last they were called back to the fire by Eput, and the sky was dark above them.

Now the three Eskimos had finished their meal, and night fell upon them. They spoke of the hunt which was passed and there was laughter then, and singing afterwards. Eput bragged a little of the blocks of fat she had cooled and hardened in swathes of wet moss. Hekwaw and Bellikari looked at her handiwork and pretended to find bits of bone and twigs in the sweet-smelling and flawless blocks.

The fire died down and, as the boy Bellikari sat staring into the coals, his father reached into his hunting pouch and brought out the beak and the talons of the raven. Hekwaw had bound the bill and the feet in a tiny rawhide sack, and as Eput looked on with a frightened solemnity in her lined face, Hekwaw sewed the things from the raven onto the back of his son's parka.

Bellikari turned a puzzled face to his father, and the old hunter spoke to him quietly, by the side of the dying fire.

"Son of Eput," he said, and he looked not at his son, but to the dark plains that stretched away to the north. "Son of Eput, here is a thing for you to remember all the days of your life. In the time that is yours you will listen for the voice of the Raven. When the Raven Spirit calls in the night, you will listen and do what the spirit says you must do. This day you brought down the Raven, and the Black One does not die as other birds die. In all of my time I have not heard of a man who came close enough to the Black One to strike him down from the air. I think this is a sign that the Raven Spirit will help you, has chosen to help you. So you must not again lift your hand to the Black One of Air, but listen instead to the voice of the Raven in the long hours of darkness and do what his voice shall tell you to do."

Hekwaw finished speaking but Bellikari did not reply. He felt of the tiny packet sewed to his parka and he was a little afraid. Later that night, when the three of them lay under a fresh hide by the failing warmth of the fire, he snuggled close to his father and, when an arctic fox chose to bark from the hill, Bellikari listened and his heart thumped in his breast, for he was listening for the voice of the Black One of Air.

And so the first day of this story comes to an end. Beyond it lay the time when the snows came and the River of Men lay hidden under the sheath of white ice. The deer disappeared to the south, and Hekwaw and his family gave up the skin tent by Ootek's Lake and built their igloo by the nearby lake where Alekahaw—the Lame One—had his winter camp. The snows grew deeper and the cold sharper. Then one day Hekwaw's neighbor, Alekahaw, set out with his family to visit a distant camp of the People far to the north on the banks of the River of Men. The second of the three days tells of what came to pass during that journey.

The short winter day was half over, and Alekahaw was in a hurry. He waved the dog-driving stick over his head and the tail bones of a wolf which were tied to the stick rattled loudly in the still air. The dogs heard, and bounded forward again, and the twenty-foot *komatik*—the sled—creaked over the exposed black rock of a ridge and careened off into the snow-packed gulley below.

Kaluk, Alekahaw's wife, sat on the sled with her children, her six-year-old daughter Kowtuk and her three-year-old son Kelaharuk. Alekahaw ran beside his dogs on the upgrades, but on the down slopes he flung himself on the back of the komatik, for he had a leg that was crippled from an ancient thrust of a wounded musk oxen's horn, and he could not run so well as other men.

The sled charged down the slope and the dogs curled up their tails and drew in their rumps as they scampered to get out of its way. The snow lay like a pavement of quartz and no wind blew over its burnished white face. The sun hung pendant on the rim of the sky and it was a cold, dying flame, though it stood at the peak of its rise for that day. Under the

hides on the sled, the woman sat still as a dead thing, for she had no motions to waste in her struggle to protect herself and the children from the cold which beset them.

Now from a valley ahead there came the discordant wailing of dogs. Alekahaw's team broke into a gallop and the man leaped from the sled to run limping beside it, shouting the time-honored greeting of the Ihalmiut at the top of his lungs.

"*Aija!*" he cried. "Look up you of the People and see us! For we come from the right side—from the right side of the ridge!"

And from the domes of three igloos men and women crawled out into the thin light of day and waved their arms and shouted cheerfully at the newcomers.

The dogs threw their necks against the thongs and the big komatik bounced wickedly over the drifts to be halted only when Alekahaw jumped on the back and threw out the brake. This was a section of caribou antler, cut in such a way that its prongs could be pressed into the snow with one's foot and so bring the sled to a halt.

The brother of the woman Kaluk, whose name was Katelo, now dragged his sister from under the hides and she rolled, shrieking happily, in the snow while her stiff limbs recovered their powers of motion. Her two children crawled out from under the robes and dashed for the entrance of an igloo, like rabbits caught in the open by hounds.

A second man took the dogs and led them off to the picketing place, while Alekahaw went with Katelo to a thick, packed bank of hard snow nearby. Here Alekahaw thrust his long, willowy snow probe into the drift, feeling the firmness of the snow underneath. He tested, then he laughed with satisfaction and drew out his snow knife.

The place was noisy with voices, for those in the camp had gathered to greet the recent arrivals. Onekwaw's wife was shouting to all of them to come and eat in her igloo. Alekahaw answered that his belly could wait, for there was work to be done. The rest of the people gathered under the low dome of Onekwaw's igloo and heard the new gossip which was to be told.

Meanwhile Alekahaw and his brother-in-law dug out a circular pit in the chosen part of the drift. Alekahaw stood in this hollow while Katelo cut thin blocks of hard snow, beveled them at top and bottom, and handed them to Alekahaw who used them to build the first circular tier of the wall. He began with one triangular block and as his second row reached this block it was slanted upward so that the work formed a continuous spiral. It went very quickly and as the tiers rose, the beveled edges of the blocks slanted them inward until a dome began to shape.

In less than an hour Alekahaw stood under the dome and carefully trimmed the key block so it slid into place at the top of the igloo. When it was done, he took his snow knife and cut a door in the south side of the dome and crawled out to help Katelo stuff up the chinks with soft snow and to build a long, arched tunnel of snow blocks away from the door.

A high, keening sound in the air was growing steadily louder, and the two men hurried to finish their work. They built up the sleeping ledge that covered half the floor space of the igloo, and they brought in Alekahaw's scanty belongings.

The sun was now only a memory and no twilight showed. Overhead the green shimmer of the aurora flickered nervously, and the high, distant note of the blizzard grew louder. It struck with no warning of wind, except for a distant whine. But in the instant of striking it transfigured the land with a mad, roaring agony. The drifts which had appeared to be as hard as the rocks they covered were scoured by the wind until they gave up sand-like fragments of snow which whirled and cut at the two men who stood by the new igloo with their backs to the gale.

White darkness closed in on the camp. The two men bent double against the wind and worked their way to the tunnel of Onekwaw's igloo, and there they stripped off their outer garments and placed them in a niche.

The broad sleeping ledge of Onekwaw's home was crowded with people, for there were three families in the camp, and all three were here to welcome the family of Alekahaw. There had been much drinking of cold soup, and much talk, while the feeble fat lamp flickered from a ledge beside the tunnel entrance. But the best talk was yet to come, for Alekahaw had driven for many days over the Barrens from the camp of Hekwaw the great hunter, and he had a remarkable tale to relate.

With a soup bowl of musk ox horn on his lap, Alekahaw settled himself on the ledge. Outside the igloo, the gale snarled and shrieked, but inside the gale was only a shadow, less than a shadow, over the minds of the People. There was talk, there was laughter, until after a while Alekahaw shouted:

"I have a tale to tell!"

And the many voices fell silent, and Alekahaw's voice contended alone with the scurrilous fury of the wind's voice outside the igloo.

"Well, now," he said, "that was indeed very good soup as my belly will tell you"—and he burped loudly to show what he meant—"and perhaps it is too good for a fool like me. But listen, for I shall tell you about this fool, Alekahaw, who sits on the fine sleeping ledge of Onekwaw and his wife." He paused and looked around the igloo, which was a sphere of darkness with a thick, white, luminous cover. He began:

You have all heard how Bellikari, the son of Hekwaw, found the Black Spirit of Air in the fall of the year that is gone? Well, I too heard the story from old Hekwaw himself, but you know, I have a powerful spirit of my own called Atinhuit who looks more like a bear than a man, and who I always thought was stronger than any bird spirit could be.

Now when Kaluk, this woman my wife, and I decided to travel north to your camp, old Hekwaw asked if I wanted the good wishes of Kaila, the God of All Weather, to help us along. One does not refuse such a thing, so I asked Hekwaw to speak to Kaila through the spirits he knows, but the old man instead called on Bellikari, his son, to speak to Kaila for me.

Being very much of a fool, I didn't think so highly of that, for Bellikari is not yet a shaman like his father old Hekwaw. But I was a polite fool, and so it happened that Bellikari was called to the task of his father. He stood in the center of the igloo and he called loudly to the Black One of Air, the Raven, and after a while he collapsed on the floor and, to my surprise, the great harsh voice of the Raven came out of his throat, and it called five times. I was a little afraid, but still I did not think the Black One was as strong as Atinhuit, my own personal spirit.

When Bellikari recovered himself he said that he had not spoken to Kaila at all! Only that he had seen the Raven Spirit and it had warned him not to travel out on the plains for the space of five days, else he would meet the great winds of Kaila and not return to his igloo again.

It was all clear enough, but then I am a fool. I thought that if the boy had not spoken to Kaila, then his spirit must have been weak. I trusted in Atinhuit, *my* spirit, and that very day we packed up and drove off for the north, though old Hekwaw was angry when we ignored the words of his son.

As we drove off, Bellikari gave me a wing-feather of the Raven and he told me that if I came into trouble, I should ask it for aid. And he passed his amulet belt under my arms and spoke to the sky, saying:

"Watch this man who is blood of our blood! Speak to him with thy voice which is as harsh as the rocks, if he has need! Come to his eyes and show him the way he must go, if he calls for your help!"

Then away we went northward, and we had traveled the lifeless plains for only a single day when we were met by the great wind of Kaila, as the Raven Spirit had said. We tried to make camp but we could find no snow fit for an igloo and at last I turned the dogs out of the mouth of the wind and let them run straight before it, while we all sat on the sled to keep each other from freezing.

But that wind was a real devil wind and it changed its direction so many times that I, being very much of a fool, was quite lost on the plains. At last we were forced to make a rough camp in the lee of the sled, and here we hungered and froze for the five days of that wind. Really, I was frightened, for we had only a little food left. But then when the storm at last came to an end, this woman here, my wife, remembered what the boy Bellikari had said, and she told me to go stand on a hill and speak to the Black One and ask him for aid.

I was frightened, so I went and stood on the hill and I could see nothing I knew in all the land, and that made me more frightened. Atinhuit had not offered to help me, so I cried:

"Listen, you Black One of Air! Listen to the cry of a fool who is lost, and come from your place in the dark sky and show him the way!"

There was no answer in all the land that was so still after the blizzard, so I turned and walked down toward the place where my dogs and my wife waited. But suddenly Kaluk screamed out to me, "Look over your shoulder!" and when I looked, there was a great black-winged Raven and it flew straight towards the horizon from the hill where I had stood!

Well, we turned our dogs and we followed the way of the bird and in two days we came over the Little Hills to your camps. And so you see what manner of fool is this fellow Alekahaw! But not so much of a fool that he will forget to give a small gift to the ravens when the deer again come to the land!

After the story was told, everyone in the igloo spoke at length of the thing which had happened, and all were pleased with the tale. And many resolved, in their hearts, to give a small gift to the ravens when spring brought the return of the deer.

Then Onekwaw brought out his drum and someone took it and the singing began; and it lasted until the new day dawned feebly over the land. The gale was dead and forgotten and the sun again hung coldly on the rim of the winter sky. And so the second day that I tell of came to its end.

Now that was the first winter Bellikari trapped foxes all on his own, and his father had given him five traps to set where he chose. Since it was his first season as a trapper, he made his mistakes, and not the least of these was that he delayed too long in the late winter months and could not pick up his traps before the spring thaws had come to the land.

It had been a bad winter. Before spring there were deaths in some of the camps, though in Hekwaw's igloo there was enough food for life. It had been particularly hard for the woman Eput, wife of old Hekwaw, for in the time when food was the scarcest, she gave birth to a son who was the brother of Bellikari.

The birth was hard. Bellikari watched it and he was frightened. He watched while one woman grasped his mother's outstretched arms as she lay in her agony there on the ledge. He watched as the second midwife grasped Eput about her broad belly and forced the unborn one down out of the womb.

Then there had been a month when Eput was unclean after the birth, and neither Bellikari nor his father could enter the igloo at all. For a month, Eput could not be permitted to leave the snow walls of her prison and all her food had to be prepared out of doors and brought to the mother and child in special vessels which no one else dared to use. The man and his son Bellikari had known what real hunger was during that time, until the days suddenly changed and grew warm and spring returned out of the south.

Now the winter was done with, and on the third day of my story Bellikari had gone to reclaim his traps, to spring them and to cache them high on the hills where he could find them when another winter had come.

It was June as we walked over the long roll of the hills which lie to the north of the river. Bellikari carried enough food for a week; that is to say he carried a handful of dried meat. But it was enough, for already the birds were flocking into the plains and the little streams of the muskegs were thronged with fat suckers, anxious to spawn. This was the fourth day of Bellikari's journey and it had taken him that long to cover, on foot, a distance dog teams in winter could have covered in half a day. There was a particularly rocky ridge which lay between two little lakes and in this place the boulders were so huge that an igloo would have been dwarfed beside them. Winding among these great rocks were the trails of the deer and it was beside these trails that Bellikari had set some of his traps.

His sodden skin boots slipped on the rocks as he climbed the steaming slope of the sun-drenched ridge. Behind him the wet plains wavered and shook under the heat waves. Green mosses flared on the boulders and the lichens were thrusting their gray-blue fingers out of the gravel.

Bellikari came to his first trap and found it had been sprung. A wisp of white fur told him he had caught a fox but the tracks on the sand showed that a hungry wolf had come past after the trap had been sprung.

The second trap lay as the boy had set it. Now he tripped it, put it in his pack and went on. Ahead of him the great rocks had parted to form a deep gulley, and as Bellikari passed into its mouth, two big arctic hares leaped from the darkness under a rock and fled like gray wraiths out of sight of the boy. Bellikari was angry that he had not been prepared for them, so he slipped his bow out of its case, fitted an arrow to it and was about to go forward when the voice of the Black One spoke out of the warm silence ahead.

The Spirit spoke in the tongue of the bird, a harsh, terrified croaking so charged with alarm that it needed no words to carry its message of fear into the heart of the boy.

Bellikari stood still for a moment, in the deep shadows of the canyon, and his heart raced like the heart of a hare in flight. He was frightened and unsure of himself. There was no doubt in his mind that the Raven Spirit had spoken to him, warning him of a danger which lay in his path. But what danger? And what should he do? Was it the Inua, the Ghost of the Rocks, who lurked at the end of the canyon? Was it Paija, the one-legged devil who feeds on men's blood? Bellikari had no way of knowing, and now he backed cautiously out of the rocky ravine, the way he had come, with his musk ox horn bow half-bent and the arrow still held to the string.

He backed out of the canyon, then he climbed cautiously to the top of one of the rocks which hemmed in the dark gully, and from this vantage point he could see ahead to the exit of the ravine that had been hidden from view. He looked, and the blood coursed savagely into his throat—for there on the ridge, a stone's throw from where he would have emerged from the gully, was Akla, the great bear of the Barrens!

Akla, the frightful brown bear who towers twice as high as the white bear of the arctic; Akla, the mysterious monster few white men have even heard of; Akla the terrible, whose paw-prints in the sand are as long as the forearm of a man; Akla, whose name is the best synonym for *fear* in the tongue of the People!

He is rare, so rare that many men of the Ihalmiut have never even encountered his footprints, and for that they are grateful. Yet in truth, he exists, this grizzly bear of the Barrens. Now Bellikari saw him and recalled the tales he had heard of the fierceness of Akla, and now he knew what the Raven Spirit had warned him against. But with the foolhardiness of youth, Bellikari drew back the gut-string of his bow and let the thin arrow fly.

The Black Spirit was indeed kind to the boy for he made sure that the arrow fell far short of the brown bulk of the bear. And so Akla did not notice the puny shape of the youth on the rock, and he ambled over the ridge with a ponderous grace and went on his way, unaware of the boy.

It was a full hour before Bellikari dared come down from his rock, and he was trembling as he circled the canyon and came at last to the place where his third trap had been. It had been dragged from its anchor, and the chain that held it had been snapped like a twig of green willow. About it there was a ring of black feathers, and fresh blood smeared both the trap and the rocks. But of the trapped raven who had called out the warning, nothing remained but a claw and the upper part of the beak. This was the bird which had come to the bait Bellikari had left for the foxes, and had been itself trapped. It was the one which had cried out in terror as Akla approached it. And Bellikari had heard the warning, and had not come suddenly on the bear as it fed. And so the boy lived—though the raven was dead.

Bellikari completed the trip to the last of his traps, though he was greatly afraid. He moved very quickly, and did not linger long at his work. When the last trap had been found, he turned back, and if he did not quite run, he walked exceedingly fast. Yet he had time to stop and pick up the claw and bill of the raven, and to add these to the little amulet pouch he carried on the belt round his shoulder.

He was still half a day's walk from the camp when he

saw the ravens again, but this time he was not at a loss for their meaning, nor was he frightened, but instead he was wildly excited.

They came out of the south, like flights of black clouds. Two hundred ravens perhaps, in flocks of a dozen or so. They came steadily on into the north flying very high in the sky. The leaders of the flocks tumbled and rolled like clowns at the head of a parade. And in fact, these ravens were indeed leading a mighty parade.

From a hill near at hand, Bellikari watched the ravens swing by, then he looked down at the hosts which were coming. Far to the south, the dun-colored face of the land was in motion. It rippled, not with the rise and the fall of heat waves, but with the swaying backs of the deer!

Forgetting Akla, his fears, and the winter behind him, Bellikari ran down the hill like a mad thing, and as he came in sight of the camps he was shouting so loudly that all in the tents rushed out to see what was the matter.

"Tuktu mie! They are coming!" he screamed. And those who heard knew that the deer had again returned to the land.

So the third day—the third memory—is brought to an end.

These are only three days chosen from the thousands that have passed into story, and that are relieved about the campfires which glow on the plains drained by the River of Men. And these things which are of the past shall not be forgotten while voices and memories still remain in that land.

XII

The Shape of the Law

Throughout June of 1948, while we were still at Windy Cabin, Andy so conscientiously pursued caribou in the name of science that I was forced to remember I too was a biologist of sorts. I salved my conscience by amassing a collection of the small mammals that lived in the mosses and lichens of the plains. My collecting equipment consisted of three dozen ordinary mousetraps, widely dispersed and marked with little flags of red cloth so they could be found again.

One day I casually asked Ootek to check some of the traps while I looked at the rest. An hour later, when I had finished my part and was heading back for the cabin, he joined me. He carried his skin pack-sack and as he jog-trotted across the tundra he held the bag well away from his side as if it contained something far too precious to be subjected to bumps and jiggles.

Curious, I asked what he had found, but for once he was taciturn, refusing to answer except with muffled grunts. He seemed preoccupied, so I did not press the question.

At the cabin I unpacked half a dozen mice and lemmings from my specimen bag and laid them out on the table while

155

Ootek watched me with a puzzled frown on his face. At last I inquired whether anything had been caught in his share of the traps. He came to life suddenly, pulled open his sack and after delving into its murky depths for a moment or two produced a little bundle carefully wrapped in moss. This he handed to me without comment and watched intently as I unrolled it. The bundle contained a single mousetrap lying on a large piece of chocolate-colored peat which bore the clear and unmistakable imprint of a wolf's foot.

Somewhat taken aback, I turned to Ootek and asked him what this odd combination was supposed to mean. But Ootek became dreadfully embarrassed and refused to open his mouth. When I tried being stern, he began to stutter and at last he turned and fled to his tent.

Later on, Ohoto, always the most direct and unabashed of the Ihalmiut men, paid me a call. I showed him Ootek's strange trophy and asked him to explain its significance. He too seemed to have some difficulty in finding his tongue, but at last he told me what I wanted to know.

It was a shining example of the "oblique mind of the Eskimo," if you want to put it that way. But to me it was a prime example of the tremendous delicacy the Innuit can show when they feel called upon to give advice to a white man who, poor fellow, has more wealth than sense. Ootek had looked at my mousetraps and it had been painfully obvious to him that I was not going to catch any foxes or wolves. And not even in his most lurid dreams had he thought that white men put value on lemmings and mice or that I would deliberately try to catch these little beasts. So it seemed to Ootek that I was just incredibly naive in the arts of a trapper. Being my song-cousin, he felt it was his duty to show me the futility of my trapping methods but in such a manner that I would feel neither resentful nor foolish. Ootek hoped that when I saw the big wolf's track beside the frail little trap, I would get the point without any words being spoken.

When Ohoto explained all this I was annoyed, for I felt I was being treated as a somewhat backward child. Calling Ootek to the cabin I went to great lengths to explain why I wanted mice, not wolves; and Ootek, sensing my indignation, listened with grave concentration as I tried to explain about museums, and science, and other inexplicable phenomena of the white man's way of life.

When I finished, Ootek picked up a bundle of my traps

and walked off with them into the Barrens. The next morning there were five mice laid out on my skinning table, but Ootek never again spoke of my mousetrapping, nor did he show any further interest in improving my trapping technique. In interfering—no matter how hesitantly—with what I was doing, he had contravened a basic code of his People, and it may be he was ashamed of what he had done.

This is the first great law of the land: that a man's business is sacred unto himself, and that it is no part of his neighbor's duty to interfere in any way unless the community is endangered. However, this does not mean that assistance is withheld in cases of need. In fact, the second and perhaps the most important law of the land is that while there is food, equipment, or bodily strength in any one of the tents, no man in another tent shall want for any of these.

This belief has led to a communization of all material things in the most real and best sense of the word. Nevertheless, individual ownership still exists in the camps, and this paradox may seem hard to grasp. Put it this way: every item of equipment is the personal property of one person, or of a family group. But if a stranger in need of a spear should come to the place, any spear is his for the taking. He does not necessarily need to ask permission of the owners, though he usually does, and no direct recompense is expected or offered. He may or may not return the spear when he is finished, for the spear is now *his* property, and is not just something he borrowed.

Obviously the system is not abused. Used with discretion and only under pressure of real need, it has greatly assisted in making men's existence possible in the Barrens. The man who requires a spear will always, if he has time and materials, make one for himself. However, the man who needs a spear urgently, takes one from a neighbor, and it is given to him with good will.

This unusual approach to the problem of ownership was a source of annoyance to me until I grasped its significance. When I first came among the Ihalmiut, they, with their limited knowledge of white men, treated me as they would treat one another. They were not aware of the gap in law and usage which separated us. For instance, I had a rifle, a souvenir picked up during the war, which I treasured. It was an excellent deer gun and it went with me wherever I went and at night it stood close beside me. I seldom used it, for I do not shoot for amusement, or sport, and the occasions when Andy and I needed meat were few, since the Eskimos kept us well supplied.

One day a party of five Ihalmiut men walked down from the Little Hills country to visit us at the camp by Windy River. The weather had been exceptionally bad and the trip took nearly three days. These men had not brought rifles, for they had no ammunition. During the three days of the march they had existed on two little suckers they caught with their hands in a stream. After some sixty miles of the most devilish walking in all the world, they arrived at our camp, thoroughly tired and hungry, and yet they did not ask us for food.

To ask outright would have been a breach of good manners. One does not ask for food in the Barrens; it is automatically offered to a visitor on his arrival. But I was busy with some trivial chore. I greeted the visitors abstractedly and went back to my job while the five hungry men sat and waited with the most perfect patience.

Then Owliktuk saw a deer on the slope across the river from camp and he at once seized my rifle from its place by the side of the cabin and ran off to intercept the animal. He was gone well over an hour and long before he returned I had missed the rifle. Without thinking, I flew into a rage and stormed over to the waiting Ihalmiut demanding the instant return of my gun. It must have seemed like an incredible display of bad manners and infantile rage to those men, but they humored me. Ootek smiled reassuringly and explained that Owliktuk had only borrowed the rifle to kill a deer with, because they were all very hungry. Then, believing he had adequately explained things, he began to chat cheerfully about the bad weather. I was not in a mood for amiable chatter. I was bad weather myself, for I was thrice damned if any Eskimo who felt a casual urge was going to trot off with my treasured rifle under his arm.

Owliktuk came back at last, using the rifle as a shoulder stick on which to sling most of the edible portion of the deer he had shot. The barrel was drenched in blood and the stock was scratched where it had banged against rocks. Owliktuk flung his load to the ground and came into the cabin carrying the tongue and the brisket—the choice parts of the deer. He leaned the rifle against the door, handed me the meat and smiled pleasantly. And then I blasted him.

Poor Owliktuk! During all the rest of the time I knew him he was never again fully at ease in my presence. After that day, he approached me as if I were a potentially dangerous animal to be humored and placated constantly. Later on I did my best to remove the bad impression I had made, but I never succeeded completely. Now, when I remember how the Ihalmiut feel about these little things, I can understand why I failed.

The Ihalmiut forgave me, or rather they never judged me for my infantile outburst of selfishness. But in the future it was understood that I was an unfortunate barbarian who was as wildly jealous of his possessions as a wolf bitch is of her cubs. There was no retaliation, and I was at liberty to borrow, and keep, any possession of the People that I might fancy I needed. If I didn't care to play the game as it was played in the Barrens, that was my privilege and I was not to be penalized for it.

The two unwritten laws I have mentioned are loosely combined with all other laws of the land into a code of behavior known as the Law of Life. All of the delicately balanced minor and major restrictions which go to make up the law are flexible, and yet they impose barriers beyond which an Ihalmio does not dream of stepping. Very probably it is the flexible nature of the laws, their openness to individual interpretation, and their capacity to adjust to individual cases, that accounts for the remarkable absence of what we know as "crime" in the camps of the Ihalmiut.

Of all the stories written about the Innuit, as a whole, the majority have dwelt with a morbid and smug satisfaction on the Eskimo deviations from the moral codes we white men have developed. Tales of cannibalism, wife-sharing, murder, infanticide, cruelty and theft appear with monotonous frequency in arctic stories, where they not only serve to supply a sensational element, but also provide the popular justification for the intrusion of the self-righteous white men who would destroy the laws and beliefs of the People in order to replace them with others which have no place in the land.

Take murder as an example. If you examine the Royal Canadian Mounted Police reports for the last twenty years, and compare the number of murders committed by Eskimos with the number of murders recorded in a corresponding numerical segment of any Province of Canada, or any State of the Union, you will discover that murder is a rarity in the Innuit camps, a phenomenon. Furthermore, many of the so-called Eskimo "murders" were not murders at all, but mercy killings dictated by dire necessity. Of the homicides

which remain, the balance are concerned with the killing of
white men when the murderers were under implied or direct
threats from the visitors, threats which brought an unreason-
ing fear to the Innuit, for they were threats which could not
be understood by the Eskimo mind. I do not know of an
authentic case of an Eskimo killing a white man for motives
of revenge or of gain, but only from motives of self-defense,
mistaken or real. The basic motivation of such killings has
always been fear.

There are other causes for the rare murders which are
committed, and of these blood revenge must be mentioned,
though there are only a very few authentic cases of it in all
the annals of the North. There is, too, the case of the "amok"
killer in the grip of a strange malady called "arctic hysteria."
This form of temporary insanity is, of course, not restricted
to the Eskimos. In the past few years there have been
numerous "amok" killings in the United States and Canada,
and in many cases these resulted from a religious mania.
However, such derangements among Eskimos are seldom
traceable to the native religious beliefs of the Innuit. The
most notorious case of a mass killing among the Eskimos
followed hard on the visit of a missionary to a native village.
When the R.C.M.P. investigated rumors of murder in this
village they found that one man who had been impressed and
frightened by dimly conceived and misunderstood aspects of
our Christian dogma had become extremely morose and had
finally gone mad. He believed that he was the reincarnation
of Christ, and when he announced this fact, a wave of
hysteria swept his village. The madman murdered several
people before he was finally executed by an old Inuk who,
almost alone, had remained aloof from the white man's
religion—and so, in this case, had alone managed to remain
sane enough to deal with the murderer.

The point I wish to make is that murder for motives of
gain, or for other cold-blooded reasons of self, is foreign to
the mind of the Ihalmiut. With them the killing of a man may
be sanctioned only as a solution to a situation where other
men's lives are threatened. In all the folk history of the
Ihalmiut there exists only a handful of memories of homicide,
and most of these were brought about as the sole possible
means of removing internal dangers which threatened the
People. There is, for example, the case of one man who
became mad during the long arctic night and killed two of his
brothers, who he believed were plotting against his life, then

threatened all those in the camp. He was a victim of arctic hysteria and he was himself killed only after a consultation of all the remaining men had resulted in the decision to destroy him, for the good of the group.

Infanticide is another favorite bogey of the missionaries and a stand-by of sensationalist writers. The tragedy is that it most certainly does occur, and will continue to occur while there is need for it. That is the point—there is an inescapable need for it at times, and nothing we can say will change the need; nothing we can preach to the Innuit will alleviate that tragic necessity.

The need for infanticide produces the most terrible situation an Eskimo can be forced to cope with, for all Eskimos—and the Ihalmiut in particular—are passionately fond of their children. Their young ones receive more deep-rooted affection, and are shown more tolerance and kindness than many of the children of our homes ever know. To have children and to raise them to maturity is a passion even stronger in the Ihalmiut than in us, because the People are much closer to the primeval drive towards reproduction of the species than we are. But despite the love they bear for their offspring, and despite this consuming desire to see children grow into men of their blood, there are times when a more desperate emotion overwhelms the parents.

To understand what infanticide really means in the Barrens, you must first understand that in those hard lands all human life is valued according to a fixed-priority system that may seem callous to us who can afford to oppose sentimentality to reality. The unwritten order of survival places the man, the hunter, at the head of the list as the most indispensable member of the family group. He is the provider and should he die it does not greatly matter whether or not the rest of his family lives through the immediate crisis, since they cannot live for long afterwards without a hunter's help.

Next to the man stands his wife. If there is more than one wife, the youngest stands next to the man. From her womb the continuity of new life will be maintained. Yet even she is not irreplaceable, for there is a surplus of women in this land where many men lose their lives simply in the course of their everyday efforts. Old wives quickly lose their priority, for their wombs become sterile and they can give little more to their race.

The children must stand below both the man and his

wife. This is a cruel thing indeed, but the cruelty is not the work of the parents. It weighs more heavily upon them than it does on the children. But new birth can replace sons and daughters and so their loss is tragic only in terms of emotions; for while wombs remain fertile and loins remain potent, children may be born again.

The old people stand at the lowest point of the scale. The men whose arms are no longer strong and the women whose wombs are no longer fecund—these live on the thin edge of time, with death always before them. When the choice of living and dying comes upon a camp of the People, when starvation announces the coming of death, then the aged ones must be prepared to go first, to seek death voluntarily so that the rest of the family may cling a little longer to life. The old ones seldom die a natural death and often they die by their own hands. Suicide is not lawful in our eyes but as it comes to the People it is a great, and a very heroic, sacrifice—for it is the old who fear death most and who find it the hardest to die.

Put coldly like this, the value placed on the lives of men, women and children seems like a harsh, unnatural thing, but there is nothing else to be done. Who can care for helpless old people when their sons and daughters are gone? Who but the wolves? Who can care for children who have not yet been weaned, when the mother is gone? Only the wind and the snow. What can the wife feed her family when there is no man to bring in the meat of the deer? Only tears and the hard taste of dying.

The logic of the order of death in the Barrens is more inexorable than death itself, and as inescapable. Yet there are few of the People who, when the time of decision is on them, do not try desperately to escape the horror of seeing a loved one go into the night of the winter. Love overcomes logic. Many families have perished because love was too strong to let logic save the lives of all but a few.

Yes, infanticide happens. I have seen Ootek with his fourth child, Kalak, and I knew his other three children did not live their first year to its end. I have seen the overmastering devotion Ootek feels for Kalak, and I have seen the frantic desperation which fills him when danger threatens the child. But I should not like to know or feel what Ootek felt as he watched his first children die, unable to help them in the face of the grim trickery death played upon him.

Let the moralists peddle their wares to those who would

think of the Innuit as barbaric and bestial people who destroy
their own children. Let them preach the white man's love
which must be brought into the dark, savage hearts of the
Innuit. But let them keep their sanctimonious mouthings from
the ears of Ootek and those of his race, who alone know what
it is to assist death in his work.

There is a place in the great plains called the Lake of the
Dead Child, and on a promontory of this lake stands a small
cairn of stones. Through the interstices of the rocks you can
see the tiny bones of a child, and on the grave are the
decayed remnants of many things, robes of the best deerhide,
gifts of meat, toys carved from scraps of wood, and kamik-
boots sewed for a child's foot with infinite care. There are all
things needful for the living—or for the dead.

The story of that grave concerns a family of three who
lived alone by the lake during a winter long past. On a certain
year the father was stricken down with a strange illness so
that he was unable to complete his fall hunt and did not make
a large enough kill to last through the winter. It is told how
the blizzards came early and hunger followed. It is told how
the dogs were eaten and how, at last, the woman understood
that only if she made her way for ten days' travel on foot
over the winter Barrens, to the camps of her kinsfolk, could
her family survive.

The Ihalmiut do not say what the woman's thoughts
were as she saw the decision she must make. She knew she
must go alone, and could not carry a child with her. She
knew too that she could not leave the child behind, for her
husband was too ill to attend to it and there was no food he
could give it, for the child had not yet been weaned. Nothing
is said about the thoughts of the woman, but it is told how
she left that camp after coming to her decision. The few
scraps of food which remained she placed by her husband on
the sleeping ledge, and the child she placed under the snow.

It took the woman nearly two weeks to reach the igloos
of her people, and for five of those days she walked in a
blizzard. She walked almost a hundred miles without food,
but she arrived safely at her kinsmen's igloos. In a few days
the dog team of her brother took her back to the shores of
the Lake of the Dead Child. The sick man was rescued and
lived. In the years that followed, this couple had many
children and some of these still live in the land. But each
year, while they lived, the woman and her husband returned
to the shores of the distant lake, in the first days of spring,

and placed fresh clothing, food and toys on the grave of their first-born.

Truly, infanticide does exist in the land of the People.

There is also the crime of sexual promiscuity, which is almost as abhorrent to the men who carry the Word into far places as is the crime of murder. But I know from my experiences with the Eskimos that promiscuity in the world of the Innuit does not compare with its sordid prevalence in our lands. True, erotic play among children is common, but never hidden or driven out of sight to become something dirty and obscene. Apart from this, wife-sharing, as it is called, is really the only manisfestation of sexual promiscuity in the Barrens. Women for hire, clandestine sexual experiences, the thinly cloaked extra-marital relations of those who have been joined by the Church, all these belong to our race and not to the Ihalmiut. Wife-trading, in the Ihalmiut way of life, is a voluntary device which helps alleviate the hardships of the land. To begin with, only song-cousins or other close friends would normally consider the exchange of their wives. Contrary to popular opinion about Eskimos, a stranger is not expected to leap into bed with the wife of his host. That is a stupid lie with no basis in fact. . . . Well, perhaps it *has* a basis in fact, for many of the white men who have come to the land have demanded just such an arrangement, and, because the Innuit will go to great lengths to meet the wishes of a guest, it has occurred.

When a man must make a prolonged trip on a musk ox hunt, or on a visit to a distant relative, or for purposes of trading at some distant post, he often leaves his wife at home because of the dangers of travel. If there are children it would be foolish to risk either the wife or the children where there is no need. So it happens that when the man arrives at his destination his song-cousin may, with the wife's full consent, volunteer to share his wife with the visitor during the time of his stay.

This is contrary to the law of the white man, but to my unsubtle mind it seems a perfectly sane arrangement, particularly since there is no problem of illegitimate children in the Barrens, nor any jealousy of paternity. To the Ihalmiut the children themselves are what matter, and a child from any source whatever is as welcome as any other child in the camps. Paternity is unimportant. A man who questioned the paternity of his child would be thought mad. It would be the opinion of those in the camps that he ought to be grateful for the presence of any child. A child sired by a visitor is as much the son of the man of the family as the children he sires for himself.

Now this may be uncivilized behavior. But is it as barbaric as our repudiation of bastard children who must bear the stigma of their parents' "sin" throughout their lives?

As for theft and dishonesty, before the coming of white men the Ihalmiut were unaware of the meanings of these words. Obviously, theft can hardly occur in a land where the rules of ownership are those I have already described.

Unfortunately, cannibalism, like infanticide, does sometimes take place. But if it can be called a crime to eat the flesh of the dead in order that death may not claim those who still live, then our race and every race has been guilty of that crime. Many expeditions of white men into the arctic have come to know the same appalling needs which come to the Innuit, and not a few of these expeditions have saved lives at the expense of the dead. Yet though we condemn other peoples as cannibals, we pity these men of our own race, and we think of their acts as the ultimate bravery of which man is capable, for to force one's self to eat of the dead demands a courage few of us have.

I have spoken to an old woman who now lives near the coast and who in her youth survived a terrible winter by eating the flesh of her parents after they had died of starvation. The marks of that experience still lie on her though the event is now three decades in the past. She is an object of sympathy to her people and is cared for and helped by all manner of men who have heard her grim tale. As for the woman, she never recovered from the mental ordeal she had faced. Though she lived on in the body, in her heart death has lived for full thirty years.

Cannibalism does happen, though rarely. The wonder is that it does not happen more frequently and that murder and cannibalism do not happen together. There is no doubt at all but that the eating of the flesh of the dead is as abhorrent a thought to the Ihalmiut as it is to us. The difference is that the macabre decision must sometimes be met by the Ihalmiut, while we are spared.

Now I have mentioned many of the "crimes" of which the Innuit, as a race, are accused by those who seek an excuse for interfering with the ways of the People. The Ihalmiut, who must share this condemnation, are only men, after all, and not infallible. Therefore there are deviations from law, and there are crimes in the land; for no race of men can be free of these things. But there are also certain forces which the People control and which in turn direct the actions of men, and these forces keep the law-breaking within narrow bounds. To understand these forces is to realize why the Ihalmiut have no need of our laws to maintain the security of their way of life.

There is absolutely no internal organization to hold authority over the People. No one man, or body of men, holds power in any other sense than the magical. There is no council of elders, no policeman. There are no assemblies of government and, in the strictest sense, the Ihalmiut may be said to live in an anarchistic state, for they do not even have an inflexible code of laws.

Yet the People exist in amity together, and the secret of this is the secret of co-operative endeavor, limited only by the powers of human will and endurance. It is not blind obedience or obedience dictated by fear. Rather it is intelligent obedience to a simple code that makes sense to those who must live by its rules.

Now and again a man may willfully step over the borders of the unwritten law. Perhaps he may refuse to share his deer kill with a less fortunate neighbor. Let us look at the result.

Does the starving man revenge himself by killing the one who refused him, and then take what he needs from the man he has killed? Not at all. He goes elsewhere for help, and never by word or deed does he show any overt resentment or anger toward the man who turned a deaf ear to his plea.

This is so because there are certain things the Barrens do not allow to co-exist with men, and foremost among these is anger. Anger in the heart of a man of the Ihalmiut is as potentially dangerous as homicidal madness, for anger can make him overleap the law and endanger not only himself but the rest of his community. It can lead him to ignore the perils which beset him, and so bring him to destruction. Anger is a luxury in which the People dare not indulge, and, apart from these physical reasons for its absence, the Ihalmiut have always looked upon anger as a sign of savagery, of immaturity, or of inhuman nature.

Children alone are permitted brief outbursts of temper, for a child is not held responsible for its actions. But when a man gives way to anger it is something of the deepest shame to the beholders, for anger is the only really indecent thing in the land.

And so it is that a man who breaks the law is never punished in anger. The man who refused meat to his fellow may visit the camp of the aggrieved one, if he wishes, and he will be well received. The resentment felt against him will not be allowed to appear naked, and so provoke an outburst of physical violence.

However, methods of punishment do exist. Should a man continuously disregard the Law of Life, then little by little he finds himself isolated and shut off from the community. There can be no more powerful punishment in the lonely wastes of the Barrens, and in fact it is a punishment which can easily be fatal in a world where man must work closely with man in order to live. A small dose of ostracism usually brings the culprit to an acute awareness of his defects and he ceases to transgress the law. Thus while there is no overt act of justice or of social revenge, nevertheless the object is achieved and the wrong-doer almost invariably returns into the community once again, with no permanent stigma attached to his name. The law does not call for an eye for an eye. If possible the breaker of law is brought back to become an asset to the camps. His defection is tacitly forgotten, and to all intents and purposes it never happened at all.

Such is the punishment for most major offenses. Minor offenses are dealt with by enjoying the powerful weapons of ridicule, and the Ihalmiut are masters of that art. A man capable of doing his own hunting, but whose family must be fed by other hunters because he is lazy or simply indifferent, is made the subject of the drum-dance song and an object of biting laughter. Only a very callous man can face that sharp laugh for long. However, he knows that when he returns to his duties, the songs about him will disappear, and in time all memory of the incident will be washed from the minds of the People by common consent.

On the other hand if a man is prevented from doing his work because he has been crippled, or because he is one of those natural incompetents who botches whatever he puts his hand to, then the Law makes an exception. In our society, such unfortunates may become embittered, or may even grow dangerous as a result of the treatment meted out to them. In the Ihalmiut camps, those who are physically or mentally unable to cope with the problems of living are treated with inexhaustible patience and understanding. Poor, dull-witted

Onekwaw, for instance, never managed to succeed in a single deer hunt during all the time I knew him. He tried hard enough—but it was always someone else who had to keep Onekwaw's family from starving. And yet, as far as I know, no one ever seriously rebuked Onekwaw for being a burden to his People. True, everyone made fun of his efforts to be a great hunter, but this was good-natured fun and Onekwaw joined in it himself. He even seemed to extract some sort of compensation from being able to provide a source of amusement for the other men. He was the butt of innumerable good-humored jests—but he was never exposed to the bitter ridicule which is the punishment of those who are capable of obeying the law, but who refuse.

The only physical punishment in the Barrens is death, but the death penalty is not the same as with us. It is not intended as an act of social revenge or even as a warning to other potential wrong-doers. It exists only as a means of releasing a man who cannot live in the land he has defied, or as a means of releasing the People from an added danger to their lives.

When a man becomes mad (and only a madman kills, according to the beliefs of the People) and murders or threatens to murder those who live about him, then, and then only, the sentence of death is invoked. There is no trial, no official passing of judgment. Perhaps three or four men, usually those most closely related to or most closely concerned with the murderer, meet and speak indirectly of the problem which faces the entire community. One of their number is usually designated as the executioner. But he is not an instrument of justice as we know it, for his task is not to punish, but to release the soul of the madman from a physical life which can only end in agony of the flesh if it is prolonged. The executioner does his duty quickly and humanely—for the idea of physical or mental torture is simply not known to the Ihalmiut. When the deed is done, the executioner obeys the spirit laws and begs forgiveness from the ghost of the dead man. If he is lucky and the white men do not hear of it, that is the end of the matter. But in not a few cases Eskimos who have had the terrible task of destroying brothers, fathers, or sons, so that the rest may survive, have been brought to the bar of white man's justice and rewarded for the mental sufferings that they have endured by being hanged by the neck until they were dead.

XIII

Kakumee

Partly because the story of his life outlines in minuscule the tale of his People, and partly for other reasons, I give Kakumee,* the old shaman of the Barrens, a greater place in this book than I give to any other man. His story is one of disintegration and of degradation and this is also the tale of his People. His life is bitter and tragic, the more so because it is not his alone, but also the tragedy of his race.

It was a long time before I came to know much of his story, for the name of Kakumee is an anathema in the mouths of the Ihalmiut. When they can be brought to speak of him they speak shortly and with the bridle of fear on their tongues.

Even Ootek, who was my song-cousin, spoke of Kakumee only when I begged him to speak and he grew visibly uneasy whenever I mentioned the name of the old shaman. Ohoto too, that brash man who claimed to fear nothing,

---

*The name Kakumee is a pseudonym for a man whose real name was Pommela and who died in 1958, as described in the sequel to this book, *The Desperate People.*

would not tell me much of Kakumee but would deftly switch the subject and talk instead of the deer or of the land.

Franz had known him well, yet even in the stories Franz told I detected an undercurrent of tension and of uneasiness. Eventually it dawned upon me that Franz, who believed he was gifted as white men are with superiority over the primitive natives—Franz too was afraid of Kakumee!

Because I could at first gather only vague clues to the reasons which led the Ihalmiut to fear the old man, my curiosity grew. In the early summer of 1948 I even began to prepare for a journey northward to the shores of Kakumee Kumanik, where the two tents of the shaman stood apart from the rest of the People. The preparations were needless, for this man who had brought a great fear into the land had heard much of Andy and me from some of the other Ihalmiut, and had developed plans to bring us into the orbit of his influence.

One summer day I looked casually from the window of Windy Cabin and saw a stranger approaching. He came up and stood by the door, not offering to enter unbidden, as the other Eskimos always did. So I went out to meet him.

He was not a tall man, yet he was even more massively built than old Hekwaw. His great legs were bowed slightly apart, supporting a square body almost as broad as it was high. But it was his face that caught and held my attention. I shall never forget the face of Kakumee.

When I think of him, I remember those magnificent yet hideous masks the Iroquois used to carve to portray the faces of their devils. Kakumee's face was like a masterful devil-mask that had weathered and cracked through the centuries under the storms and the sun. It was ancient, not in terms of mere years, but ancient in time long since forgotten by men.

Two or three clumps of straggling hairs hung from his pointed goat-chin in the shadow of a bulbous lower lip. That great lip splayed downward to expose a broken, outpointing row of dark-colored teeth, each as massive as the tooth from the jaw of a fossil. A sparse fringe of hairlets was permanently cemented to his upper lip by an unchecked dribble of mucus. His eyes were tiny black marbles sunk deeply under the thrust of his brow and folded under taut curtains of skin, yet they glistened out from their crevices as the black eyes of great spiders shine from their shadowed caves under rocks. His forehead was itself a great rock, cut by ten thousand crevices left by the weather. Above his face was a wild mane of rough, graying hair knotted and twisted in confusion.

That was our first meeting, but many more followed as Kakumee sought by all the cunning he knew to turn Andy and me against the rest of the People.

He was the first Eskimo I had met who deliberately lied, and for a while I almost believed the slanderous stories he told us about Ootek and the others, for I was not prepared to find an Ihalmio who did not speak the truth. Kakumee did more than try to alienate us from the others with lies—he threatened them directly, and us indirectly; and it was only because we refused to be intimidated, and so set ourselves up against him, that the other men dared to remain our friends. Kakumee wheedled me, bribed me, lied to me, threatened me, and revolted me. Yet despite it all I grew fascinated by the character of the man, and increasingly covetous of the incredible store of knowledge he possessed of days lost to all memory but his.

He was a master of indirection, and his subtlety was often too much for mine, but after a while I began to understand him a little. In time, too, I managed to get at some of the stories about him which were known to the rest of the People.

Kakumee was born on the River of Men not far above the Little Lakes where the People now live. His father was Ajut, a shaman whose fame had spread beyond the limits of the plains and who was known even to the distant folk dwelling by the sea. In these days of his childhood, Kakumee was one of more than a thousand Ihalmiut who lived along the banks of the river and on the lakes thereabout.

Ajut's three wives had given him other sons and of these the eldest was Kakut, who lived to be a great man and the enemy of Kakumee. When Kakumee was born, about 1880, no white man had yet entered the land of the People. But in the spring of 1894 two canoes came down the river from the south bringing the first white stranger into the land. This man was Tyrrell, and though Kakumee was but a youth at the time, he can still recall every detail of that visit.

Tyrrell stayed only a day at the camp, because he was anxious about the future, and he did not know where the river would lead him. As a good host, Ajut undertook to accompany Tyrrell down-river and show him the way out of the Ihalmiut country. When the canoes moved off, they were accompanied by the kayaks of Ajut and of his eldest son Kakut.

When Ajut and Kakut returned to their home, nearly a month later, they brought extravagant tales of what they had seen of the fabulous things the white man carried in his canoes. Kakumee listened avidly to these tales of the wealth of the stranger, and he harbored them in his mind.

All of the Ihalmiut spoke of these things with much wonder, but though they saw and appreciated the worth of Tyrrell's belongings, they did not envy the white man. The People were not greedy for change and so remained content with the life they had always known by the River of Men. In a few years the little gifts Tyrrell had made to them were lost or broken and the memory of the white man's wealth grew dim. It was this way with all of the Ihalmiut save one alone.

Kakumee did not forget. He remembered the goods of the white man as if they had been, in fact, the goods of Kakumee. He dreamed vivid dreams and these remained in the daytime to haunt him. He was filled with a great longing he could not describe, for there were no words in the language of the Ihalmiut to describe the insatiable yearning that had come over him to possess material things. But he kept his dreams to himself, for he knew they were evil according to the Laws of Life in the land. So he spoke no word of the visions which were hidden deep in his mind.

In the winter of the year when Tyrrell passed down the river, Ajut decided his two eldest sons had crossed the threshold from childhood to manhood. During that winter both Kakut and Kakumee began to receive instruction in the shaman's secrets known to their father, for long ago it had been decided that these two sons of the shaman would follow in the path of old Ajut.

Ajut revealed to his sons all that he himself knew of the spirits of the land, and taught them the magic spells which are spoken in an ancient language. He explained the manner of calling on Kaila, the Wind of the Sky and the great God of all men. He warned the youths of the dangers of Paija, Apopa and other inimical spirits, and explained how they could master these beings.

Before the coming of spring there came a time when Ajut could teach his sons nothing more. Now it was left to them to find their own way. It is the custom for a youth who wishes to become a shaman to seek out seclusion far from all other men and there know such suffering that he may meet a *Tornrak*, a good spirit, who will speak to the novice as he lies or sits in a trance. This Tornrak then becomes the guiding spirit of the new shaman and is the strongest and most potent force the shaman can call on for aid in the future.

Kakut, being the eldest, was the first to set out alone from the camps. He was gone nearly two weeks and he carried no food for his trip nor did he eat during that time. It was a period of great storms and though he had no shelter from the driving winds, Kakut survived to return to the camp of his father and to tell of what he had found.

Five days out from the camp he had been halted by a blizzard and had squatted in the lee of a rock which thrust out from the snow. Here he stayed for a week or more—he could not tell how long it was—and he did not move nor did he eat. About the fifth day he thought he had died, yet in death he beheld a huge crooked stick pushed out of the snow at his feet. He listened with terror while the stick spoke strange words. Then it grew arms, long knotty arms, and from its lower end thrust out a spidery tangle of legs. Kakut was filled with fear, but all the same he drew out his snow knife and made a lunge at the Thing. His knife was twitched from his hand, so he flung himself on the being and grappled with its twisting body of wood until at long last he subdued it. Then he rose to his feet and said:

"Kaitorak—you, the Spirit of Forests! Now you are mine! You shall do my word in all things, and never again go free in the forests far to the south of this land!"

Kakut broke a twig from the back of the spirit and sewed it into his amulet belt, and then he came back to the camp. Thus it was that Kakut found his Tornrak.

It was Kakumee's turn then, and this is the tale that he tells of his search for the Tornrak:

I went forth from the camp in the morning before it was light, and I walked into the north. It was cold but I felt nothing of that. I was hungry yet I felt nothing of hunger. I was alone after a time in a place where not even a fox track crossed the snow. I came to a frozen lake and in the middle of it I built a half-shelter of snow and sat down to wait.

Nothing came for many days but the wind, then on a night there was a great crashing noise from deep under the ice. I thought at once of the Great Fish which is said to live in the lakes and I got up to run to the shore, but my legs were so stiff and cramped they refused to obey me. So I fell on the ice and lay as one who is dead.

The ice under me crashed and muttered and splintered until the cold water surged up through the cracks and filled my mouth and my nostrils. Still I could not move from that spot and at last the ice under me sank into the water and carried me down.

All was dark in my eyes and then slowly a thing began to take shape in the green mist of the water. It was no fish, but the head of a man with no body and with arms and legs springing right out of the head. But the strangest of all things was that this was the head of a white man, though not the one I had seen on the river the previous summer.

It was a strange face, heavily bearded and with cold eyes the color of sky. I knew I was drowning, and I struggled against the grip of the water and all the time that great head swam about me and laughed, making a horrible bubbling sound in my ears. I knew it was a Tornrak, and that I should grapple with it and conquer it so that it would help me in the future, but the cold water was filling my lungs and I was drowning.

I do not know how long I struggled under the ice but I believed I was dying, for all things faded from my mind. When I recovered myself, I was lying on top of the ice by a great black hole filled with water which did not wish to freeze. But my water-soaked garments had frozen hard to the ice underneath them. I was bitterly cold. I fought my way out of the clothing and it was hard as new iron. I tore flesh from my hands and my body, wriggling out of the ice-hard furs, but at last I was free and ran naked over the lake, and the frost did not touch me.

Later the People told me they followed my tracks for a full day's journey over the plains, and my bare footprints were clear in the snow. They came to the lake and saw the great hole, and my frozen clothes that looked like a dead man lying out there on the ice. But they did not go close, for no one could say how that hole had been opened through ten feet of hard winter ice.

When Kakumee told this story to Ajut, his father, the old man was greatly afraid. He could not understand what it meant. He knew only that Kakumee had failed to subdue the spirit he had seen and he may have feared that instead the spirit had captured Kakumee. But he could not be sure, and so he said nothing at all to the youth, and he told the People he believed Kakumee had captured a wonderful Tornrak.

In the summer of that year, Ajut died and was buried under rocks in the land where the frost does not leave the ground. He took with him his bow, his stone pipes, and his shaman's staff—but his magic he left to his sons.

Kakut was satisfied with his inheritance and after a little while he began to fill the place of his father. To him came those who suffered ills of the mind or of the body. Some he healed and some died, but Kakut's reputation grew steadily all through the land and he was known as a good man and as a great worker of magic.

It was otherwise with Kakumee. The restless and nameless desire of his childhood had become an irresistible curse since his novitiate on the ice of the lake. His strange dreams grew more vivid and so oppressive that even the familiar spirits at his command could give him no surcease. Often he thought of calling on the bodiless head of the white man who lived under the lake, but he was afraid, for he did not know if he could control it, and he feared that it might seize him and carry him back under the waters to die.

Kakumee's hunting did not prosper, nor did anything he attempted to do. He lost patience with his fine musk ox horn bow one day when he was hunting, for he had tried to make it kill a deer at three hundred paces, an impossible range, and so he flew into a rage at it and smashed it on a rock. He did not know why he did this. He did not know that he was remembering the rifle of the white visitor which could kill at three hundred paces.

He was content with nothing made by the People, with none of the tools or weapons, and he showed his discontent more and more as the years slipped away. Had he not been a shaman he would have been held up to ridicule, for it is often the excuse of a poor hunter that his weapons are inadequate to the task. But fear of the man was growing steadily in the hearts of the People.

This was the way of things until the fifth winter after the death of Ajut. Then came a time when Kakumee took a bride, and this was strange, for he was now twenty-two and long past the age when most Ihalmio men seek out a woman. He had been too obsessed by his dreams to want women. Now he took a young girl to wife and if reports speak truly, he loved her and found in her some measure of release from the frustration which tormented his hours. He loved her and so one night as they lay naked on the sleeping ledge of the igloo he told her the truth about his fight with the white devil he had met under the lake. She was young, not much more than a child, and she listened without comprehension to the tale and to the illusions of great wealth that Kakumee disclosed to her in his effort to rid himself of the weight of his dreams. She listened but could not understand, and one day she turned on her husband when others were near and openly ridiculed him in their hearing.

"You are a dreamer of dreams!" she cried. "But I am heavy with child, and I cannot suckle a child on the dream-stuff that fills your head and your heart. Give me something to fill these soft breasts of mine that I may know I married a man and a hunter."

Who knows what happened then in the mind of Kaku-mee? I think the love for his wife died as a hare dies when an arrow splits it from end to end. But before dawn came again to that winter encampment, Kakumee had vanished out of the land. By morning the ceaseless swirl of the drifts had filled up the tracks of his dog sled so that no one even knew which way he had gone. He had told no one of his plans, for not even his wife would have believed he was mad enough to set out alone to seek the place where the white men dwell beyond the frozen wastes of the plains.

The place of the white man, of the traders, was unknown to the Ihalmiut men at the turn of the century. It was as distant and unreal a place as the bland surface of the white moon. The People knew of the white men only through Tyrrell's visit and through the magnified and distorted tales of a man called Angyala who had once passed through their land, and who had lived on the coast and knew something of the white man by hearsay. He spoke of the place called *Iglu ujarik* (which is "the Stone House"), where the white traders lived.

Iglu ujarik is Churchill, and it takes its Eskimo name from the sullen piles of gray rock which are all that remain of the fort built by Samuel Hearne in the days of the arctic wars with the French. And Iglu ujarik was the goal of Kakumee as he drove his long sled to the south, though he had no notion of how far it was.

It was an epic journey. Three days of hard traveling took him out of the land of the Ihalmiut, into the forests. These lands are forbidden to the men of the People, because they are the homes of the hostile Indians who have held a blood feud with the inland Eskimos since time beyond knowing and because the country of forests is filled with demons and spirits who side with these Indians.

Nevertheless Kakumee left the hard-packed snows of the plains and entered the forests and now his long, narrow-runnered sled so well suited to the icelike snows of the Barrens became an encumbrance to him. In the soft drifts under the black roof of the spruces the sled sank to its crossbars and the dogs could not pull it until he had gone on ahead and broken a trail.

Snowshoes were unknown to Kakumee for there was no need of them out on the hard snows of the plains, but in the forest a man breaking trail for his dogs must wear snowshoes. Now here is the measure of the tenacity and intelligence of Kakumee: it usually takes a race of primitive people many long generations to evolve and perfect a new piece of equipment, yet Kakumee not only solved the problem of snowshoes, but in a single day he constructed a pair that, while they were rough, were adequate to his purpose. They served, these hooplike things he had made, and so the heavy sled with its load of deer meat for the dogs and the man drove on deeper into the forests.

The forests are believed to be evil, and it is thought by some of the Ihalmiut men that the trees themselves live, and resent the presence of Eskimo men. If an Innuit must travel and sleep in the forests, he has a grace of five days during which he is safe, but should he linger longer under the shadow of trees, the trees will conspire to destroy the intruder.

Kakumee had now been in the forests for almost five days, and only the compulsion which drove him enabled him

to bear the mounting terror the forests brought to his heart.
On the afternoon of the fifth day he came to a great lake with
many rocky islets which were free of trees, and on one of
these islets Kakumee made his camp for the night. There was
no wood for a fire so he sat in the shelter of a low wall of
snow blocks. He shivered with fear and with cold, and a
desperation began to possess him. At last he sprang to his feet
and cried wildly on the spirit he had met in the waters under
the distant lake on the Barrens.

For Kakumee was lost in space and in terror. His supply
of deer meat was nearly exhausted and he was afraid to go
on, but he could not turn back. He feared many things, but
most of all he feared the Indian devil called Wendigo who
eats the flesh of travelers. The ghosts and demons of the land
had voices that came through the darkness out of the forests
surrounding the lake. The five days were done, and to
Kakumee it seemed as if the black spruces had begun to grow
more closely together, obstructing his terrified path. He
thought that in the course of another day they would have
grown so close he could not pass between them, and they
would not let him withdraw, so that he would be held like a
beast in a deadfall until Wendigo claimed him.

He did not know how far or in what direction lay Iglu
ujarik, and he did not know when he might come unexpectedly upon a camp of the Indians—who would probably
murder him.

All these things passed through his mind as he stood
shivering by his sled and screamed a summons into the
darkness to the spirit he had once seen under the water.
There was no answer, but the aurora flickered with sudden
violence, bathing the desolate land in a violet light, and
Kakumee took this as a sign.

He had no fire that night and yet he was able to sleep
alongside his sled with only the dogs, curled up against his
back, for warmth and protection.

A lesser man—or perhaps a saner man—would have
turned back. Only a brave man or a madman, inexorably
driven, would have continued into the unknown which
stretched darkly ahead. Before dawn on the sixth day in the
forests, Kakumee hitched up his dogs and drove southward
again.

Though he could not know it, he was now two hundred
miles off his track. Iglu ujarik lay far to the east, and to reach
it he should long since have swung eastward along one of the

mighty rivers which run to the sea. But his track had been too far inland and so he had missed these waters, and now he came instead to a great frozen river that ran to the south into the forests. He could only travel where the rivers ran, for the forests were too thick to admit his long awkward sled, even had he dared the ominous darkness under the trees.

On the afternoon of the tenth day he rounded a bend in the river and came unexpectedly on the log shanty of a white man. It was no more than ten feet square, yet to Kakumee it seemed immense and pregnant with menace.

The place was silent and the snow about it unbroken. No smoke came from the tin pail which served as a chimney. Only the thunderous roll of the frost-riven ice splitting on top of the river could be heard. Kakumee halted his starving dogs and fingered his amulet belt as he looked fearfully at the cabin. At last he walked stiffly forward on foot, came up to the door and found it swinging ajar.

Snow had banked thickly into the windowless shanty, but on one side of it a high wooden bunk was above the reach of the snow. Kakumee saw that something rested silently there. His heart was a tremulous thing in his chest, but his courage had not yet come to its end. He walked into the cabin, staring with wide, frightened eyes, and beheld a horrendous sight.

He looked down upon the bearded, frozen face of a white man, and into ice-cold eyes like the blue of the sky.

To Kakumee's overwrought mind his face seemed to be one with the face he had seen during his novitiate. He could not believe that the thing he was looking at was a mere corpse. He saw it instead as the spirit he had called upon, by the shores of the lake. Though he was horribly frightened, he nevertheless saw in this macabre encounter a second chance to grapple with the Tornrak who had once eluded him.

Words came to his lips, garbled, gibbering words. He leaped forward and seized the head by its stiff, frosty hair. Now he grappled with the spirit, seeking to master it. The room roared with sound. Dimly Kakumee heard his own voice screaming questions at the thing he fought with, as it lifted and wavered in front of his staring eyes. The thunder of nameless noises seemed to take on a palpable form until the room became darker than darkness and suddenly vanished from the Eskimo's sight. The head of the white man grew larger until it was as large as the world, and suddenly its frozen lips parted and the cataclysmic sound split and shattered into words!

Kakumee heard, without hearing through ears, the words of his Tornrak, and they told him that he must travel on into the south, into the forests. They told him no more, and there is nothing else of that day in the memory of Kakumee. He knows only that he found himself lying on his sled while the dogs labored along the rough ice of the river. He was never to know the truth that the Tornrak he saw was no more than the corpse of a young white trapper—a man still remembered at the trading post—who was the first to enter this region, and who had died of disease during the winter.

Kakumee has little memory of the rest of the journey. Only dim flashes remain, until the day when his sled swung out on the bay of a huge lake. Across the bay, in the distance, many dogs broke into voice, and Kakumee saw the smoke of wood fires and the outlines of many buildings and tents.

His journey was done. Before him lay what was then the most northerly interior outpost of white men in that part of the arctic. Already his strange sled had been seen and men ran down the high bank of the shore to receive him.

Of those who witnessed the arrival of Kakumee, an Indian and two white men are still alive. One of the whites is a priest and the other a trader, long since retired, who lives now only in the days that are dead.

But the Indian and both these white men remember Kakumee. The white men speak with awe of his journey, for he had come through the heart of the Indian country where he would probably have been shot at once had he been seen.

The priest and the trader each had his motives for making much of the stranger who had arrived from the unknown lands to the north. The priest looked upon Kakumee as a contact with men who had not yet heard the call of the Lord. The trader quickly grasped the fact that in the desolate depth of the tundra there lived a hitherto unknown race of Eskimo hunters whose land was filled with the fabulously valuable white arctic fox.

Both of these men wanted Kakumee to make a safe return to his People and persuade them to visit the post, or at least they wanted him to act as a liaison agent between the post and the Barrens. The trader had once lived on the coast, and knew a smattering of the Innuit tongue. Now he took great pains to learn the strange dialect of Kakumee. Also he fêted the Eskimo. Taking him into his own cabin, he gave Kakumee many valuable presents, and so at last the nebulous dreams which for so long had tormented the Eskimo were brought to fruition.

The trader allowed Kakumee to wander at will through the store and the storehouse where he displayed a never-ending succession of marvelous things before the gleaming eyes of the man from the North.

The priest also worked on Kakumee. Though he could not speak the tongue of the Innuit, he too made gifts of small images which the Eskimo took to be amulets of great power and tied to the sorcerer's belt at his shoulder.

Now the winter was drawing to its close, and there was a long road ahead of Kakumee. Both the priest and the trader were anxious to see him start north.

Kakumee was called into the storeroom again and was given a large quantity of trade goods. The things he was given made him sick with desire, yet he was told they were not his own but were to be traded for furs with his People. It was made clear to him that when he returned with the furs on the following winter, he would receive for himself much more than lay on his sled.

On the books of the trading post the name "Kah-Koom-ee" was written and after it the words "Engaged as native trader to the Eskimo lands." And in the mind of the priest was engraved the name of Kakumee and the thought "This is the first of my converts amongst the many poor heathen children who live to the north."

Both white men had worked hard, with good plans to work from. But this time the plans failed, for though they had reckoned with Kakumee the man, they had not reckoned with the devil of Kakumee the shaman.

It was only three weeks before break-up was due when the Eskimo left the post for the North. He drove his well-fed dogs up the river and he carried a brand-new .44–40 rifle strapped to his back. The sled was so heavily laden that he could not ride on it but had to walk ahead or behind. This small thing gives some indication of the man's depth of purpose, for it is almost axiomatic that an Eskimo will not walk when he can ride, even if it means jettisoning part of his load.

Kakumee jettisoned nothing—and walked.

The great sled creaked heavily over the rough ridge ice of the lakes on the river, and the dogs spread out in the harness and stretched forward with their heads almost touching the snow under foot. Progress was desperately slow, but Kakumee cared nothing for that. He was not afraid any more, not even of the ghosts of the forests, for did he not carry the amulets of the bearded white man? He was not afraid of the Indians, for did he not carry a fine rifle strapped to his back? He sang the songs of the shaman as he walked to the north, and there was a fierce exultation that sat in his heart and burned as hotly as the passion for wealth had burned in his soul. His devil—his Tornrak—was a great devil indeed, and the man was as great as his devil.

No one knows for certain, for the Indians never spoke of the affair afterward, whether the five toboggan-like carioles, which went north a few days after Kakumee, were driven by men with an evil purpose in their minds. Probably not, for these were good children of the white priest and they would have heeded his warning not to injure the Eskimo.

Still, it is possible that the five young Indians intended to take some of the wealth from this outlander who had come empty-handed into their land and was leaving it richer than even the chiefs of the Idthen Eldeli. I do not believe they carried murder in their hands, though they may have had it deep in their hearts, for the blood feud between the two races is more ancient than any man knows.

I can only guess at their intentions. But this is what happened.

Kakumee traveled upriver, and he left a clear track. He built great fires at night and gorged on the unfamiliar foodstuffs he carried on his sled. He had no fear of the land, of its spirits or of its people, and so he traveled with no caution at all.

Ten days away from the post he came to the south shores of Nu-elthin-tua (Nueltin, we call it) which in the Indian tongue means Lake of the Island That Sleeps Like a Man. Kakumee camped on the wooded foreshore and not on the barren rock of an inlet. Before he lay down to sleep he made careful beds of spruce boughs for each of his dogs, since his power to carry his fabulous wealth depended on the well-being of the beasts. Then as the fire burned down, the man stretched out under his robes. Even in sleep he was aware of the hard, powerful presence of the rifle which lay with him under the skins. It was more wonderful than a woman, and Kakumee's contentment was as great as if he were sleeping with his wife.

The fire was still smoldering when five dog teams came down the dark and blue-shadowed shore of the lake. Kakumee's dogs heard the approach and howled their alarm and surprise, but the man, secure in the fantastic riot of his wild dreams, did not heed the cries of his dogs. He thought they were merely howling at wolves.

He awoke only when the five carioles careened off the ice, up the low shore and into the camp. Five dark, lithe men leaped from the carioles and came quickly up to the fire. Only one carried his rifle, for they expected no trouble from a lone man.

Kakumee did not understand the guttural words they addressed to him as he sat up and stared at the strangers. He did not move but sat like a frozen image of death, and the Indians did not understand what was in the image's eyes.

One of the Indians started to unhitch his team while the others walked over to the spruce beds which the Eskimo had made for his dogs, and pushed the Innuit dogs to one side so the lean mongrels of the Indians might have the beds. For an instant no eyes were watching Kakumee, and in that instant he acted.

The .44-40 was out and red flame was in its mouth before it was seen by the Indians; and three of them were crumpled up on the snow before they knew what had happened. The heavy lead slugs of the rifle caught them before they could move, and a man who is hit by the massive bullet of such a rifle does not move again.

The two men who were lucky ran frantically to their carioles and were away down the lake in the instant, with the dull roar of the rifle still in their ears, and the high whistle of the lead slugs splitting the frozen stillness of the lake.

In the morning Kakumee moved on. Three lightly loaded toboggans and dog teams followed on a lead rope behind him. But three men slept by the black coals of the fire on the shores of Nu-elthin-tua, the Lake of the Island That Sleeps Like a Man. Thrown carelessly on top of their bodies were three or four little images, cast in soft metal, for Kakumee had noticed that each of the dead men wore such an image about his neck; and so Kakumee plucked the amulets which the priest had given him from his belt, and flung them with contempt on the bodies. The charms of the priest had not protected these men from the fury which was the gift of the Tornrak of the shaman.

Kakumee drove on, and that day he left the forests behind and headed out into the rolling plains. He did not care that he had killed out of fear for his wealth and not for his life.

XIV
The Breaker of Law

The first days of thaw had brought wet dissolution into the land before Kakumee and his train of dog teams came again to the River of Men. He crossed the cold surface water which lay above the old ice of the river and he came in sight of the igloos he had left behind months before.

A child saw him first, and ran screaming into an igloo, crying:

"Itkilit! Itkilit kiyai!" (The Indians come!)

It was an ancient warning, which had not found a use for a generation of men but was still preserved in the bloody tales of those days when the Itkilit bands used to fall on isolated Ihalmiut camps and butcher the People.

Now the old cry brought men tumbling out of their igloos, fitting arrows to bows and tearing the rawhide caps from the sharp points of deer spears. They came out to meet a great danger and a sudden attack. What they saw was no band of Itkilit, but only a single man clad in the skins of the People, and they lowered their bows, and let the spears sink to the ground, for they did not know that the danger which was coming upon them was more to be feared than the attacks of the Itkilit had ever been. And they were partly reassured by the familiar formula the stranger called out.

"I come from the right side—from the right side of the

186

ridge!" Some of the men recognized the voice of Kakumee who had disappeared so suddenly in the early days of the winter. Kakut had said then that the Tornrak of Kakumee had come for him in the night, and had carried him into the life beyond life. Now those who recognized the voice grew afraid, and the huddle of men on the high bank overlooking the river grew tighter. One whispered the thoughts of them all.

"Ino! A ghost comes on the river! The spirit of him who is dead—what do we do?"

Kakumee saw the knot of armed men, and so he cried, "Ai! You on the bank! It is only Kakumee who comes! And I return from the lands of Kablunait, bearing gifts for the People!"

It was to have been his great moment of triumph. He who had dared the indescribable terrors of that long journey was returning laden with much more wealth than even the white man who had visited the river had carried in his canoes.

Again and again he called out, but the cluster of men stood silently on the bank and no one acknowledged the hail of Kakumee. Women peered furtively from holes melted in the igloos by the thaw. The huskies stood about, growling deep in their throats, for they had caught the unfamiliar scent of the Indian dogs and they too were alarmed.

Then Kakut came from his igloo, which stood apart from the rest. Kakut, the shaman, was a wise man, wiser than many of the old ones in the camp, though he himself was still young in years. He stood on the shore looking steadily at his brother, who had halted a few hundred feet from the shore. At last he turned to the men who watched from the cliff and chided them for their fears.

"This is the *man*, my brother, and not his spirit! When did you ever hear of a ghost who drove dog teams up the River of Men?"

The tension dissolved. Women and children poured out of the igloos and their hurrying feet rustled over the brown clumps of brittle, dead moss on the snow. The dogs broke into long wavering howls as the camp came alive. Kakumee reached the edge of the shore and a dozen men sprang down to untether his dogs as he stepped forward and solemnly touched noses with Kakut, his brother.

People clustered about the man who had returned from the dead, and they cast curious glances at the long, skin-covered sled which held the balance of the wealth he had

brought. Now he cut the thong lashings of the skins covering
the load. It was his moment, and the cries of amazement as
the People looked on the fabulous things on the sled were
sweet in the ears of Kakumee.

Five rifles, a case of black powder, a box of bar lead, a
shotgun, three cases of tea, bags of flour, salt and white sugar,
bolts of cloth, axes, snow knives, and kettles—these were but
a part of the load. It was wealth unbelievable. For a few
moments fear returned to the hearts of the People. It was
beyond comprehension how a mere man could have come by
such things.

Yet flesh and blood is real enough to the touch. Kakumee was real beyond doubt. The things on his sled were real
too, and fear ebbed away from the People to be replaced by a
mounting excitement, and an overwhelming curiosity. The
close circle of men, women and children began to give free
rein to the fascination which gripped them. They closed in on
the sled as one person, and their curious hands clutched, tore,
picked up and discarded the things which they saw. Things
were passed from hand to hand, boxes were pried open,
things were spilled and dropped in the snow. It was careless-
ness that caused a sack of flour to spill; it was not envy that
made men handle the rifles, and it was with no thought of
possession that they exclaimed over the razor-sharp steel of
the short-handled axes.

Kakumee must have realized all this, for he had been
gone from the river for only five months of his life. Yet if he
did realize what this attack on his sled really meant, the
realization was not enough to stifle the unease of his devil.

He fought his way into the center of the excited mob of
his People and tried to restore his things to the sled. But as
fast as something was returned, someone else would seize it
and pass it about, and Kakumee, working at an impossible
task, began to lose his control. He kicked a child who
plunged its finger into the torn sack of flour, and only because
the excitement was great did this unforgivable act go unchal-
lenged. Desperation rose in the mind of Kakumee. He forgot
that these things were to be traded for furs. He knew only
that the hands of other men were grasping what was his—*his!*
His bargain with the white trader was forever forgotten. He
screamed imprecations into the unheeding ears of the People,
and his face was set in the mask of rage which was never to
leave it again.

Then it happened.

Kakut, who had been quietly watching from a few feet away, now stepped forward and picked up a rifle. He looked at it with pleasure and then with the nonchalance of a man who knows the law and respects it, he turned from the sled and began to walk off to his igloo with the rifle held in the crook of his arm.

It was no more than his right. A rifle would be of great aid to him in supporting a family swollen by the addition of the wife and child of Kakumee. Kakumee himself had a rifle—five rifles, in fact—and a man has no need or desire for more things than he can use with his own hands. It was the creed of the People that what a man had he shared with his neighbors.

Kakut had not taken more than a dozen steps when Kakumee saw what had happened. He acted with such speed that no one could have stopped him, had any dared to try. He seized one of the axes and, leaping after his brother, caught him a slashing blow on the shoulder with the keen edge of the ax.

Kakut spun about and his free hand clutched the wound while blood poured out between the gaps of his fingers. He stared into the face of his brother and for a long moment there was a terrible silence. The mob by the sled was stricken into a quietness which was heavy with foreboding. There was no sound but the labored breathing of Kakumee.

Then he cried out in a great voice so all the People might hear, and these were his words:

"All this that I have is mine—and mine only! Hear me well, Kakut, for if I must argue with you about this, then I shall argue with a man who is dead!"

Now a sense of sacrilege possessed the watching People, for they were beholding the flagrant violation of a law as old as life. This thing was without precedent in the memory of the Ihalmiut. Yet not only was the law of material things being openly flouted but Kakumee had also broken another law, for he had struck a man in anger, and that man was his brother. This was madness!

Kakut was a brave man and one who did not shrink from danger. Perhaps it was an awareness of the madness of Kakumee that made him act as he did. Or perhaps, since he was a shaman, he knew the true strength of the devil shining from the eyes of his brother. Kakut let the rifle slide to the snow and walked slowly away to his igloo. The devil had won. Now it was free of all need to hide behind the face of

Kakumee. It was free now to work its full will on the People by the River of Men.

When Kakumee came back with the rifle, he did not seem to notice that the People had all disappeared and the shore was deserted. Carefully he packed up the scattered things and replaced them on the sled. He hitched up his dog teams and when all was ready, turned his leader out on the ice and drove his teams up the river. Behind him in a silent camp fear was beginning to quicken.

Of all living things, the Ihalmiut most fear a madman, and it is the rule that such a one must die, and his name must never again be spoken by living lips. But in the camp of Kakut there could be no such easy release from the danger of one who was mad. Kakumee was a shaman who could not easily be harmed by human hands. Moreover he had gone from the camp and not even Kakut had the courage to follow and to face the evil spirits Kakumee would unleash against a pursuer.

Yet if men could not follow, words could. Early the next day the word began to pass up and down the length of the river, as dog teams drove out from the camps of Kakut. "Kakumee, son of Ajut, has come back to the land—and he is filled with the madness!" These words branded the shaman as an outcast. A wave of uneasiness swept through those camps where there dwelt over a thousand men, women and children who now heard of Kakumee's return, and feared for the evil that he might do.

It was barely two weeks before those fears were realized. A strange sickness broke out in the camp of Kakut. Three women sickened at once, complaining of a Great Pain that sat on their chests and denied them air for their lungs. The magic of Kakut was helpless against this new evil and in a little time those women died. Then the Great Pain, as it was called, swept on up the river, into the hidden camps by the lakes, and all over the face of the land.

Before the end of that spring more than a third of the People were dead, and the disease had broken the People. In many camps by the river no living men were left to bury the dead. The wolverines, foxes and even the dogs which had been abandoned by death grew fat on the flesh of the Ihalmiut. Only small, fleeing groups of living men remained, and those were scattered out over the length and breadth of the plains in their attempts to escape from the killer against which they had no defense. In those isolated places, cut off from their fellows by fear, the survivors waited for death and cursed the name of Kakumee.

The winter before the coming of the Great Pain had been a hard one, for it had been long protracted. But there had been no deaths from hunger that winter, though the Ihalmiut had been weak and lacking in strength, when the coming of spring, and Kakumee, brought the plague to their land. The killer which Kakumee had brought with him from the place of the white men, perhaps even from that little cabin where he had believed he looked on the frozen face of his devil, struck down the hungry folk of the Barrens.

When summer was old, the land was not as it had been in the first days of spring. The River of Men was deserted, and only hasty graves on its banks remained to mark the habitations of men. In the years to follow, the river never again saw the great camps of the Ihalmiut, for now it had changed its nature, and had become the River of Ghosts.

Though men sickened and died in all the camps, Kakumee, who had brought the Great Pain, did not sicken, for he was well fed and lacked for nothing. When he saw what had happened and knew that all living men laid the blame at his feet, then he was filled with the savage pride of a man who knows he is a master of life. He came out of hiding and passed through the tents of the dying like a spirit himself. He went without fear into those camps where the stench of death filled his nostrils, and as he passed, he took all things he desired, even unto the belongings of the dead which had been placed on the new graves by the survivors. He took three women, and these came with him without struggle, for their fear of the man stifled all thoughts of resistance. His wife, who had gone to Kakut, had been one of the first to die of the disease, and Kakumee was glad it was so and to his new wives he sang songs of the power of the devil who was his Tornrak.

That year, just after the turn of the century, was the most evil year in all the time of the Ihalmiut, nor will it be forgotten while men still live in the Barrens. Yet it does not stand alone, for, in the years which followed, disaster after disaster came to the People who had survived the Great Pain.

Along Tulemaliguak Ku, a little river which leads into the immense Lake of the Heaped-Up Rib Bones, were five igloos in the third winter after the plague; but by spring all five of those igloos were empty, for the deer had not come that way in the fall. It is told how a man came there in the days before spring to visit his brother. He found only naked, frozen bodies of the people he sought, and these were scattered far out from the igloos. This happened because of a merciful madness which sometimes intervenes to bridge the last gap between starvation and death. Then the dying ones tear off their clothing and with the last of their strength, run into the snows that their death may be quick and the long agony ended.

This one episode was repeated year after year over the face of the plains, for the People were separated from one another, and one camp could not extend aid to another which was in peril, for often they did not know of the peril until it was too late to help.

But despite famine and plague, the Ihalmiut nevertheless slowly began to recover their numbers. They might have made good their losses in the time to come had not the fates seemed angered to see their resurgence.

Although Kakumee never returned to the trading post, his visit was not forgotten. The traders remembered, and they though of the untapped wealth of the Barrens as miners think of a rich lode hidden deep in the mountains. So the traders pushed to the north. Slowly their posts crept up to the edge of the Barrens, and here at last they renewed the lost contact with the Eskimos of the plains.

It was in the second decade of this century that a band of the Ihalmiut, driven south to the edge of timber in search of the deer, came on the most northerly outpost of the traders.

Now the contact was renewed and expanded and trade with the People began. Many of the men procured guns and bought flour and lard and for a while all those who went to the tiny outposts of the traders were secure from famine— though not from the hidden starvation and so also disease, which became increasingly virulent as their contacts with white men increased.

In the years which preceded the first Great War of the white races, the value of white fox pelts shot rapidly upwards, and the trading concerns did their utmost to encourage the Ihalmiut into an almost exclusive pursuit of fur. Then the war came, and with it there came a drop in the value of fox, and an abrupt discontinuation of the activity of the traders on the borderlands of the Barrens. With the sudden withdrawal of the white traders and the cutting off of supplies of ammunition, the brief rally of the Ihalmiut came to an end.

By 1926 only three hundred of the Ihalmiut were left alive. One by one the little camps had disappeared. Year by year the number of new graves increased while the number of children born in the starvation camps grew fewer. As the survivors failed, year after year, to meet the grim challenge, so failed their hearts and so failed their will to survive.

At last loneliness drew the handful of living People together in the age-old heart of the land under the Little Hills. The great loneliness grew more oppressive until even Kakumee came back to the lakes of the Ihalmiut, and established his camp a few miles away from the remnants of the race he had helped to destroy.

But in the postwar boom years, in London, Montreal and New York, the price of white fox fur rose again, and this time soared to a new record of value. The traders again remembered the People who dwelt in the plains, and they returned. From 1926 until 1930, no less than seven fly-by-night trading posts operated for varying periods of time on the edges of the Barrens. Once again the traders handed out rifles and shells, flour and tea to the Ihalmiut. Once again the little band of survivors did as the traders desired.

This time the blow fell quickly. The traders withdrew once again, and by 1938 barely a hundred survivors were left in the camps of the People, and in 1947 only forty-six still remained.

This was the pattern of life and death from the day of Kakumee's return to the land from the South. During all of this time the Ihalmiut received no more aid from us than we might extend to rats haunting a refuse pile. Not until the year 1947 was any real effort made to investigate or to alleviate the conditions which prevailed in the Barrens. Not until 1947 was any step taken to forestall the inevitable end of death's labors in the camps of the People. Not until 1950 did we really attempt to rectify our remissness, and that attempt was short-lived. Now, when less than twoscore of the People exist and when there are all too few women left of an age to give new life to the Ihalmiut, we say we are ready to redeem our sins of omission, though in fact as I write this we have still done little but talk of what we will do for the Ihalmiut.

I do not know why we waited so long. It was not that we had no word of the existence of the Ihalmiut. Tyrrell, who was an employee of the Canadian government, had told us about them in 1894. Traders have permits, and permits are issued by the government, so the authorities must at least have known of the existence of the Ihalmiut as early as 1912. Certainly many people, both white and native, who lived along the coast had heard of the presence of the scourge which was sweeping men from the Barrens. As early as 1921 a coastal missionary at Churchill reported rumors of the death of nearly five hundred men, women and children in the interior during the course of one winter, but his report sank into limbo and was ignored. No, those who were responsible for the welfare of the Innuit could hardly have been completely unaware of the facts, even though these were so long hidden from the general sight of the world.

In the black years following the coming of the Great Pain, men had many things to contend with in the Barrens, and not least of these was Kakumee the shaman.

During the times of famine, Kakumee always had food, rifles and shells. If it did happen that he ran short of meat, then he drove his dog team to the camp of some fortunate man who had made a lucky hunt and took what he wanted. No one could resist. How does a man resist another who is not of this world but of the world of devils and spirits?

Although Kakumee had several wives and he fed them all well, they gave him no children of his own, and so he knew the savage despair of one who believes he is impotent. Bitterness lived in his loins, and this bitterness added new strength to his devil, so that he even stole children and called them his own. A few times starving men came to the place of Kakumee and, humbling their pride and bridling their fears, asked him for meat. But this son of Ajut knew nothing of giving. He turned the starving ones away, and they made their ways back to their camps or died on the trail. After a time no one came near his camp and Kakumee was alone with the women and children he had stolen; hated and feared by all those who still lived.

Kakumee not only stole for pleasure or need, but from malice as well. I have heard a tale of a time when a man whom we shall call Anga set out in winter to go to the coast hoping to obtain a rifle and shells. He was a brave Ihalmio and a stubborn one, and he would not bow to the dictates of fate, so he made the long trip, taking nearly two months to complete it. He brought back a rifle and two cases of shells and, for a season, his family and all the families under the

Little Hills had meat in plenty. Then one day in the winter, Kakumee drove his dogs to the house of Anga, and entered the igloo. He spoke no words to those who were huddled within but picked up the precious rifle and disappeared into the darkening snows.

The next day Anga, despite the pleas of his wife and the advice of his neighbors, set out for the shores of Kakumee Kumanik. He swore that when he returned he would bring his rifle safe on his sled.

The day was dark, for snow fog was lying low over the hills. Anga and his dogs vanished quickly from the sight of those who stood outside their igloos to bid him good luck. The wife of Anga wept, and let her hair down from the tuglee as women do when they mourn for the dead.

When spring came Anga was found. His body lay in a crevice of a rock near the south end of Kakumee Kumanik, and it was said he had been killed by the she-devil, Paija. But—there was a bullet through the bones of his chest.

In the later days of my last year in the country, Kakumee became my frequent companion, for he believed that the prestige of showing himself to be at least my equal would strengthen his hold on the Ihalmiut. But perhaps more important to him was the irresistible fascination our belongings had for the devil who dwelt in his heart. One day Ohoto warned Andy and me that we too courted death from the hands of the devil Paija because of the riches we owned. But that was not true, for though Kakumee might have welcomed our deaths, he would hardly have had the courage to kill us.

I did not repulse him, partly because I never quite mastered the cold chill I felt in his presence, but mainly because he was a rich source of stories about the Ihalmiut. However, in the last few weeks of our stay in the land, we visited his camp and what we saw there changed my relationship with old Kakumee.

His two tents—one for himself and a young wife, and one for an old wife and two adopted, or stolen, children— were enormous, but filthy, and in a poor state of repair. We were invited into the main tent and its contents were as unbelievable as if we had found a pawnshop dropped down in the heart of the Barrens. The place was packed with rusted and useless items of white men's goods. There were parts of at least a dozen rifles and shotguns, all heavy with rust except for one or two kept in use. There were countless tin cans, an old cast-iron stove with no bottom or top, tin pails which could no longer hold water, boxes of scrap bits of metal and clothing, an ancient Edison gramophone with one cylindrical record, rusted and broken tools and an endless profusion of

other things, most of them ruined by time and neglect. There was also a great collection of tools, weapons and even toys made by the People.

I was appalled, for it was not simply the material wealth of one man I saw, but the wealth of a race, piled there to decay and to pass into dust that one man's passion might be well fed. Useless junk, most of it, that in its time might well have helped the Ihalmiut to delay their progress to extinction. The tents of Kakumee were filled with the sterile wealth of his race while the tents of that race were silent, and empty of men.

A few weeks later Kakumee came to see me at Windy Cabin, for he knew we would soon depart and he wanted to take possession of anything we might be persuaded into leaving behind. I was not glad to see him, for at last I was sickened by the incredible greed which had made him prey on his People even in death. I ordered him away, and told him bluntly not to come back. I spoke in the presence of other men of the People and the blow to Kakumee's prestige must have been severe. However, he went only as far as his travel tent, pitched a few hundred yards away, and there he remained while our preparations to leave were completed.

But on the last day of my stay, I began to see Kakumee with a clearer perspective. At last I began to understand something of the tragedy which underlay and partly explained the apparent malice of the man. Now that my anger was gone, I was aware of the unexpected presence of pity. The curtain of evil, which hung around Kakumee like a cloak, became threadbare, for I had begun to see the depth of the calamity which had long ago come upon him. So I went to his camp, and from his parting words I learned what I should have guessed long before.

Kakumee was squatting on his sleeping robes in the gloom of the tent. When at last he spoke, his head was turned from me and his eyes fixed on a slit of white light showing along one of the seams of the tent. He spoke strongly, and savagely, of the days when his People had been happy, and many. Then he faced me.

"Now where are my People, you white man? When you went down the banks of the River of Men, did you not see my People? Did you not see the graves of the dead on every side of the land until the graves were as many as the hills that rise from the plains? And did you not listen—and hear the voices of the People, as they spoke of how it was that they died?

"Those ghosts speak much of the Kablunait, the white men, who have all things in this world, but being greedy for more, took also the deer who were our life—and gave us back only the Great Pain which sits in our chests till we die!

"You are rich! You are very rich, white man! Richer in tea, and in rifles and shells than we of the People. And yet we too are rich! Richer in graves, and in ghosts—and this is your doing."

These were the last words I heard from the lips of the son of Ajut. And only then did I understand the full powers of the devil of Kakumee and know the immensity of the deception it had practiced upon him. I left his tent knowing what the old man himself will never know, such is the cunning of the devil who drove him: that the evils which were the gifts of the white men had been brought to the land and to the People in the body and in the mind of a man of the Ihalmiut.

XV

Stone Men and Dead Men

The end of June in 1948 saw the last stragglers of the spring deer migration passing out of the Windy River country, thereby bringing Andy's caribou studies to a temporary halt. We decided to follow the deer into the northern Barrens, and our choice of a destination was Angkuni Lake.* Angkuni—the Great Lake—lies halfway down the River of Men and we chose it for two reasons. In the first place it was once the scene of the greatest deer concentrations known to the Ihalmiut, which would make it rewarding for Andy. And in the second place it lies in the very heart of the interior plains

---

* *Angikuni* on current maps. I have used the original Eskimo version of the name.

and thus it offered us an excellent base from which I could continue my investigations into the history of the inland people.

Tyrrell was the first white man to reach Angkuni, and since his visit in 1894 it has been seen by only two or three other white men. Very little of its contorted shoreline has been mapped and no one knows the lake's true extent, though I should think it must be at least forty miles in length.

When Tyrrell passed across the lake he saw, but did not visit, one camp which may have held two hundred Eskimos— and this was only one of many camps along the bays and inlets. From stories told to me by Hekwaw and Ohoto I knew that somewhere near the turn of the century Angkuni had probably been the site of the largest Eskimo encampments ever known throughout the arctic regions. Those camps are all empty now and no man lives beside Angkuni's shores, but I hoped a visit to the lake might still reveal the answers to many unsolved riddles about the old days of the People.

With much hesitation Ohoto had agreed to accompany us as guide, but his emotions as he contemplated the trip were mixed. In more than thirty years no Ihalmio had visited the Great Lake nor had anyone dared travel down the river, for these waters no longer knew the tents of living people. Only shallow graves and restless spirits remained along their shores. Ohoto and his dead father Elaitutna had been born in one of the largest camps of the Angkuni group and so the land was dear to Ohoto's youth and he felt drawn to it, though at the same time he was repelled by his fears of a dead land and its unseen inhabitants.

It would be tedious to write at length about the river above the Great Lake, for graves, rapids and falls are all of a kind, even when they stretch for two hundred miles. I shall begin the story of our visit to Angkuni on the day when our canoe came in sight of the famous hill called Kinetua, which guards the western entry to the lake. Ohoto was in the bow that day and when he identified the looming majesty of the great hill we knew we had achieved our goal, in space at least. We bore down on Kinetua and the river flung us angrily from side to side in a rocky gorge before it gave up the war it had waged against us and the mutter of its tormented waters ceased.

The current sank away and dissipated its strength in the still waters of Kinetua Bay. Kinetua itself hung over us and cut off the sinking sun so that we moved in shadow, although on the distant north shore the sun still flung a clear yellow light over the old encampments of the *Kinetuamiut*—as the Angkuni group of the Ihalmiut had been called. The long hills rolled up green from Angkuni Lake, which stretched to the horizon ahead of us. The canoe drifted idly on still waters and nothing in all that vast world moved or lived save we three intruders and a white-winged gull. The Kinetuamiut were gone; the living men were gone; and yet the land was not quite so deserted as it seemed.

We landed at the foot of Kinetua and climbed its receding slopes until we stood on the bank of the mounded giant. From the crest we looked far out over the sodden muskegs; past ridges, eskers and little lakelets, and as far as the most distant glitter of the Great Lake's southern bays. We looked out over a dead land—but not a deserted one, for our eyes quickly discovered the shapes of men standing in monumental immobility on every side of us.

They were men. But men of stone! Insensate little pillars of flat rocks piled precariously atop each other, they stood on every hill, by every lake and river, as they have stood throughout the long ages of the People who created them and called them *Inukok* (semblance of men). They are such puny monuments, these lone inhabitants of emptiness, it seems inevitable that they must topple into the anonymity of the rocky slopes from which they sprang. And yet they will not fall. They stand immutable, contemptuous of the winter gales and of the passing years, imbued with an essential quality that belies their faceless forms and gives to them more than a semblance of reality as men. More real, more vital, are these shapeless things than the cold-eyed statues of our great museums. This is because they were not built to keep some memory green, nor to express the hidden passions of a sculptor's hands. The Inukok have being because they were created as the guardians of living men against a loneliness which is immeasurable.

When the first man came this way, restlessly probing into unknown lands, he paused upon some hill before he ventured further into the obscurity ahead, and here he raised the figure of an Inukok. Then, as he went forward into the boundless distances, he retained a fragile link with his familiar world as long as he could still discern the dwindling figure of the man of stone. Before it disappeared behind him, the traveler paused to build another Inukok, and so another and another, until his journey ended and he turned back, or until he no longer needed the stone men to bind him to reality and life. The Inukok are not signposts, just simple landmarks as most white men have thought. They are—or were—the guardians who stolidly resisted the impalpable menace of space uncircumscribed, which can unhinge the finite minds of men. From the crest of Kinetua we looked out and saw these lifeless beings and were comforted to see them standing there.

For a long time we three were silent as we gazed out over the Angkuni hills studded with their motionless sentinels. The light was going and the bay lay motionless below us when at last Ohoto broke into our thoughts.

"This is the place," he said. "Here stood my father's camp—and it will not be strange if he should come to me and if I again hear his voice that has been silent for two winters past."

It was a true prophecy he made, but on that evening Andy and I paid it little heed. Descending the hill then, we paddled across the bay of Kinetua and pitched our tents on a sloping shelf along the northern shore. Andy and I were very tired, but there was little rest for us that night. We lay sleepless for hours, listening to the voice of Ohoto as he sat in the darkness outside and chanted the thin, lugubrious songs which are sung only for dead ears.

In the morning our little travel tents were filled with a fresh and boisterous breeze. The mood of the previous night had vanished. I stood outside the tent and looked at the spacious and aloof beauty of the country as it lay revealed under a brilliant sun. Northward the great bare hills rolled into a white sky only faintly touched with an ephemeral blue. The soft and flowing colors of the lichens and the grassy swales seemed to assume the properties of motion as the wind hurled itself up the valleys and over the far crests. The wind brought a measure of life to a lifeless land; and while the wind blew, the loneliness was held at bay.

Below our camp the clear waters of Angkuni flickered under the wind's touch as the seas built up and drove toward a dim line of ridges on the southern shore. At our feet was the broad low path of a huge isthmus cutting across the lake to lose itself in the bright distance.

There were no trees nor other ragged, upward shapes to break the smooth contours of the land—the swollen continuity of curving space. But hidden in some favored valleys were a few tiny "forests," each consisting of a dozen or so scrawny spruces, none of which stood more than a yard high. Poor, ugly little things, they thrust their heads upward until they were on a level with the shoulders of the shallow valleys, then they were caught and cut down by the scythe of the winds. Held down by that invisible barrier of air they spread outward, growing like plants beneath a pane of glass.

The wind is master in that land, but we blessed it for its simple presence since while it blew, the haze of flies was held impotent in the shelter of the lichens. Breakfast was mercifully free of flies on our first day at Angkuni, and afterwards we took advantage of the wind's kindness and went exploring. Ohoto was the first to leave the camp and he went inland, ostensibly to scan the wastes for signs of deer. I watched him idly as he grew smaller in the distance and then I saw him pause. Lifting my binoculars I watched while he heaped up a little pile of rocks upon a ridge. In a few moments it was done and Ohoto passed out of sight over the rise, leaving yet another Inukok to stand against the Barrens' sky.

We had brought with us a copy of Tyrrell's sketch map, the only existing map of Angkuni, and while Andy went to examine and measure the antlers of some long-dead deer, I set off along the shore of Kinetua Bay to try to find the Eskimo campsites Tyrrell had seen and recorded fifty years before. Half a mile away I came to a rocky point which was labeled "Eneetah's Camp" on Tyrrell's map. Little triangles printed on the sheet indicated that three tents had stood here in Tyrrell's time.

I cast about and at last came upon three circles of boulders, half hidden in the moss and lichens. I walked into the center of one of these tent rings, for such they were, and found the hearth and in it the blackened embers of a fire which looked to be so recent it startled me. For a brief moment I almost believed this camp had been deserted only yesterday and that its owners might return at any moment. I raised my eyes and searched the glittering surface of the water, but nothing moved and the illusion passed.

Only then did I remember that decay and rot are almost strangers to the Barrenlands. In this world of clean sun and wind both wood and things of bone seem to possess a strange immortality so that after centuries they still retain the form they had when they were first brought to rest amongst the boulder heaps. I particularly remembered finding a roll of birchbark some three hundred miles north of the forests where the last birch trees grow. That bark, intended for the repair of some Indian canoe, had faced the hunger of the years for at least three generations, and when I found it, it was still sound and untouched by rot. This relative absence of decay is an important thing to men who are driven to pry into times long past. The tent- and igloo-dwelling Barrens peoples left little enough to mark their passing, but because of this victory of matter over dissolution, what little did remain has been miraculously preserved to tell its tale with a clear tongue.

Examining Eneetah's camp more closely, I came upon part of a human skull lying in a little bed of dark, coarse hair which had once cushioned the skull from snow and sun, and which now cushioned it against the weight of years. There was no grave nearby and so the skull suggested that when death came to this camp he took all men, leaving none to obey the law which says men must have a sufficient burial. There was further evidence of sudden tragedy, for near at hand were the precious poles which had once held up the tents. The tents themselves had long since vanished into the bellies of mice and wolverines, but the poles remained; and tent poles in that land of "little sticks" are not abandoned unless no man still lives to use them any longer.

The thick moss within the boulder rings veiled other things as well: a copper fishhook, a ladle of musk ox horn—and a wooden spool which had once held white man's thread. The spool alone was of our time, and may have been one of the gifts Tyrrell left with the people whose fleets of kayaks welcomed him under Kinetua. All of these things that I had found, mute in themselves, created voices in my mind. They told me that death had struck Eneetah's camp after its first visit by a white man, but before the goods of traders became common in the land. The sun-whitened cylinder of wood, and the fragments of tools, told me who Eneetah's killer was, for I knew that the Great Pain of Kakumee's bringing had come into the land less than two decades after Tyrrell—and before the Innuit met the traders on the borders of the Barrens.

I left Eneetah's camp and walked westward along the shore, passing rows of miniature Inukok set up by children at their play—pathetic little products of dead hands. After a time I came to a shallow inlet backed by a massive cliff and in this sheltered place I found a soft green swale running down to the only sand beach I saw on the Great Lake. It was an oasis; a warm and gentle place, and on that grassy meadow I found the tent rings of a mighty camp.

There were perhaps thirty rings scattered here and there and at least eighteen of these had been in use when last the site was occupied by man. But like Eneetah's place, this site had also been deserted suddenly. In and around the rings I found the tools of Ohoto's people. Here was a wooden tuglee from a woman's hair—this precious ornament discarded in the moss. There lay a section of a bow with a good spring still retained in its ancient fibers. Nearby was a stone meat cache filled with the bones and hair of many deer which had been left to rot away, unused. Down by the sandy shore immense square blocks of stone had been upended to form winter resting places for kayaks where they would be secure from the ever-hungry dogs. No dogs had found them—but time had taken them instead. The frail bones of the little vessels were complete and only the skin coverings had vanished, leaving the naked frames to look like the skeletons of slim and graceful beasts, denuded of all flesh.

The sunlit meadow seemed to darken as I walked among these somber relics of an unknown tragedy. I seemed to hear the echoes of that fatal tale, and a confused babble of soundless voices filled my ears, trying desperately to tell me of what had come to pass in this lovely and hidden place. They spoke of the nemesis which had fallen upon this camp with such savagery that men gave no heed to their most precious possessions as they fled. But—had they fled? What terror could have made a woman abandon this elaborately carved meat tray—a thing of enduring value—to split and whiten under the long summer suns? And how could men flee when their kayaks and winter sleds remained in the deserted camp?

At its last life the camp must have held many people, for the tents had been immense, many of them twenty feet across the base. Most of the present tents of the Ihalmiut are dwarfed little cones, half that size, and yet they shelter families of seven or eight, and sometimes more. The great tents by Angkuni could each have held a dozen people comfortably, and this one camp may have contained a hundred souls who appeared to have mysteriously vanished out of time. Vanished, yes—but where?

The question was soon answered. A few hundred feet behind the camp there was a broken outcropping of black rock—and here I found the people whom I sought. Each lay in an igloo-shaped stone crypt; each in his ageless home, surrounded by some few tools which he had used in life. The graves were so closely crowded, in the limited space suitable for making tombs, that many overlapped and some had been forced to house more than one occupant. I counted thirty-seven in one place, that had all been built hurriedly and at the same time—or at least within a few weeks of each other. The scanty nature of those structures and the paucity of tools within them proclaimed that death had allowed no time for careful ceremony. Evidently whole families had perished at one time, and the few tools and weapons belonging to the family had been thinly divided amongst many souls who would have need of them in the world of Kaila—God of the Skies.

Not yet surfeited with horror, I searched farther afield, and beyond the main graveyard I found where the dwindling survivors of the terror had abandoned all efforts to give the dead their due. Here the bones lay in shallow hollows scraped in the moss and no one had bothered to provide these ghosts with the tools they would need on their eternal journey. The terror must have been nearing its peak when these naked ones were buried, and the camp must have been all but deserted then. Certainly if any had still lived on they would have been quick to move away as the graves multiplied, for it is an inflexible rule amongst the people that tents must not be pitched near where the dead lie at rest. The dead had come to occupy the place and the camp was given over to them, while the few surviving Kinetuamiut attempted their escape.

Before I left that camp the dead spoke to me and told me of the terror. Though there was no other sound than the harsh piping of the wind, the voices spoke in such a way that I could not misunderstand. I knew how the Kinetuamiut had died. It was not from starvation, for there had been funeral presents of deer quarters on many of the graves. It was not from violence, for the bones of the dead were unscarred and whole. The Kinetuamiut died because they had received our gift. It was the Great Pain of Kakumee's tale.

Perhaps, I thought, a few had escaped; but where had they gone and what was their ultimate fate?

I found the answer to those questions, too, as I walked away from the sunlit meadows, out into the browning plains which stretched away inland. A few miles from the shore I stumbled on a tiny tent ring consisting of half a dozen stones, barely sufficient to anchor the flimsiest shelter; and in this circle lay one who had fled the terror. The wolverines had given him what burial he needed. Twice in the next mile I found rock crevices into which men's bodies had been roughly stuffed to find what protection there might be from the weather and the beasts. These were the men who had fled the camps beside Kinetua Bay—and they had not escaped.

I walked back to the shore and followed it to the mouth of the river, a distance of ten miles. And I found three other great camps that had died under the plague. Beyond the last of these was an ancient burial ground which had existed long before the Great Pain came, and in it I saw the manner in which the Kinetuamiut cared for their dead when death gave them the time. A tall gray pole marked one burial mound whose roof had been constructed of the owner's long winter sled. The openings had been neatly filled with rocks and thatched with willow, and the whole was so well made that the crypt had remained almost intact. Beside the grave were deer spears, a snow knife, bow drills, arrows and a stone lamp containing five wonderfully made stone pipes and many other needful things to show that this man had left the world well prepared to face the next. This was a peaceful grave, and it was in startling contrast to the ones near the plague camps.

When I turned back I found myself hurrying and I felt an almost hysterical desire to see living men again. I almost ran the last few yards to camp where I was greeted by Ohoto, and in turn greeted the Eskimo with an effusiveness which startled him. Ohoto told me he had found no deer, but he said the land to the north appeared to have been one of the greatest highways the deer had ever used. This was small comfort, for we had expected to find the deer themselves at Angkuni and we had counted on stocking up with meat so we could continue our explorations into the unknown lands to the northwest. Our food supplies brought from Windy Camp were almost exhausted and we did not care to risk missing the deer by starting off to a distant part of the Barrens which the deer might never visit.

So we began a period of waiting that stretched into days, then into weeks. As patiently as possible we waited for the deer, but patience was soon exhausted by the hordes of flies which also waited hungrily, but that were willing to accept us as substitutes until the deer did come. For days on end we three were forced to stay in our tents while viscous masses of mosquitoes and black flies hung like living tapestries on the outside of our mosquito nets. We partially escaped the blood-hungry throngs by keeping inside, but we had other tortures to contend with, for the sun was without pity and the tiny cube of motionless air enclosed by our tent was often heated to the point where our water bucket grew surprisingly hot. Those were not pleasant days, but perhaps one day in three would bring a wind and then, as if by some benevolent sorcery, the flies would vanish and our imprisonment would be briefly broken. On one of these days I wandered for almost twenty miles along the shores of Angkuni looking for signs of living things; and I saw not a bird nor an animal. On another day I did manage to surprise a covey of half-grown ptarmigan in a swale and once I saw a single gyrfalcon, a great, gray-winged shadow that swept low over the crest of a hill, cried piercingly, and vanished swiftly. But there were no deer, no arctic hares, no ground squirrels, no foxes, and almost no other birds.

Deserted and empty as they were, the Angkuni plains did give me one rare gift and that lay in the opportunities I found for long talks with Ohoto. As our enforced idleness dragged on, Ohoto became almost garrulous and I had the unusual good sense to take advantage of it.

Just before dusk one day a strong south wind sprang up. Ohoto and I sallied gratefully out from our prison and climbed the crest of a high hill to scan the distant plains for deer. As usual we saw no sign of Tuktu, but it was a pleasant evening so we sat amongst the broken rocks of the hilltop, smoked our pipes and waited for the low sun to pass from sight. It was then Ohoto told me the Ihalmiut story of genesis and something about the early days of men.

"Things were not always as you see them now," Ohoto began, then paused to drag furiously at his pipe. . . .

In the beginning there was no sun in the sky, and the land of those far times was warm and dry. No snow lay on it and no rain fell. And it was so when Kaila, he who is Thunder in gray skies, knew it was time to bring life into the land.

First, Kaila made the hare and ptarmigan and sent them down through darkness and bade them multiply until their tracks covered all hills and valleys of the dark and hidden world. So the ptarmigan and the hare went into darkness and did as they were told.

There came the time when they were many, and Kaila saw that they were many, and he knew the land was ready. And Kaila took the first woman and the first man, and these two he sent into the world which lay ready to receive them.

Yet Kaila, who sees without eyes, in darkness as in light, forgot that men see nothing in the dark. But it was so, and the man could not see, and hunger came upon the first man and woman, for though the hares and ptarmigan were many, the first hunter could not see to make his kill.

Then the woman stood on a high place and cried out to Kaila, begging for his aid. And Kaila heard, and he sent fire into darkness, and then there was both light to see by, and heat to cook upon.

It became the woman's task to keep the fire alive, for it had been her gift from Kaila. But the man thrust his forefinger deep into the coals so that it caught fire and became a flaming torch. Then with this torch to light his way, the first man roamed the hills, and many were the hares and ptarmigan that fell beneath his hand.

So for a long time the man and woman lived in peace, and with full bellies. But at length hares and ptarmigan grew wary of the hunter's torch and they fled into ground and into air. Hunger came again to the first man and woman. Once again the woman stood on a high hill and cried her sorrows, and once more Kaila heard and answered her. He heard, and spoke, telling her to dig a great hole in the ground, so deep that none might see its bottom.

When the hole was dug, Kaila bade the woman make a strong line from the plaited sinews of many hares, and a sharp hook from the wing bones of the ptarmigan. And this too was done as Kaila said that it must be.

Then Kaila bade the woman try her skill with the hook and line, in the deep hole that had been dug. The woman sat beside the hole, holding her line, while the man stood beside her letting the flame of his great torch send shadows dancing into the hole. Then came a sudden tug on the line. Quickly the woman hauled it up and dragged the first wolf from the bowels of the earth. But the wolf was an eater of meat, and no giver of meat, and so the woman cast him loose, bidding him multiply and to become many over all the land. The wolf heard the woman, and obeyed her words.

Again and yet again the woman flung her hook into the hole and always when a weight came on it, she drew it up. In this way she caught all the beasts of land: Amow the white wolf, Kakwik the gray wolverine, Akla the great brown bear, Hikik the red-haired squirrel, Omingmuk the shaggy musk ox—and all other beasts which walk the world. And yet it happened that none of these was what the woman desired, and after speaking to each as she had spoken to the wolf, she freed them all, and cast her line again.

After the land beasts came the beasts of air: Tingmea the white goose, U-ulnik the long-tailed duck—and all the lesser beasts of air. But none of these was what the woman sought and so she freed them into darkness, speaking to them as she had spoken to the wolf.

After the beasts of air there came the beasts of water: Ichloa the red trout, Atnju the soft sucker—and all the lesser beasts of water. But still not one of these was what the woman sought, and so she freed them into lakes and rivers, speaking always as she had first spoken to the wolf.

Now came a time when no new weight fell upon the line, and the man grew weary of his vigil by the hole. He would have slept, for the world was filled with many kinds of game, and he was satisfied. But the woman rebuked him, for she was as stubborn as all her daughters have been ever since—and she had still not caught the one thing which she sought.

We do not know how long the woman lingered by the hole, for then there was no winter and no summer, no day or night. But in the end there came a great jerk on the line so that it was almost torn from the woman's hands. The man sprang to help her and together they pulled the sinew rope out of the pit. It was a mighty struggle, and yet man and his woman triumphed and so they at last beheld the antlered crown of Tuktu—first of all the deer!

The woman cried out with joy and flung her hook away, and the deep hole closed up and vanished. Then the woman spoke to the first deer, saying:

"Go out over the land and become as many as all other things which live in water, land or air—for it is you and your kind who will feed me and my children and my children's children for all time that there is yet to come."

The first deer heard, and heeded what the woman said, and so it came about that there were many deer. . . .

Ohoto ceased his tale, and together we looked out over the broad isthmus where the gravels and lichens bore the trails of many deer. Those trails were so many they were like a close-knit web covering all the land. We looked in silence,

until at last I asked, "What of the first woman, and her
man?"

For longer than I know [Ohoto continued], the first man
and woman lived in the dark world. Yet though Tuktu was
there and hunger had been banished, still the man's loins
stayed dry and the woman's womb was empty as an ancient
skull. So might it always have remained had not it been for
Hekenjuk the sun, the giver of new life. And Hekenjuk came
to us because of a great battle fought between the wolf and
the wolverine in times long past.

Of all beasts in the land, Kakwik the wolverine is
strongest and most cunning. Because of his great cunning,
Kakwik learned to hunt in darkness. But Amow the wolf
could never learn and often enough he blundered into rocks
while the deer he chased so blindly laughed at him and fled
away.

In those times Kakwik and Amow lived together in a
cave sunken deep into the rocks, and once when they were
digging at the back of the cave they chanced to uncover the
bright face of Hekenjuk, who had been buried by Kaila at the
first of things.

Amow was happy then, and cried, "Let us free the sun,
for then there will be light in darkness, and I shall see to
make a mighty hunt!" But Kakwik had no desire to see the
wolf become a hunter of great skill, and he would not agree
with the white wolf, but kicked the dirt back over the
gleaming sun.

This was the beginning of the battle, but in those days all
animals spoke the same tongue with man and when they
fought, they fought with words alone. So Kakwik fought with
the first wolf, and the sound of battle echoed over all the hills
and was as loud as thunder. Amow was clever, yet Kakwik
was more clever; and so at length the wolf was beaten and
fled back into the cave, while Kakwik went out to hunt.

But when Kakwik was gone, Amow quickly uncovered
Hekenjuk and freed him from the grip of rocks. Flaming, the
sun rose to the peak of the black sky and all darkness
vanished. Kakwik was filled with rage, a rage so great that
even high Hekenjuk trembled; and to placate the wolverine,
the sun agreed to go back into hiding for part of every day.
And thus it is we have the change from night to day.

With the coming of the sun, the seasons came, and now
in the summer, when the hunting is not hard, the wolf grows

strong and so the days are longer. But in winter, when the hunting of the deer is hard, Kakwik is stronger and the sun must hide, so that the days then are short.

Now when Kaila saw that Hekenjuk the sun had been freed without his knowledge he was mightily enraged. His lightning shattered the sky, and his storms blew over the breadth of the land. The skies grew as angry as foam at the foot of the rapids, and Nipello the rain first fell over the world. So also came Aput and Hiko, the snow and ice, and also the blizzards which live in the long winter nights.

And because of these things, Kaila is known to this day as the God of All Weather. Even today his anger lives, and our world is only a toy for his anger to crush.

Ohoto paused again. In the evening sky the dark rage of Kaila was massing and the sun was shrinking before it. Flames roared down from the zenith, to lose themselves in the angry black clouds which poured up from the horizon like coils of thick smoke, and spread out over the pallid face of the sky. Then somewhere in the storm-darkened hills a white wolf howled sadly, and the echoing cry wavered over the lake like the voice of the first of all wolves, bewailing the loss of the sun. The long echoes shattered and died as Ohoto once again took up his tale.

After a time the woman grew big in the belly for with the coming of Hekenjuk, the Giver of Life, the loins of the man had grown heavy with seed. The woman gave birth to her children, and these were not men as we know them—but dogs!

From her womb came forth litters of dogs. Yet in those times all things spoke the same tongue with man, and so all things were brothers, even with man, and the dogs were man's brothers too.

Now in those days the man and woman lived in a camp by a vast inland sea which lies far off to the west. But soon that camp by the sweet-water sea was filled with the children the woman endlessly bore. At last there were so many the man could not hunt for them all. He grew weary and even the woman, their mother, grew weary. So on a day she took off her deerskin boot and blew into it, and by her magic it became a great boat. Then she launched the boat on the waters of the sweet-water sea, and in it she placed most of the children she had borne. When the wind came out of the

north, the woman pushed the boat free, and the wind took it
southward until it was gone from her sight.

The boat sailed on into the south until it passed from the
lands of our people into the deep, hidden lands where the
forests cover the world. Here the boat entered the mouth of a
river and ran aground on a shoal.

Many of the dogs in the boat were hungry and were sick
of the water, so some of them swam to shore and entered the
forests, and here they have lived ever since, for they became
Itkilit—the Indian peoples.

But still the wind blew from the north and at last the
boat slipped free of the shoal and drifted on to the south.
How far—no one knows. When it at length came to rest, the
remainder of the dogs entered into an unknown land, and
here they became Kablunait—the fathers and grandfathers of
you and your kind.

Not all of the dogs were sent away in that boat, for some
remained in the camp by the inland sea, and these were the
ones the woman favored over all of the others. After a time
these became the fathers and grandfathers of me and my
kind, for they were the first Innuit—the first Men.

As Ohoto finished speaking, the sullen darkness of the
storm swept in over the Great Lake and the long moan of the
coming wind rose above the cry of the distant wolf.

All along the stark and rocky shores which lay beneath
us were the old camps of the Innuit, and they were as silent
as the dead soul of the land. Dimly I saw the stone circles
which marked the places of tents, with the lichens growing
high amongst them. Beyond the stone rings, up on the ridges
where the frost-shattered rocks of the slope stood upended
like tombstones disordered by earthquakes, there were the
people.

Little rock mounds rose above the stone surface like
gray boils on the bones of the land. All along the darkening
shores the little mounds rose. And under each of them slept a
son of the woman, with the tools he had used in his life by his
side.

XVI

From the Inland Sea

The succeeding days at Angkuni brought no sign of the deer. While we waited impatiently for their arrival, I took advantage of the windy days to explore the high plateau north of the lake, and in many places among the mounded gravel ridges I found further traces of the men who were gone. One day I picked up an oddly shaped fragment of wood, and when I asked Ohoto to identify it, he replied that it had been part of a crossbow.

Now this was a startling discovery because, as far as I knew, no Eskimo people had ever used this weapon. When I questioned him more closely, Ohoto told me that the Ihalmiut of the previous generation regularly made crossbows from the springy horn of the musk ox, and used them extensively in hunting Tuktu. The remnants of the bow by Angkuni Lake were proof of the truth of his words, but to this day the Ihalmiut occasionally make crossbows of spruce for the children to use in hunting ptarmigan and small animals.

There could be no doubt that the crossbow was as old as the People, but where, I wondered, had they acquired the art

213

of making such a weapon? Was it on the far steppes of Asia? And if so, why had the Ihalmiut retained this art, which had evidently been lost to all other Eskimo peoples?

The ancient history of the Ihalmiut is shrouded in mystery, but the legend of genesis which Ohoto told me has in it many hints about the nature of that mystery. Ohoto's curious reference to the "inland sea," where the first woman lived, probably applies to the real inland sea we know as Great Bear Lake. There are many things in the folklore of the Ihalmiut to indicate that Great Bear was once the home of the People; and there is nothing at all to indicate that the Barrens race ever dwelt by the ocean. The whole spoken history of the Ihalmiut belongs exclusively to a people who have not the faintest folk memory of life beside the salt water. The language and customs of the inland men give further evidence of a broad and ancient split in the proto-Eskimo race, for almost all the religious and magical tabus of the Ihalmiut deal uniquely with an inland culture based solely on Tuktu the deer. The language, too, is widely divergent from that used by the sea peoples. It differs not only in minor ways, but it lacks the very words which are specifically related to knowledge of the sea.

Knud Rasmussen, leader of the Fifth Thule Expedition, 1921 to 1924, who was himself half Eskimo, guessed the probable meaning of this chain of differences between the coast Eskimos and the plains dwellers. Rasmussen traveled a little way up the River of Men, from its mouth at Baker Lane, and he encountered an inlying group of former coastal Eskimos who had met and assimilated a small remnant of the inland people who had been driven north by the plague. The culture of this bastard group was predominantly coastal in folklore, though inland in practice. However, Rasmussen, who was an observant man, detected signs of an unusual antiquity of race in them which went far beyond anything to be found among other Innuit. From his brief but intense contact with this group, he concluded that they represented the last surviving link with the proto-Eskimo stock from which all modern Eskimos are descended. But Rasmussen never met the Ihalmiut, and never even suspected their existence.

Let me turn back the blank pages of a history which will never be written, and tell you how I would explain the coming of the crossbow to the great ridge beside Angkuni Lake.

In an age long forgotten, thousands of years before Christ, a new movement among the constantly shifting races of northeastern Asia brought an irresistible pressure against the men who were then living in the eastern peninsula of Siberia. The pressure was applied slowly, but it was inexorable, and the men who were to be the fathers of the Innuit were forced ever east and north. Some of them perhaps emerged on the Arctic Coast of Siberia, for there, to this day, lives a race of men, the Chukchee, who are much like our own coast Eskimos.

However, the balance of the fugitive Asians, who had continued eastward, at length found themselves hemmed in on the narrowing apex of land which is now the Chukchee Peninsula. There may well have been a complete land bridge to North America in those days, but this is of no importance, for there was certainly a chain of islands crossing the Bering Strait, and it would have been easy then, as it is now, to go from Asia to Alaska by island-hopping. The spreading pressure area in Siberia now forced the fugitives to cross the continental strait.

Probably the new land of Alaska was already occupied by the forebears of the Indians, and its coasts may even have been in the hands of the Asiatics who had earlier been forced to the Siberian coast, and who had there developed a sea culture and spread eastward. The new migrants from the west would thus have been forced to move through the interior until they found unoccupied land. Probably they worked through the Brooks Mountain barrens in northern Alaska—a devilishly inhospitable area—until they reached the true, flat Barrens, near Great Bear Lake. These rolling plains would have been like home to the wanderers, for the tundra to the north and east of Great Bear is very similar to the northern treeless plains of Siberia. On their Ameican Barrens these peoples from the west would have found a familiar world of rocks, muskegs and lichens. And not only the land, but its beasts too would have been familiar. The white fox, the lemming and the wolf, as well as many other animals, are virtually identical in both Siberia and Northern Canada. As for Tuktu the deer—in those distant ages mighty herds of both wild and tame reindeer roamed the Asiatic plains, even as their close relatives, the caribou, roamed the Barrens of North America. Thus, an immigrant race who had lived on reindeer would find no serious difficulty in building a new life about the caribou. They would naturally use the same weapons and much the same techniques that they had learned in Asia—and the crossbow was originally an Asiatic weapon.

As they spread out from Great Bear, two new influences would have begun to make themselves felt. The caribou made their annual migrations north each spring to the Arctic Coast, and over a period of years beginning perhaps two millenniums ago, some of the inland dwellers must have reached the coast in seasonal pursuit of the migrating deer. These people could have acquired a knowledge of the sea, and perhaps developed a mixed sea-and-caribou culture such as persists to this day with the Bathurst Inlet Eskimos. Caribou provide the staff of life in summer for these people, but in winter they depend on the sea for seals and other aquatic mammals.

The second factor to disturb life about Great Bear Lake may have been of a more recent nature. It is known that, many centuries ago, centers of human population pressure developed on the prairies lying south of the Canadian forests. This pressure was exerted northward, in succeeding waves. In relatively recent times the proto-Cree Indians were pushed out of the plains and forced high up into the forests, where they in turn pressed against the south flanks of the Athapascan Indians, of which the Chipewyans are one group.

The Athapascan people were unable to stand firm against the pressure of the Crees, for they were poorly organized, or not organized at all. They could not fight except through the medium of quick raids and ambushes, and so they moved north to escape. They moved right out into the Barrens at last, and in time they suited their way of life to the deer and became almost as migratory as the deer herds themselves.

It was inevitable that they should encroach on the lands of the inland Eskimos near Great Slave Lake, and it was inevitable that blood would be shed. Samuel Hearne, writing of his search for the Coppermine River in the year 1771, tells of the massacre of an Eskimo band by Athapascans at a place now called Bloody Falls. This is a famous tale, but it was only one isolated incident in a war of attrition and of survival which must then have been very old, and which was to continue almost to the end of the nineteenth century.

As the Athapascans were unable to stand against the inroads of the Crees, so the unwarlike inland Eskimos were even less able to withstand the recurrent Indian invasions. Eventually the men of the plains were forced eastward away from the Great Freshwater Sea.

There are Ihalmiut folk memories of the trek in search of new lands where the Itkilit had not yet penetrated. Some of the fugitives, probably those who had already been to the sea in pursuit of caribou herds, seem to have fled northeastward, and it is probable that these people came to the Arctic Coast from Coronation Gulf to Chantrey Inlet. These northern fugitives also developed a new culture adapted to the demands of the sea. But the rest of the plains dwellers went east into the widening angle of the Barrens, and remained an inland people.

The sea culture came to have a complex structure, built up of many layers of change, migration, and the intermixing of local groups. The original offshoots of the proto-Eskimo stock, who had learned to live from the sea, spread eastward as far as Greenland, and westward again back into Siberia. But the men who had steadfastly remained with the plains since their arrival on the continent stayed in the plains. Stubbornly they clung to the old things as they fled eastward where the depths of the Barrens are greatest. The inlanders eventually reached the spreading plains of the Keewatin Territory on the west coast of Hudson Bay, a north-south stretch of tundra vast enough so that it was at last possible to avoid the thrusts of the Indians. And in this new land, good fortune came to the fugitive descendants of the first Eskimo stock.

When white men came to the prairies and the forests of Northern Canada in force, the pressure of the Indians into the Barrens ended. With the decimation by disease (mainly smallpox) of the Idthen Eldeli about 1780, the Eskimos were able to push southward, up the River of Men, until they established their southernmost camps on the very edge of the forests. Now the entire length of Innuit Ku was theirs, and more and more camps came into being.

No one will ever know with certainty how many Innuit lived in the interior tundra plains in the good years of the early nineteenth century. There must have been more than a thousand, and perhaps twice that many in 1880, before a new evil came upon them from the South and accomplished that destruction which two millenniums had been unable to achieve.

I well remember the whitened fragments of the crossbow I found in the Angkuni hills. But at the time of its finding, the crossbow meant little to me, for it was then only another sad relic to handle and wonder about, and to put aside. We had little interest in meditating on such ancient history then, for we were becoming increasingly worried about our own immediate future. The deer still had not come and we could no longer wait for their life-giving flow into the barren hills of Angkuni. It was time we took active steps to find other food.

We tried fishing, but though we set our nets in picked places along the lake shore, we caught nothing. And this was not only strange, but a little frightening, for all the other great lakes of the Barrens swarm with whitefish, lake trout and pike. Only Angkuni inexplicably refused to give us fish.

There remained the birds, but despite many heartbreaking hunts after ptarmigan we managed to kill only three or four in a week. Truly, the land about Angkuni was dead in every sense of the word. There was nothing alive that could be eaten; there were only eaters—the flies and ourselves.

It was then almost August, and at last we decided we would wait no longer but would set out in search of the laggard deer. Very early in the morning of a bright day when no puff of wind ruffled the stiff crests of the gray-green lichens on the hill slopes, we packed out gear into the canoe and set out to find Tuktu. And we were all glad to go, for the atmosphere of Angkuni, which had become increasingly oppressive to Andy and me, had an even more deep-seated and ominous effect on Ohoto.

We paddled westward from Kinetua Bay until our way was blocked by what seemed to be a great isthmus. After a search we came to a passage, very shallow, but with enough water to allow us to drag the canoe over the barrier and into open water beyond. At this point Tyrrell's map became useless. We could no longer identify his landmarks or his route, perhaps because we had passed through the isthmus by a different channel. Now we were off the narrow lane of known territory which Tyrrell had explored. Instead we swung to the west into another vast bay of Angkuni which Tyrrell had missed.

The sky was flawless and the sun fiercely hot. The cold waters of the lake grew misty under the pounding heat. The lowlands under the hills became an undulating phantasmagoria, as mirages flickered endlessly before us.

There was an absolute and tangible silence, broken only by the fluid dip of paddles and the gentle mutter of water underneath the bow of the canoe. The lake itself was frozen in the dead, unearthly grip of perfect calm.

Islands rose suddenly before us, like surfacing sea monsters soundlessly appearing. They lifted clear of the horizon, then floated faintly in the sky as their mirage images dissolved. The shore drew away from us and twisted so that its low, uncertain progress gave us no clear conception of whether it was one mile or ten miles away. Angkuni lost all semblance of reality and of concrete form. Its shores and islands had an amorphous quality which defied the eye and left the mind with no clear memory of what had passed astern of the canoe.

The hypnotic atmosphere seemed to transform all our efforts into a nebulous and ever-changing dream. Then suddenly Ohoto pointed into the waters beneath us.

"*Kuwee!*" he cried. "Here flows a little river!"

With some sense unknown to us, he had detected the invisible presence of a slight current in the bay. At his direction, we turned the canoe towards the shimmering and elusive shore. We closed in on the land and it resolved itself into a contorted jumble of smashed rocks. We let the canoe drift. Then, when we were so close we could have touched the boulders with a paddle, we heard the stream for which we were seeking.

It was hardly a river, this secret water flashing momentarily against the lake before losing itself in the still depths. Yet Kuwee, as Ohoto named it, seemed a friendly and delightful being. It ran from the northwest, out of the heartland of the Barrens where no white man had ever traveled, and it ran out of the direction from which the deer should come. Because of these things and because we hoped for fish under its rapids, we began the ascent of Kuwee and left Angkuni behind.

Kuwee had little depth. Like most Barrens rivers it simply ran at will over the boulder-laden land, for it had not yet dug itself a bed. We scrambled up and our progress was a constant struggle with shallow but active rapids. During the first day's travel we were plagued by a sense of frustration, for only many days of tortuous progress could tell us with certainty whether or not we were following a blind alley.

Towards evening of that day, we rounded an abrupt angle of the river and came upon two stone men by the shore. I cannot express the magnificent sensation of relief they gave us, but for the first time I felt the true power of the Inukok. I knew then why they had been built everywhere across the land, and I understood the mute role they played. The oppressive sense of our unimportance, and the nagging fears that we were being sucked into a dead vacuum somewhere beyond the scope of life, were banished instantly when the stone men appeared. We smiled at them, and at each other, and we waved our paddles cheerfully at those silent beings who have vital force without the gift of life.

By noon of the second day we had progressed well into the land to the west, and Kuwee was growing stronger and more clearly defined as we moved up it. This was strange, for rivers usually grow weaker as you near their headwaters. At last the little river opened into a lake and we went ashore to climb a ridge and see if we could discover the inlet to that lake.

From the ridge we saw no opening along the tenebrous line of undulating shore, but far off to the west was the minute projection of another Inukok upon a hill. With perfect confidence we headed into the open water and set a course for the distant stone man.

We were only a mile from shore when, with no more warning than an artillery shell is likely to give, the still lake erupted into a cataclysmic sea. The wind did not "rise," it simply was in being! The soporific and somehow frightening calm of the preceding days was not broken, it vanished instantly. No clouds showed anywhere upon the unchanged sky and yet from somewhere, as if generated on the exact spot where the canoe was moving, a wind that was almost a hurricane was born.

The lake was shallow, and in a minute it had been whipped to white-tipped breakers which lifted us, then flung us down again with calculated savagery. Ohoto worked frantically with the teapot to bail out the solid sheets of spray, while Andy and I drove the furiously active craft towards the nearest shore.

There was an unconcealed and bitter animosity about that wind which brought a greater terror than the elements had ever instilled in me before. It lay, I think, in the unexpected nature of the attack, whose unprovoked violence had come upon us so quickly that the mind hardly grasped its reality until the storm was threatening to sink us. We survived it, but I never again walked the Barrens, or paddled a canoe upon the lakes and rivers of the plains, without a sort of

Ancient Mariner complex, peering back over my shoulder as it were, so that the unseeable and vindictive presence would not again take me so nakedly unaware.

We made the shelter of a reef, and here the canoe pounded viciously until the wind vanished as inexplicably as it had risen. Then we scuttled feverishly along the shore, hugging the coastal rocks as a rat hugs the walls of a broad room.

For five more days we traveled up the river, and where the falls were too angry we portaged our gear over the flat, sodden world around us. The hills and ridges were all gone, sunken into a morass so that only their black spines remained in sight, like buffaloes wallowing in a swamp. Water seemed to have risen up through the earth's crust to drown the country in one great, quaking bog. It was no place for men, but it was built to order for the flies, and these rose to a crescendo of hungry activity so that they crawled over our bodies like a living cloth.

At every rapid Ohoto showed his skill as a fisherman, using a short length of twine and a hook baited with a bit of shiny tin. Standing on a rock near the foot of the rapid, he whirled the hook about his head, let it fly into the deepest pool, and with clockwork regularity hauled out the great red-fleshed lake trout. At night we sat about the fire—when we could find fuel enough to build one—and ate the boiled heads of the trout. Nor were we too delicate to eat the firm red meat raw when no fire could be had. Our slim rations were almost gone, so we gorged on fish. But though we consumed tremendous quantities, we seemed to extract no stamina, no strength and staying power from this food. It was a firsthand demonstration of the inability of fish to meet the dietary needs of men in the arctic plains.

On the fifth day we came upon a low-lying point that almost bisected a little lake on the river's course. There we found a tent ring, the remnants of another camp of bygone men. But this ring was very small and not quite round. Even more baffling were the nearby ribs of a boat, which were much more like those of our canoe than like a kayak's.

Ohoto muttered, "Indians camped here. See—here is their *umiak*, their canoe!"

It was almost incredible that forest Indians could have found their way through the hostile lands of the Innuit to such a distance. But Ohoto was right, for this was indeed an ancient camp of the Idthen Eldeli, built in the days when those Eaters of the Deer used to follow the great herds northward even as we were following them now. For us it was a heartening find. That camp, and the Inukok we had seen earlier, made it certain that Kuwee must lead to some major river course, or lake, where the deer might be expected. Yet it was also a mystifying find and my imagination dwelt on those distant days when the birch canoes of the Idthen Eldeli penetrated the Barrenlands and when butchery and massacres were known on many lakes and rivers.

Kuwee left the little lake and pointed to the north. Another day, and we heard the heavy, sullen roar of a big rapids, and went ashore to have a look before proceeding into the maelstrom.

Once on the high bank of the shore, and raised from the downward-sloping surface of the river, we saw stretching to the horizon on the west the clear, livid blue of open water under a blazing sun. Here was a vast unnamed and unmapped lake that no white man had ever looked upon before. This lake, whose western shores lay below the line of the horizon, was an irresistible magnet to our restless curiosity. Where it should have shown upon the maps there was nothing but blank white paper. The desire to sketch in a crude black outline on that virginal expanse of map was, I suppose, the essence of the desire which makes most men yearn to push beyond known limits, whether in the flesh or in the mind.

But Ohoto did not share our desire. For a long time he stared moodily out over the gleaming waters. When at last he spoke, it was to show the first signs of fear we had seen in him.

"It would be well if we turned back," he said. "Better to camp among the dead we know, than venture into this place where men have never been!"

We questioned him and discovered that he had no knowledge of this place where we now stood. Ohoto's fears were natural enough, yet he stifled them when we insisted on pushing forward, and when we reminded him of the friendly presence of the Inukok. But before we climbed into the canoe, after portaging around the rapids to the lake's ragged shore, Ohoto stopped to gather a handful of small pebbles. Once in the canoe, he tied these little stones together with a length of rawhide line. We paddled out over the translucent waters and when the bottom of the lake had dropped and disappeared from sight, Ohoto carefully slid his string of pebbles overboard and let them go, soundlessly, into the deep waters.

It was his gesture of appeasement toward the unknown beings who might lie hidden under the glaring surface of the lake.

XVII
Ghosts, Devils and Spirits

It is time now to speak about the ghosts and devils who share the Barrens with the People and the deer, for in the days which followed the discovery of the nameless lake, these things loomed large in our experiences.

In the world of the Ihalmiut, the Law governs both man's social and his spiritual life, and applies with equal force not only to the absolute realities but to the abstractions of the supernatural. There is but one Law for man and for the spectral entities whose name is legion. These "other beings" are so numerous and have such varied forms that the Ihalmiut do not know them all by name or even by description, and they can hardly gauge the full potentialities of those they know. It follows therefore that a man must be exceedingly careful to observe the most trivial instructions of the Law which can alone protect him from both the known and the unknowable.

It was through the fine mesh of the Law of Life that I saw and came to have a limited understanding of the hierarchy of the Barrens' demiworld. Kakumee was my principal instructor and he knew whereof he spoke, for he was closely in league with many ghosts. He showed no reluctance in discussing these things with me, nor did I encounter that reluctance among any of the People, perhaps because they

224

have not yet heard that the beliefs are abhorrent to white men, and must be hidden from us.

At the peak of the hierarchy of spiritual beings stand those elemental forces of nature which have no concrete form. At their head is Kaila, the god of weather and of the sky. Kaila is the creator and thus the paramount godhead of the People. He is aloof, as the mightiest deity should be, and man is no more than dust under his feet. He demands neither abasement nor worship from those he has created. But Kaila is a just god, for he is all things brought about by the powers of nature, and nature, who is completely impartial, cannot be unjust.

It is permissible to appeal to Kaila, yet there is no implicit belief that Kaila will hear or respond to prayers couched in the midge-like voices of men. This quality of impersonality, of detachment, in this god of the Ihalmiut strengthens the majesty of his power. Kaila is no simple creation of men's imaginations shackled to the whims and fancies of human minds. Kaila, to the People, is an essence. Kaila is not spoken of with fear, nor yet with love. Kaila *is*. That is enough. What man may do or not do is of no more direct concern to Kaila than the comings and goings of ants under the moss. Kaila is not a moral force, because the Ihalmiut have no need of a spiritual magistrate to administer the moral law. Kaila is essential power. He is the wind over the plains; he is the sky and the flickering lights of the sky. Kaila is the power in running water and in the motion of falling snow. He is nothing—he is all things.

The amorphous quality of Kaila makes it difficult for an outlander to understand the Ihalmiut's real concept of their god, but the lesser deities associated with Kaila are more readily comprehensible. Of these, the most important are Hekenjuk the sun, and Taktik the moon. Both are real in the same sense that the world is real, and it has happened that shamans in trances have visited Taktik and found themselves in a land not unlike the Barrens.

However, though they have a concrete existence, both Taktik and Hekenjuk exist also as primeval forces which are manifestations of Kaila. This dual concept allows for the parable of Hekenjuk being released from his imprisonment deep in the bowels of the earth by Amow the wolf; and this parable is no more difficult to reconcile with modern religious thought than is the parable of Adam and Eve. In fact, most of the spiritual beliefs dredged up by anthropologists from the folklore of native peoples are nothing *more* than parables. This point is worth remembering when we tend to pass superficial judgments on the religions of native races.

The demiworld of spirits, ghosts and devils is much easier to understand. These spirit beings are either devoted to the cause of good or evil or to an admixture of the two. For the sake of clarity I have divided them quite arbitrarily into three groups. The first of these, the supernatural entities who devote themselves to evil, are fantastic and often horrible apparitions, which are in some ways no more than elaborations of the ultimate evil in man or the ultimate destructive power in animals. Those with a human form kill by human means, but those that resemble animals destroy by means of teeth and talons.

Of those evil spirits the foremost is Paija, an immense female devil. She is a giantess who has but a single leg, springing from her generative organs, and who is clothed only in flowing black hair. Paija stalks abroad in the winter nights, and her single track is sometimes found in the new snow, an immense, twisted impression of a human foot.

No man can tell you much of Paija, except from hearsay, for to see Paija is to die with the sight of her frozen in the mind, forever beyond the reach of words. I once heard of a man called Jatu who lived near the Hudson Bay coast and who met Paija. One winter night he was coming home from his trap line, a blizzard blowing in his face. The swirling clouds of gray snow were like shadows seen by the light of a misted moon on a black night. Jatu had reached his igloo and was pulling up to a halt when those of his family who were inside the snow house heard him scream above the whine of the wind. He cried out a single word before his screams ended, and that word was "Paija!"

It was hours before anyone dared venture out to see what had happened. Then a brother of Jatu, who wore an amulet belt and was something of a shaman, took his spear and went out into the night. He found Jatu standing by his sled. The snow was drifting steadily so that it had already risen above Jatu's knees—and he was dead. Frozen solidly there, yet he still stood and his open eyes stared into the smoke of the drifts—and in his eyes was the image of Paija. So the brother of Jatu came as close as any man ever has to seeing Paija and remaining alive, and he saw only the horror reflected in the eyes of the dead man in the snow.

This is a well-known story, and both Jatu and his brother were well-known men along the river where I heard this tale.

Paija is the most feared of all devils, yet she is but one of many. Another of these unpleasant beings is a troll with a huge and hairless belly which drags on the ground. The tips of this devil's fingers are armed with wicked knives which grow from the flesh. He is said to lie in wait for men in the high hills of the land and to tear the flesh from the body of a victim with such exquisite deliberation that the victim lives for many hours.

Another, called Wenigo, is a notorious cannibal who haunts the forests. Wenigo is also known to the northern Indians and he is the most feared spirit in their land, where he is called Wendigo. There is no doubt that these two devils are one and the same, and this is very interesting, for it illustrates one of many affinities between the culture of the Indians and the Ihalmiut, who are blood enemies of each other.

These three unpleasant demons, like dozens of others in this group, serve a useful purpose. Wenigo was a very powerful influence in dissuading the Ihalmiut from venturing deeply into the timbered areas, where they might have been massacred by the Idthen Eldeli. Paija keeps men from making unnecessary journeys in the winter darkness, when the blizzards are awake, and that is a good thing, for many men have not returned from such dangerous journeys. As for the troll of the hills, he too acts as a deterrent to those who would try to penetrate the dangerous rock heaps where he lives.

His value was demonstrated to me once when I took Ootek with me for a trip into the Ghost Hills near Windy Bay. Ootek was loath to go, but rather than admit his fear he came along. We made progress only with the most heartbreaking efforts, for the overburden of immense glacial rocks was so heavy that horizontal travel was worse than mountain climbing. We leaped from rock to rock, and even with rubber-soled boots I took several painful tumbles. Ootek had deerskin *kamik*s on his feet which gave no grip at all on the smooth and moss-encrusted stone. After two hours, in which we had gone only three miles, Ootek slipped and caught his leg between two rocks.

He did not cry out with the pain, but tears were in his eyes when I reached him and he could hardly bear to stand. With Ootek limping painfully, supporting himself with a rifle for a crutch, it took us seven hours to retrace our path. Had he been alone, Ootek would still be in that vicious labyrinth of shattered rocks, and the troll might well have claimed another victim. As it was, and with all the help I could give him, he barely made the shore of Windy River without collapsing. And all he was suffering from was a badly bruised ankle!

Whether they exist or not—and I will not argue the point—the demons *do* represent manifestations of real and potential evils, and so they are not without value.

The second of my arbitrary groups includes those unpredictable spirits who may be benevolent, neutral, or actively evil—more or less as the mood strikes them. Of these, the most interesting is Apopa. Apopa is the Puck of the Barrens, a little dwarf devil shaped like a man, but grossly deformed. He plays malicious tricks on the People, but not all of his trickery is completely objectionable and so the Ihalmiut regard him with tolerance unless he carries his jokes a little too far.

The trick Apopa played on me is still something of a puzzle.

One afternoon in the fall of my second year in the country, Andy and I were sitting quietly in the cabin at Windy Bay, drinking tea and chatting. Then without warning the little shack was violently shaken, much as a rat is shaken in the jaws of an angry dog. We both jumped to our feet and rushed out of doors, certain an earthquake had struck us. But as we stood on the bank of the river, we could see nothing amiss. A small herd of deer rested contentedly by the far shore, and the September day was drowsy and quiet.

Baffled and a little uneasy, we went back to our tea. But we had barely seated ourselves when the shaking was repeated! Tin mugs bounced off the table and stretching-boards fell with a great clatter from the rafters. This time we were thoroughly excited. Once again we ran outside, and again we could find nothing to explain the sudden vibrations in the cabin.

Some Ihalmiut who had come down for a visit were camped near at hand, and in search of an explanation of the strange tremors I walked up to their tents and described what had happened. They looked at me quite blankly, and showed no signs of comprehension. In some exasperation I asked if they had not felt the vibrations too, and I even suggested that they were playing a trick on the white men. They only looked more puzzled than ever. Then Ohoto brightened a little.

"Kakumee is camped just over the hill," he said. "Perhaps he will know what happened, for it sounds like the work of a devil."

I went on to Kakumee's tent, and when I put my question to him he answered at once—almost as if he had been expecting my visit and knew its reason.

"It was Apopa," he told me. "Apopa—the mischievous one. He flew over this place, for I saw the air shake as he passed, and so I knew he was near. No doubt he glanced down at your igloo and saw the two Kablunait drinking their tea. Apopa would laugh to see such a ludicrous thing, for his sense of humor is keen. So you see, when he laughed he shook the walls and the floor, and that was what you felt."

That was that. The matter was settled, and the Innuit paid no more attention to it, except to chuckle a little at the exquisite sense of humor of Apopa who was so uproariously amused by the mere sight of white men. Well, I suppose that Apopa too has his value, for a sense of humor is a hard thing to retain in that land.

Apart from Apopa and one or two other particular devils, there is one large group in my second category of spirits that can be collectively referred to as the *Inua*. They comprise not only the actual ghosts of dead men but also, to some extent, the spirits of such inanimate objects as rivers, rocks and plants. The Inua come in two sizes: *Inua mikikuni*, the little ghosts; and *Inua ungkuni*, the great ghosts. Inua of both sizes vary from active hostility to active benevolence toward men. The dangerous Inua are those who come from the land of the dead, because of failure to give them proper burial; because of some crime they have done, or because of evil which was in their hearts when they died. These spirits are not content to remain in the land of the dead. Instead they return, to pass through the lands of the living, and they may come in the actual guise of a man. They are fond of the rough hill country, and so are another good reason for giving the rocky hills a wide berth. However, they do not restrict themselves to the hills, but may come wandering over the plains in search of a living being whom, by treachery or through terror, they can possess and thus manage to return fully into the land of the living.

One of my most vivid experiences in the Barrens was when an *Ino*—the singular of *Inua*—chose to attack my song-cousin, Ootek. Here is the story just as it happened. I did not see the Ino myself; nevertheless I am convinced that as far as Ootek was concerned, this Ino existed in an unpleasantly material sense.

Again the incident took place at Windy Cabin, but this time in June, when there are no nights but only the coming and going of twilight. It was very late, and I was trying to catch up on my notes while Andy was occupied with some little task at the back of the cabin. Ootek was staying with us, and this evening he was busy carving a new pipe from a piece of black spruce.

Casually, Ootek glanced up at the window to see if the moon had risen yet. What he actually saw caused him to explode into a perfect frenzy of terror. He shrieked like a woman in childbirth, leaped to his feet, and shot out of the door of the cabin.

Andy and I were both so startled by this inexplicable eruption of our midnight quiet that it was some time before we could get up steam enough to see what had happened to Ootek. When we did move, we found him standing near the doorstep, gibbering wildly and staring at the slopes of the Ghost Hills. He tried to tell us what he had seen, but nothing came from his mouth except garbled noises and a thin trickle of saliva that ran down his trembling chin. Andy pulled him into the cabin, while I had a look around, a cocked rifle in my hands. Nothing moved except for a flock of late ducks which came whistling down the river.

When I went in, Ootek was squatting on the floor. He had recovered some of his self-control and was able to make us understand that he had seen an Ino—an Ino wearing complete winter clothing—that had fixed Ootek with the eyes of a dead man. Now Ootek was certain this spirit had determined to possess him, and he was not unnaturally terrified at the prospect.

We told him he had seen no more than the flicker of wings as a late bird went by the window, but Ootek would have none of it. At length it became obvious to us that this was no imaginary terror which gripped him. So we changed our tactics and I offered to mix up a particularly powerful *kabluna* potion that would keep the Ino away. Ootek's gratitude was pathetic. I went to the table, poured some harmless chemicals into a vial, then added a scrap of paper on which I had written—with my usual lack of imagination—the first line of "God Save The King."

When I brought it to Ootek, Andy had just finished giving the Eskimo a rough physical examination. He told me, with a worried note in his voice, that Ootek's pulse was nearly twice as fast as it should be. In addition the Eskimo was sweating so heavily that his clothing was soaked. He seemed to have all the symptoms of severe physical shock, even to a shortness of breath.

I handed him the vial, and he grasped it with a pitiful eagerness, but the reaction was hardly what we had hoped for. His eyes suddenly rolled up until the pupils were hidden. He gasped once, fell over on his side, and his limbs kicked uncontrollably, while his breathing seemed to stop completely and his lips began to turn blue!

At this point I suspect we were sweating as freely as Ootek, for we were not looking forward to explaining the presence of his corpse to his friends when next they visited our camp. And a corpse he would certainly have become had not Andy, acting on pure intuition, pried open the clenched jaws to find that Ootek had literally swallowed his tongue! My friend got his hand bitten, but he managed to crook a finger around the tongue and restore it to its proper position. It was bad luck for the Ino, who had come within an ace of finishing Ootek completely.

Ootek recovered quickly after that. He was almost normal again in an hour, for his faith in the charm we had given him was boundless, despite its first effects. Later on I asked him if he had ever had a seizure like this before, since I suspected it might have been some sort of epileptic fit. But he swore that this was the first, and he intimated that he would be quite happy if it was also the last. I have no doubt his condition was simply one of severe shock, brought on by a serious fright. By an Ino? Well, whether it was a bona fide ghost or not, its effects were only too real.

Ootek sewed our vial into his amulet belt, where it hung as a mute reproach to me during the rest of my time in the country—for I, who take a dim view of people who perpetrate superstitious humbug on the natives, was now guilty of the same crime.

The amulet belt brings me to the last of my three groups of spirits. These include the *Tornrait*, whom we have met earlier, and who are the chief aides of men in their struggles with the elements and the unfriendly devils; and a lesser breed of good spirits who have no inclusive name and who are perhaps better described simply as forces, rather than as supernatural entities.

These latter beings are attached to a man by virtue of an amulet he has acquired, preferably in his youth. When a child is born, his parents at once attempt to enlist certain animal forces to aid him through life. The amulets, or tokens of the chosen spirits, should preferably be "things of the earth." Thus even small insects are believed to be efficacious, for they come from the earth. Beetles and bugs are thought to have a specific value as defenses against the more gruesome trolls and dwarfs who live under the ground. Amongst the other charms worn at the amulet belt are the talons and beaks of birds, the dried skins of small mammals such as weasels and lemmings, the teeth and the ears of larger mammals, such as wolves and foxes and in some cases even the scales of fishes. I should add that man does not necessarily acquire the physical attributes of these things. A weasel *tapek* or charm, for instance, does not endow the owner with the strength or speed of the weasel, but acts instead as a specific deterrent against some form of evil. Halo, one of the Ihalmiut who claims rather extensive supernatural favors, wears a miniature parka and a pair of tiny kamiks on his amulet belt, and these ensure him against accidental death from freezing or drowning.

It is best for the owner to acquire amulets by purchase or as gifts. The more distant their source, the greater their power. Halo purchased a seal-tooth amulet from the Padliemiut to the east, and they in turn had obtained it from the Dhaeomiut on the coast. The tooth came a long way, gaining power as it came and its ultimate purchase price, when Halo bought it, was one new kayak! The value of a good amulet is not insignificant.

Probably connected with the amulets are the particular tabus called *pewhitu*. These tabus are laid on a child at birth, and they usually forbid him some specific form of food, or they may forbid him to kill a certain species of animal. Thus Ohoto is forbidden to eat the flesh of the great northern pike; Anoteelik may not shoot nor eat a loon; Hekwaw must never touch the liver of deer, and Tablu must not kill a lemming. The penalty for disobedience is the possibility that the law-breaker may become an Ino after death. The practical value of these tabus is purely disciplinary, as are many of our religious prohibitions.

As for Tornrait, they are not to be acquired so easily

as are the amulet spirits, for they are the most powerful forces for good in the Barrens. They are positive beings who not only defend their owners—or rather, their friends—from evil, but who can attack actively and accomplish great things. Tornrait may be acquired in a variety of ways, although usually a man must seek them out by enduring physical hardships. So the shamans expose themselves to the weather, to hunger and thirst, until they fall into a trance. Then, and then only the really great Tornrait appear, and a struggle between the wills of the man and of a particular Tornrak ensues. If the man wins, he secures the lifetime services of that Tornrak. If he loses, he seldom returns from his ordeal.

The lesser Tornrait may be encountered quite by accident, though. Thus it happened that when Hana was out hunting one day he met what he believed to be a demon. He describes it as a rather squat, animal-thing, with immense hairs on its snout and with a single paw that extended half the length of the body. This apparition attacked Hana, who bravely flung down his bow and grappled with the monstrous being. After an exhausting fight, the Tornrak—for such it was—gave up the struggle, and ever afterwards served as the personal Tornrak of Hana, to the man's great advantage.

There is a revealing sidelight, both on the Tornrait and on the minds of the Ihalmiut, in the relationship maintained between the helping spirits and men. If it happens, as it sometimes does, that a Tornrak is incapable of assisting its friend, then the man assumes that the spirit is simply bone-lazy, and with no further nonsense he sends it packing and the fallible spirit goes weeping off into the plains, out of a job.

It is impossible to talk about the Ihalmiut spirits and devils without also talking about the shamans. These dedicated men are the chief physical defense of the People against evil spirits, and so they must be particularly strong and well-armed. As an almost invariable rule they are the most intelligent men of each generation, and so they supply whatever nebulous leadership is present in the Ihalmiut society. They are not sorcerers, as many missionaries would have us believe, for, at least in the Ihalmiut country—Kakumee excepted—they work no evil but concentrate on assisting the People for the People's own good. And they make few extravagant claims. They do not say they can provide good hunting, for the Ihalmiut believe all animals have the gift of free will, and neither the wishes of men nor those of gods will influence the movements of beasts. Nor do the shamans claim to be able to control the weather, for this is Kaila's province, and Kaila does not listen patiently to the begging voices of men.

However, the shamans can, and do, assist men with particular problems. By passing into a trance and conferring with their Tornrait, the shamans can give advice on whether or not a dangerous winter trip should be attempted. They can often relieve a man of a mysterious illness and they can advise on all manner of domestic and practical problems. These things are their strength, for by virtue of their experience and intelligence they can materially assist their People, whether or not they do it by supernatural means. At the same time they are seldom so all-powerful that they come to stand head and shoulders above the rest of the Ihalmiut. A man who is too efficient, or too powerful, is not liked by the Innuit and this applies even to shamans, who exist to serve men, not to control them.

The shaman's trance provides the psychological background essential to any religion and is sometimes a formidable thing to behold, even if the onlooker is white and skeptical. There is a minimum of mummery and stage setting. While the People sit in a circle about the floor of a tent, the shaman may take his drum and with half-closed eyes shuffle about, singing a song in the ancient shaman language. The audience carries the chant, as in a drum dance, but much more softly.

At last there is a break in the drumming and the shaman collapses in a heap on the floor and a palpable silence ensues for some minutes. Then voices may be heard. The voice of the shaman is followed by the voice of his Tornrak— a strange and eerie sound which, so it seems, could not come from the throat of a man.

The awakening is sometimes exceedingly violent and exciting. The shaman may leap to his feet and be possessed with a quite inexplicable physical strength. Half a dozen men may not be able to hold him at all, and he may break through the wall of the tent and disappear into the darkness, to come back streaming with blood and in the last stages of exhaustion. In the after-grip of the trance, a shaman may do himself bodily harm which would be fatal to an ordinary man. Yet he invariably recovers from such self-inflicted wounds.

But awakenings are not usually so bloody and violent. In

most cases, the shaman returns to this life quietly, and as quietly tells his audience what he has seen and heard. If there has been trouble in the camp, the shaman may say his Tornrak has told him that someone has broken a tabu. Then there ensues a mass confession. All the onlookers confess their sins and so ease their consciences.

Certain individual shamans are gifted with unusual powers. One of these is a young man, nineteen or twenty years old, who once was of the Ihalmiut, but who now lives near the coast. He is a shaman of note, for he has the hypnotic ability to fill the tent, where a séance is being held, with deer, wolves, bears, and even seagoing beasts such as walrus and seals. On occasion he has conjured up such a menagerie that the audience has been crowded right out. It happens there is an independent trader who lives near this Eskimo camp, and one day this trader made the tactical error of doubting the shaman's ability when the young man was visiting the post. Quick as a wink, the young Eskimo conjured up the formidable steel prow of the Mission Ship, *Stella Polaris*, and brought it crashing through the wall of the cabin with such ferocious realism that the trader fled for his life, yelping with fright.

This tale is told with great gusto and joy by the Dhaeomiut, but unfortunately I didn't witness it myself. However, I did watch Kakumee at work on one of the other tasks of a shaman, the chasing away of an evil spirit.

Again it was a summer night when we were visited by an Ino, but this time the incident took place while we were entertaining Kakumee and some other Ihalmiut in our tent out on the Barrens. I never discovered just who saw what, before our quiet evening of gossip was interrupted by a startled rush of all the Eskimos, except Kakumee, for cover under bedrolls, blankets and anything else that could be found in the tent. By then Andy and I had grown moderately used to such erratic behavior, and we could observe what happened without the distraction of being thrown into a flap ourselves.

Kakumee stood his ground in the middle of the tent and stared at the doorway, mumbling like an old dog that catches the scent of a wolf. The others trembled visibly—at least the parts of them which were exposed trembled visibly—and so we assumed another ghost was in the vicinity.

The first shock wore off almost at once, and the fugitives crawled out from cover looking both sheepish and scared. Kakumee now sat them in a circle about him, and he went from one to the other holding out his outstretched hand. Each man gave the shaman some small object—a pinch of tobacco, an empty brass shell case, or a match. We contributed a pinch of sugar and a .22 bullet.

Kakumee now squatted on his hams and spread the gifts out under his parka skirts, then stood up to reveal that the objects had vanished. It was simple conjuring, and not very effective, but it was obviously only part of a ritual which must be undergone before the shaman could get down to serious work.

Kakumee's next step was to borrow a rifle from me and make a great show of loading it with an empty shell. Then he closed the breech, stepped to the door, pointed the gun into the darkness and pressed the trigger. The Eskimos knew what was coming, but we didn't, and the blast of a very live shell caused us to leap several inches into the air, to the great satisfaction of Kakumee and the other Ihalmiut.

This ended the preparatory part of the show. Kakumee now drew his knife—a long ugly weapon—and stepped outside.

He was gone for a good half-hour. Occasionally we could hear him muttering in an incomprehensible jargon. At last he returned and calmly announced that he had met two Inua—not just one—and had done them to death, killing one with the knife and strangling the other. There was great jubilation, but somehow the whole affair didn't seem to ring true. It was a good enough show, but it lacked telling effect. Some weeks later Ohoto admitted it was all a put-up job to satisfy the curiosity of the white men! As Ohoto told me, it would not do to fool about with a real visitation simply for our amusement, so the Eskimos had thoughtfully provided a synthetic example of ghost-hunting which would show us the ropes but involve no one in danger.

The tools of the shaman are simple almost to the point of nonexistence. He has a staff, a short clublike length of wood with a tapek tied to its middle; and he has something that is known to native races all over the world. Scientists call it a "bull-roarer" and the Ihalmiut call it a *memeo*. It is an oval blade of thin wood with notched edges and a cord tied to one end. Whirled rapidly over one's head, it gives off a deep-throated, mumbling roar which has the quality of ventriloquism about it, for from a few yards away it is impossible to locate the source of the sound. It is used primarily in connection with the driving out of evil from the body of a man who is afflicted with illness, or who has broken a serious tabu and feels himself in danger.

Amongst the many Ihalmiut tabus are the laws which prohibit the making of skin clothing when there is no snow on the ground; a prohibition against working with iron after a thunderstorm; the law which says no food may be eaten for twenty-four hours after a ghost has been seen, and numerous tabus covering the activities of a pregnant woman and governing the conduct in the camps when a death has occurred. A surprising number of these apparently senseless restrictions have a sensible basis in reality, and are not simply the rituals of the supernatural.

One particularly valuable possession of the Ihalmiut is a stock of potent spirit songs called *Irinjelo*. These are passed down from parent to child and their ownership is jealously guarded, though they may be used to aid any man in the camps. Most of them are specifics to aid in the cure of certain ailments believed to be caused by ghosts of evil intent towards man.

On one of my trips with Ootek out into the Barrens, I developed severe cramps in my stomach and became deathly sick. I was afraid of appendicitis, but there was nothing I could do to help myself except lie quietly in my tent and try not to groan with pain. Ootek was concerned. He brought me hot tea every few minutes and constantly inquired how I was feeling. Yet he seemed preoccupied and shy. It was only after some hours of indecision that Ootek could finally bring himself to speak of the point which was bothering him. Then, very tentatively, he asked me if he could try the effect of his own personal Irinjelo for stomach ailments on me. He had hesitated because he was afraid I would scorn his offer— being a white man and therefore a master of superior charms. Actually I had no faith in his charm, but I did not wish to repulse his kindness, and so I told him that I would be grateful.

He took a tin cup filled with fresh water and, holding it carefully in front of him, began to walk slowly around the outside of the tent where I lay. As he walked he sang his Irinjelo, a monotonous dirge in a minor key. At intervals he ceased singing and addressed himself to the cup of water, urging the evil to leave me and the good to come in. All this was continued for perhaps five or ten minutes. Then Ootek returned to the tent, gave me the water, and told me to swallow it down.

Though I was sick, I could see that he was almost abjectly afraid that I would laugh or toss the water away. He wanted very greatly to help me, but he was also deeply afraid that he was exposing both himself and his beliefs to my ridicule.

Well, I took the water, with all proper solemnity, drank it, and was at once seized with a violent urge to urinate. I barely got out of the tent in time and the urine was so hot and painful I was almost convinced Ootek had added some irritant to the water. Still, I had not seen him do it, and anyway I could not understand how any irritant could have functioned so quickly.

While I was engrossed in this problem, and with the burning in my loins, it suddenly dawned on me that my belly pains had vanished. Ootek was standing, watching me from the door, with a strained smile on his face. I gave him an answering grin, and he promptly beamed like an idiot and rushed off to cook me some supper.

I suppose it was just a happy coincidence—for it was certainly not faith that cured me . . . not mine, at any rate. When I thanked Ootek for his aid, I also asked him what had happened, and he replied with beautiful simplicity that the good had come in with the water, and the bad had gone out with the water!

Later that day he again showed the half-furtive attitude which had preceded my cure. This time I asked him what was the trouble, and he sheepishly told me I must on no account shoot a deer for five days, or I would myself experience the same agony as a deer that had been shot in the belly. Fortunately, no need to kill a deer arose during the next five days, and I did not feel much like putting Ootek's injunction needlessly to the test.

Now in this chapter I have hardly begun to delve into the spiritual beliefs of the Ihalmiut. There is a great deal more, and the whole forms a closely knit pattern which is intricately entwined with the everyday life of the People. What I *have* told you—seen out of the context by the eyes of strangers, and skeptical ones—may understandably have given the impression that the beliefs of the Barrens' People form an incubus that overshadows their lives.

But at no time did I feel they were haunted by devils and spirits, the products of their primitive minds. The closer I came to understanding and to a unity with the People, the more idiotic such rational conclusions would have become. It must always be remembered that the People are of *their* world and know nothing of us and ours, and so what seems like gross unreality to us can remain unassailably real to them. Their beliefs are a product of long centuries, and they fit the needs of their life and the shape of the land they live in.

They believe! That is the point. And it is a point we seldom consider when we decide to force our religions upon native peoples.

I knew an old white trapper who once lived on Southampton Island in the heart of the arctic. He is dead now, and probably rotting in hell, but I recall a remark of his when the question of converting the Eskimos to our religion was being discussed.

"God damn it!" he cried with quite unconscious blasphemy. "What the hell good do these sky pilots do anyhow? First they smash up the Huskies' religion, then they feed 'em a damn great Book we've been arguing and fighting over for about two thousand years. And what's the result? Why the poor buggers wind up hanging on to the worst of their heathen beliefs mixed up with the worst part of ours, and the outcome is they don't believe nothing at all, and understand less!"

Perhaps my foul-mouthed old friend has no right to be heard on a matter of religion. But I think the Eskimos themselves have that right.

Here is what a coast Eskimo said of our religion after he had spent a week under the ardent tutelage of a missionary. The remarks were made in an honest, if puzzled, spirit to the local trader, an intelligent man in sympathy with the natives.

"What a life you must lead! The *iqalua*—the priest—has spoken to me for hours of the things you believe, your God, these devils with wings, these ghosts and spirits who live in the sky and under the ground. Truly I am amazed, and afraid. It must be only because you are a white man and gifted with great strength and wealth, that you can survive all the terrors your beliefs put upon you! These laws of your gods take no heed of the hearts of their people; these devils and spirits who watch each thing you do and judge you by the terrible standards of death; these things make me shudder with horror! Yet, though I am afraid of these things, I can be sorry for you who must live under such shadows, for you also are the sons of the Woman, and the brothers of the Innuit. I wish you well in your struggles to escape from the place you call hell!"

The trader remembered that conversation in detail. He was not particularly pleased to find himself pitied by a heathen.

If you feel that neither the pagan Eskimo nor the heretical trapper has any right to be heard, then you can at least listen to the words of a missionary who represents a very great faith and who spent fifty-two years of his life in the midst of an Indian people who were pagan when he first arrived.

I came to know him well, to respect him and to feel a great fondness for him, since he was, above all things, an upright man and an honest man, and he worked as I have never seen any man work for the glory of God and of his Church.

When I knew him, his life was near its end and he died a few months after I left his little settlement. He had labored hard, with love, with belief and with severity, to accomplish his task. Now the task was done. All the Indians in his area came regularly to the Church and called themselves Christians. But in the fifty-odd years when he was the real power in the land, the old man watched a virile tribe of nearly 3000 people shrink to a passionless remnant of less than 200. Those who remained were lazy, shiftless, mentally and physically disabled men and women who lived in squalor and died in filth.

His task was done. On a midnight just before the celebration of Christmas, I was sitting in his little log home. Our talk had come to an end. The old man stared past me out the dark windows, and down his cheeks that had been tortured by frost and wizened by sun over the long painful years of his labors, tears fell slowly.

The silence was a palpable thing and I was desperately uncomfortable. Earlier that evening I had come to his house with a bitter anger against him in my heart, having spent that day in a hogpen of the people of the place, and having heard some tales that I do not care to repeat.

I had spoken bluntly and cruelly to the old man, and I

had been both unfair and thoughtless. Yet he had not re-proached me. He had not flung texts in my face and sent me away. He had listened quietly to my angry words of condemnation and when I was done he had talked, ramblingly and without evident purpose, of his life in the land. He had spoken, using an old man's disconnected words, of the memories of his long life. Then he had ceased talking, and now he wept.

I wanted to leave, for I felt sick with shame at what I thought I had done by my violent attack on the work of his years, but before I could go, his voice came stealthily back into the room. It was soft, yet older than any voice I have heard.

"It was better then?" he asked gently—"It was better that I had not come to this place—that these people I loved had not heard my voice and I had never come? You think that. And I? What do I think? I think sometimes that it was a bad thing for these people when I was sent to this place. . . ."

I left him then, left the old man with the reward of his lifetime of labor. Age and the sure face of death had left him no need to lie to himself or to me. Yet I wished desperately that he had lied, and that I had aided and abetted his lie.

XVIII
Ohoto

During our days at Angkuni Lake, and while we were traveling north and west on the Kuwee, Ohoto had been an incomplete man. He had been under the shadow of a great apprehension, greater than the depression we two white men felt at the sight of the empty tent circles and the scattered rock graves. That we had seen no deer and had found only their old tracks meant more to Ohoto than a temporary absence of the beasts from this land. He felt that he had been transported into a sort of Ihalmiut hell, a hell of the worst possible kind where there were no deer and never would be any deer.

The hell and the heaven of the Ihalmiut are real places that co-exist in this world. Thus "heaven" might be likened to the land where the deer may always be found whenever man has need of them. An actual glimpse of this paradise is vouchsafed to the People in the days when the great herds pass through their country. So "hell" is the place that knows nothing of the deer, and it too is present in reality during those times when there are no deer on the plains.

242

Inevitably Ohoto confused the nebulous concept of the Ihalmiut hell with the unreality of the Angkuni country. The impact of this lifeless land was therefore much greater on him than it was on us—and *we* felt it strongly enough. We shared his sensation of existing as disembodied nonentities. We felt, at times, as if all reality were escaping from us. We two white men were irritatingly aware of moving through an imponderable void which became more and more oppressive.

All this, I think, helps to explain two shocking things which happened to Ohoto during our voyage of exploration into the north and the west.

During our trip up the Kuwee, Ohoto developed an abscess on his cheek. With each passing day it grew deeper and angrier, but he was so engrossed in the gloom of his own thoughts that he seldom complained about it. I dressed it a few times, and after the fourth day it had become so ugly that we took a chance and lanced it. But still it persisted. At first I thought the presence of the sore was probably due to a nutritional upset, since Ohoto had never before gone without meat or existed on the devitalized foods of white men for so long a time.

By the time we reached the headwaters of Kuwee, the abscess had grown do deep and so large that Andy and I became seriously disturbed about it, and even the stoical Eskimo began to show signs of physical reaction to it. His appetite began to fail, and this is the most serious symptom an Innuit can betray, for food means more to him than almost anything else.

We made a good camp not far from the place where Kuwee left the unknown lake, and here we decided to stay until the sore began to show some signs of healing. Ohoto accepted our gesture with evident disinterest. He set up his little travel shelter, crawled into it and showed no further signs of life until darkness had come. We were all tired with the long fatigue which comes from hard travel on empty stomachs, and I fell asleep as soon as I had crawled under my fly net.

About midnight I was awakened by blood-chilling screams. They were inhuman sounds, far beyond the power of mere pain to induce, for they carried an overtone of such abject terror that I broke into a sweat without any knowledge of what had induced those fearful cries.

I lay there for a moment, but the shrieks were so

penetrating they could not be ignored. Andy was sitting up in his bedroll, and he called out to me.

"Good God! What the hell is that?"

"Ohoto, I think," I replied. Then, without bothering to put on any clothes, I crawled stark-naked from under my net, grabbed a rifle, and ran out over the broken rocks toward the tiny shelter where Ohoto lay.

The screams ceased before I got there. Instead my ears were assailed by a gurgling whimper, as if the man's voice had been overcome by sheer terror, leaving him with only an animal echo of sounds. I flung open the door flap of his tent with such vehemence that I ripped it and part of the wall clean off the poles. Ohoto was crouched inside, his body nearly filling the tiny space of the shelter, and he was staring at one of the slim poles with eyes as empty of all expression as those of a dead ox. His lips hung slack and his great white teeth shone eerily in the light of the stars.

I shouted his name, but the cringing thing on the rug paid no heed to me. Whimpers of fear still bubbled out of his throat. I became conscious of a feeling of panic, for I could see no sign of a danger capable of instilling such a fear in a man. For a moment I thought Ohoto had gone mad, and was perhaps in the grip of the dread arctic hysteria which makes insane murderers out of sane men. The potentialities of being stranded in this empty wilderness with a mad Eskimo came unpleasantly to my mind.

I acted by instinct. Dropping the rifle, I grabbed Ohoto by the hair and shook him so violently that he fell over and crashed into the frail wall of his tent. Then to my relief he made a tremendous effort, straightened up so that he was resting on his knees, and pointed a shaking hand at the blank stretch of canvas behind one of the poles of his shelter.

The gesture was a mute appeal to me, and his eyes were fixed on my face. But where he pointed I could see nothing at all except the discolored canvas and the smooth peeled surface of the sapling pole.

I still had no idea what was causing his terror. Finally, and with no coherent reason, I picked up the rifle and swung the butt as hard as I could against the slender tent pole. It was, for me, only a release of tension, but by the luck of fools and of white men I unwittingly had done the right thing.

Ohoto relaxed with the abruptness of a deflating balloon. His eyes closed and his erratic breathing sank to a long, deep rustle. He curled up like a dog, and in a moment the anticlimax of the night's work was on me. Ohoto began to snore loudly!

He snored and snored. I became aware of the multitudes of mosquitoes clinging to my naked flesh and went hurriedly back to my bed and gave a garbled account of what I had seen to my anxious companion. Then for hours I lay, and could not sleep, while the echo of Ohoto's snores sounded like a mocking denial of what had happened.

But it *had* happened, and it was no nightmare of the sleep-drugged mind but a nightmare in reality. When dawn came we got dressed and went to see Ohoto. He was sleeping gently and I nudged him with my foot until he woke, dazed by the depths of his slumber. This was itself odd, for during the previous week he had not slept except in brief naps, for the pain in his face had banished sleep.

He lay still for a moment, then his eyes widened again and stared as they had stared at me during the night. His mouth drew back in a grimace and I thought, "Oh, Lord! Here we go again!" But he only rolled over so that he could see the tent pole against which I had driven my rifle butt. Then he spoke.

"The Ino!" he cried. "Now it is gone!"

He got up then, scrambling out of the wreck of his tent, and as he turned sideways to us, we both saw with a distinct shock that his abscess was almost healed! What had been a draining wound the night before was now dry and scabbed with the healthy look of growing skin. Ohoto carefully touched the hole in his cheek and, for the first time in many days, he smiled.

"Look!" he said, turning to us. "Now that the Ino is gone the pain has left this thing in my face! Soon this will heal and I will forget it as I have already forgotten the pain!"

It seemed to be a time for explanations. I asked my questions and Ohoto readily answered them, for it appeared that he owed me a debt of gratitude. I listened to what he told us and I was of two minds about it. Under the bright morning sun, it sounded like so much supernatural gibberish, yet I could not deny the evidence of my eyes as they dwelt on that inexplicably dried-up sore. I listened and could not tell what was real and what was sheer fantasy.

The abscess had been the work of a devil—that was the first thing. This visit of a malignant Ino—and Ohoto was specific about him, telling us that it was the spirit of a man who had not been buried, and whose body had been eaten by wolves—had brought on the running sore as the first step in the destruction of Ohoto. But the devil chose to dally, and it was not until the night before that it decided to finish its job. It came with darkness. When Ohoto looked up from his pain-ridden sleep, he saw it clinging to the pole of the tent, grinning evilly down upon him.

Ohoto thanked me profusely for my intervention. According to him, it was my haphazard swing of the rifle, coupled with some blasphemy I had not realized I was uttering, that convinced the Ino I was more than a match for it. It fled. The pain in Ohoto's face vanished on the instant, and by morning the abscess was well on the way to being cured.

I must admit quite frankly I don't believe what Ohoto believed. And yet I know that in three days the abscess vanished, and that is an incredibly short length of time for natural healing to do its work.

Less than a week after the Ino trouble, Ohoto's prophecy about his father's return, made when we first saw Angkuni Lake, came true. Elaitutna returned, to the vision and hearing of Ohoto, and spoke to his son.

For a few days after his abscess cleared up Ohoto's natural cheerfulness revived, but it was short-lived. When, day after day, we still failed to meet the deer, his mood grew dark again.

Slowly we coasted along the northern shore of the unknown lake, staying timidly under the lee of towering rock dikes which the ice had gouged up and flung along the shores, for we had not forgotten the mysterious and malignant wind that had almost destroyed us early in the trip. The surrounding country was so low-lying and shielded by continuous dikes that we could not see it from the lake. Low islands swung over the horizon and tantalized us with the belief that they were mainland, before they blended with and disappeared into the rock wall which hemmed us in. The canoe was like a minute protozoan wandering in a vast saucer, aimlessly active, and blind.

Our horizon was either water or the rocky rim of the saucer. We crawled blindly along under the dubious shelter of the dikes and prayed we would not be forced to land except at places of our own choosing, for any attempt at beaching the canoe along most of that formidable coast, except in a dead calm, would have resulted in the canoe's being smashed to bits.

During three days' travel we found only five places where we could safely get ashore. From these places we could look inland and our eyes recoiled from what we saw. Beyond the dikes lay an endless cone of gray distance, a drowned and sodden land. It was a desperate sight and its most frightening aspect was the almost complete absence of deer trails. It was completely free of the intricate network of such trails which marks almost all of the Barrenlands. Only a faint depression here and there might have been made by the feet of Tuktu, a long long time ago.

After a few days of this, Ohoto was sunk into a depression that nothing could relieve. We had not only passed out of the realms of living men, but, so far as he could see, we had passed completely out of the world as he knew it. This he was certain of, for there were no deer here, and never had been any deer.

One night we found a rare, shingle beach, a few yards long, crowded into a gap in the rock barriers along the shore. Gratefully we beached the canoe and made camp—without a fire, for there was no wood. Ohoto was silent during our meal, and we too were under such tension that we made no effort to speak to him or to try to break the mood which had been obviously growing over him for days. When the meal was over, the Eskimo came to me and quietly asked me for my rifle.

I knew there was no game about that he could hunt, and anyway it was growing dark, for in late summer the nights are already long. I asked Ohoto why he wanted the gun and he answered, saying: "Give me your gun—and in the morning think of the things that I have done for you. I know you will give my body what it demands, for you know the things which must be done; nor will you leave me for the foxes and wolves—for you are a man of the Ihalmiut!"

Andy exploded. "Suicide!" he shouted. "That's all we need to make this picnic really happy!"

Certainly death filled Ohoto's thoughts, and as I realized the fact, the long tension of our journey seemed to reach an unbearable climax, and I gave way to livid anger.

I told the Eskimo that he would have no gun, and I told him to wipe the idea from his mind or I would do it for him. He walked away from us and sat down on the rocks by the shore while my companion and I rounded up the rifles, the hatchet and all the knives—even Ohoto's—and hid the lot under the bedrolls in our tent. We were bitter against the man, for it was as if he had deliberately added this last unbearable weight to the heavy uncertainty which already clouded the outcome of our journey into nowhere. We were so burdened by the strain of this uncertainty that our nerves were worn to the thin, ragged edge, and our thoughts were no longer wholly rational. We told each other we did not give a damn what happened to Ohoto, that we were angry only because we did not relish having a dead man on our hands. After we had hidden the weapons, I went to Ohoto and I beat him with words as brutally as I could in the Innuit tongue. He did not look up or answer me. After a while I felt a sense of pettiness and self-disgust. I knew dimly that this man needed what sympathy and understanding we could give him, for if we were alone in emptiness, then he was trebly alone. I caught my rage and squeezed it back into my heart, and spoke gently to Ohoto, trying to make amends and to persuade him he must not die.

If he heard me he gave no sign, and now my rage flared up anew. I stalked back to the tent, cursing him in English as I went.

Andy and I went to bed, both of us filled with a tight anger against the Eskimo. I tried to put him out of my thoughts, but neither sleep nor forgetfulness was possible.

We had not been in the tent many minutes when a pair of yellow-billed loons pierced the heavy silence with their frenetic cries. They were the first living things we had heard for days. But instead of relieving the tautness in us, they only intensified it, for their lunatic babble was not what one expects from creatures of flesh and blood.

Hardly had they begun their wailing refrain when Ohoto's voice joined them. The sounds of the loons became a maniac chorus for Ohoto's voice as he intoned the high-pitched and monotonous chant which is peculiar to the Ihalmiut who know they are about to die!

The song went on, endlessly, into the night, until I clutched the sleeping bag so tightly that my nails cracked against the rough canvas. Exhaustion eventually overcame me, and I slept, to grapple with hideous nightmares, until just before dawn I awoke. I lay there for a long time, staring up into the white mist of my net, before I realized that the singing had stopped. Then I felt sick. Nausea rocked me, as I lay there believing that Ohoto was gone.

When it was full dawn I went over to Ohoto's shelter. He was not there. I began searching, and as I failed to find him, I grew frantic and ran, stumbling among the boulders of the dike. At last I found him, lying face downward in the thick moss near the beach.

For a long time I stood over his still form, hesitating to touch the ragged fur of his old parka, but as I looked down upon him the light grew stronger and I saw that his parka was lifting and falling in the shallow, regular rhythm of sleep.

The relief I felt was utterly magnificent! I shouted at him, and when he sat up and began rubbing his eyes, I tossed him my tobacco pouch and my own pipe. If he had been standing I would have thrown my arms around his neck.

It was a penitent but subdued Eskimo who had his breakfast with us that morning. We, on the contrary, were so relieved to have him still with us that we were cheerful and even voluble. However, unlike the time he had been troubled by the Ino, Ohoto was not at all anxious to explain what had underlain his suicidal mood of the previous night. But we had forgiven him and so we felt it was our right to know the story.

Several days elapsed before we heard it all. I repeat it now. The continuity is mine but the content is Ohoto's.

When I was *nutarik* [but a child] my father often traveled on the River of Men. My father Elaitutna used to venture far down the river even as far as the lake called Hicoliguak, for he knew the land well, having lived at the Angkuni camp in the days before disaster came to that place. My father was a shaman, though only a little one. Still he had less fear of the spirits than most men have, and that was why he continued his journeys on the river for many years after men had deserted its banks. My father almost alone of the Ihalmiut visited Angkuni after the great dying there.

He had a love for the land about the Great Lake; and that love was only tempered by fear of the empty tent rings and the full graves. Many a time Elaitutna swore he would return to Angkuni, where he had seen his first deer as a child, and where his spirit would remain for all time to come.

When he died, in my tent at the trader's lake far to the east of here, I placed all things needful for a journey on his grave, for I knew he would take those things and go from the foreign place where he died, and return again to the camps which lie under Kinetua.

It was because I knew this that I spoke of Elaitutna when we first climbed Kinetua and looked out over the dead land about the Great Lake. I knew that hill; I knew that place. And I knew also that, somewhere near, the ghost of Elaitutna lingered. That knowledge gave me a happiness which was not unmixed with fear, for though I loved Elaitutna, I do not love ghosts.

We had been camped on the shores of Kinetua Bay only a few days when I knew that Elaitutna had discovered me. I could neither see nor hear him then, but I knew he was there, and his presence brought me both fear and comfort as I walked over the lands of the dead.

When we left Angkuni and traveled up Kuwee, Elaitutna was near, and as we went from the place of graves, it seemed that the spirit of my father grew in strength until at times I believed I heard the distant sound of his remembered voice. Thus it was that when we stood on the shores of this nameless lake at last, it was Elaitutna who whispered the words I said to you, saying that we should turn back from the emptiness which stretched ahead.

You would not turn back, and so we went on into the strange land of water and it happened that Elaitutna lost his powers, for this was a land where he did not belong. He could do nothing for me when the devil who haunted this river came into my face and would have destroyed me but for your magic. Still you would not turn back, though now the voice of Elaitutna was strong, and so I knew that I was passing into his world—the world of spirits. All day I heard his voice and for long hours my father spoke to me, telling me the tales of his youth and of the youth of this land.

Elaitutna spoke of the time when the tents of the People were as many as clouds on a day when the white spirits roll over the sky. My father told me of the time when the deer were so many that the Ihalmiut had no use for the word "hunger." He spoke also of the days when the great fleets of kayaks made the long journey north to the meeting place called Akilingnea, the high ridge where the Innuit of the coast came to the edge of our land to gather wood and to trade with us.

The memory of my father stretched farther back in time, and he spoke of the days when all the People who became the

Ihalmiut lived fifty days march to the west, by the shores of a truly mighty lake such as we have never seen. Elaitutna told me how the Itkilit came on that lake from the south and west and attacked the Innuit there, and the survivors fled into the east, and over the lifetimes of many men they journeyed slowly eastward to escape the Itkilit raids, until at last they found this land of the Ihalmiut.

But most of all, Elaitutna spoke of the deer. He spoke of the days when the deer needed a full month to pass by the famous crossing places. And as my father talked, I looked out from your canoe and saw no living thing in all the land, and my heart grew weak, and I grew dazed and could not tell if I had died and was already in the place where no deer are, and where the hungry spirits whine over the plains seeking the deer that are not there.

I heard Elaitutna's voice grow steadily in strength, but it was not until we reached this camp that I *saw* my father once more. He stood by me near the shore. You who are Kablunait could not see him, though he saw you, as you walked to and fro.

It was then, and in this place, that Elaitutna spoke the words which made me want your rifle, that I might seek out my rest. My father spoke no more of the old times, but spoke instead of the People, and of the land as it is now. He talked of Hunger, and of the Great Pain. He spoke of the lesser killers, and of the blood spitting which comes upon the women and children. He bade me look at you, and he said:

"See, Ohoto, these are the Kablunait who were also the sons of the first woman, even as we also came from her womb. Yet she sent them from her, and from this land which was theirs as well as ours. She wronged them in that ancient time, but they did not forget, nor did they forget that we were the favored ones of our common mother. They returned again. They returned for their revenge, and in their train they brought the Great Pain and the blood spitting. They took the deer and hid them from us so that we knew the meaning of famine. They are clever and they have come to claim the land which once was ours.

"And you, my son? Now you are here with me in the land of the dead, and that is well. In the tents you left behind upon the shores of the Little Lakes there is only evil and perhaps there will be no people left to greet you when you return. Even should those faces that you know still smile to see you come, yet remember that their time is short and I speak the truth. The day will come when there are no more faces left to greet you, when you come in from your fruitless hunts.

"I am *Angeokok*—a shaman, Ohoto, and a ghost who can see all that your eyes cannot see. What were the People in my youth but a great People who filled all the wide plains with the voices of men? You know what the People are now. But what will they be at the end of the winter which stretches ahead? A few new graves by the rivers that flow through the land.

"And Ohoto, my son, where will he be in those times? While the Kablunait remain, he too may remain, but when they are done with his help, where will he go? A time will come when he will die, and there will be no man of his People left to bury his bones. The wolves will have what is left of my son, and his spirit will find no peace in all of the world."

So spoke Elaitutna, my father. And I knew the truth of his words and wished to borrow your gun and make an end to the waiting.

But the guns were hidden, and when I came to look for my knife, it too was gone. So I went and sat by the shore, in the darkness, and sang the songs of the dying—believing the power of Elaitutna, my father, would bring me to death. Yet before morning he left me, and when I searched for him by the rocks he was gone and I was alive.

Then I had no heart left in me; and I fell in the moss and I wept, knowing that I was alone.

XIX
Days of His Father

On the day after Ohoto's decision to die, we went on from the night camp and the land changed its face. The sun rose high in a translucent sky and soon we beheld the lift of hills rising over the dikes which had enclosed our world for so long. Massive hills rose to the west and to the south. The shore now curved into the south so that we knew we had come to the end of the nameless lake.

The sight of those distant hills was like the sight of friends on the quay, at the end of a voyage, and we paddled towards them with a new strength. Ohoto was the first to see dark patches clinging in the folds of the ragged slopes on the far ridges, and through my glasses I saw, with a lifting heart, that the patches were trees.

As we swung to the south, the rock dikes crumbled and sank and were gone. Now land, real land, sloped quickly up from the shore to a line of low ridges. As we paddled under their flanks we saw with a childlike delight that they were reticulated and patterned with the myriad trails of the deer.

In the low valleys which cut into the hills were many thickets of spruce, and so we went to shore several times that morning, simply for the pleasure of building fires. Though we had nothing but a little flour to eat, we were merry as we sat near the great pyres and laughed as the mosquitoes and flies incinerated themselves.

As we sat by one of these fires, a gray, nebulous haze swept suddenly in over the lake and in an instant obscured the bleak desolation of the way we had come. The haze lasted only a minute or two, but before it had passed, a most perfect rainbow was born—grew up to the zenith and fell to the other side of its sphere so that it spanned, with one magnificent arc, from the north to the southern shore of the lake. It was only a rainbow, yet Ohoto swore it was a sign. When we pushed off into the nameless lake once more he sat in the bow of the canoe, sniffing the little wind as a dog sniffs the breeze for knowledge of what lies ahead.

We coasted along the shore until we came opposite an abrupt gap in the line of the hills. As we looked through this gap we felt a weird sensation as if this low-lying saddle was all that separated us from the actual edge of the world. From the canoe we could see, at eye level, over the flat breadth of the col, and there was nothing beyond it. Now neither the stone dikes nor the hills hemmed us in. We looked through a hole in the skin of the world, and it seemed as if we were looking out into infinite space.

We were not frightened, for around us the land had become friendly and warm. So we landed, and walked westward into the gap. Then we saw why it had seemed that the world ended here. The line of hills under which we had been paddling formed the spine of a causeway which divided our lake from an even greater one to the west. The hills ran down from the north and, as they came, they were funneled into a narrowing ribbon of land. At the point where we stood, the land was constricted to perhaps a quarter of a mile in width, and at this narrowest part the hills ceased for a while. To the south of us they rose up again, and, gaining strength, broadened the causeway until it again became a great funnel of land spreading out to the south.

We crossed the narrow neck of the isthmus and were amazed to find no connection between the two lakes. The uncanny sensation which we had felt, of coming to the end of the world, was explained by the fact that this new and mightier lake lay a good thirty feet below the level of the one we had traversed.

As we stood gazing out to the limitless west over the ice-blue water of the new inland sea, Ohoto seemed to be searching for something in the depths of his mind and in the depths of the lake. There was a startling tint to the waters, a pellucid lapis lazuli, such as I have seen in no other lake.

Ohoto was remembering that tint, for the Innuit have delicate methods of finding their ways over the plains. At length he spoke.

"This is the lake called Tulemaliguetna. The waters which lead to Tulemaliguak—the greatest of all inland waters —and the way to the ice sea in the north!"

We questioned him and it appeared that Ohoto had never seen this lake himself; nevertheless he knew the subtle distinctions which told him its name, for such things are part of the common legend of travel that still lives on in the remaining tents of the Ihalmiut. Ohoto was right. This was indeed Tulemaliguetna, and the narrow causeway on which we stood was all that divided the two major water systems of the whole central Barrens.

Innuit Ku—the Kazan—and Dubawnt River, each of them well over three hundred miles in length, run their own ways through the plains until they make a common meeting in Kaminikuak Lake (Baker Lake, we call it) at the edge of salt water. But here where we stood, in the very heart of the Barrens, the two river systems came within a stone's throw of one another, before veering off again on their separate ways northward.

Thus, from the east shores of Angkuni Lake to the west shores of Tulemaliguetna, there is an east-and-west water barrier on the migration route of the deer which is nearly one hundred miles in width, pierced only by this quarter-mile bridge of land.

As we walked over the causeway on our return to the canoe, we saw on the ground at our feet so many deer trails inscribed on the gravel that not even the hardy lichens and mosses had been able to live. Over the years, millions of deer must have converged on this little isthmus during the northward and southward migrations of spring and autumn. Here was the Deer's Way, the greatest of all roads of the deer. And, from the signs, it was clear that the deer had gone northward by this path in the spring of the year.

We also discovered a row of stone men running diagonally across the isthmus, aligned as neatly as soldiers on parade. Each man stood apart from his neighbors by the length of a canoe, and they formed a continuous front, as if to guard the isthmus against an invasion from the north; though—as we were to discover—their intended duties were quite different. Each Inukok was about three feet in height and wore on his head a patch of brown moss. They stood guard over the causeway, these squat gray figures surmounted by their brown, hairy heads, and they bore mute witness to the fact that we were not the first men to come to this place.

Ohoto smiled broadly at sight of the stone men. He knew that somewhere to the north the flood of Tuktu was even now converging, to be inexorably funneled over the narrow Deer's Way. He was a happy man when he went to bed that night, nor was he displaying any impatience about the coming of the deer. It may be that he knew when they would come, for the People who live by the deer can sense things about Tuktu which are hidden from us.

We slept on the east shore of the Deer's Way that night, but our sleep was cut short at the dawn by the hoarse voice of Ohoto.

"Tuktu! They have come!" he muttered. And as we rolled sleepily into the dawn, Ohoto had vanished.

It was a miracle of accidental timing that we should have arrived at the isthmus only a day before the deer came. We had traveled many miles through a dead land, searching for them, but not until we had reached the western limits that time and food had placed on our travels did we find that which we sought.

As we crawled out of the tent we could see the silhouettes of the Inukok against the uncertain light. Now they seemed to be imbued with a tense expectancy. As the first rising breath of the morning wind played over the dry moss on their heads, it was as if they were stirring after a long trance.

Ohoto was not in sight, so we moved to the center of the isthmus a half-mile south of the stone men. The light was growing so quickly that we could begin to see a flowing shadow far to the north, on the downslope of the hills. We sat on the rocks and waited while the light quickened and the shadows took on substance until we could pick out the clubbing, velvet-covered antlers of the deer against the pearl-white sky.

They approached slowly and easily, for they had passed this way every year of their lives, and in their time had met no enemy on the Deer's Way. The light strengthened in uneven bursts until I could see the leader, a young buck, come slowly along one of the paths until he was only a few yards from the nearest stone man. The breeze blew a quick gust, and the moss on the Inukok's skull came to life and twisted briefly in the grip of the wind. The buck stopped abruptly, planted his forelegs wide apart and stared at the stone thing. The wind was to the deer, and it brought him no scent of danger; nor did the strange shape move again, or threaten him further.

But the buck was cautious now, and alert. Stepping high over the shattered rocks, he picked his way to the east of the stone guardians and began making his way parallel to the diagonal line of the Inukok—but keeping his distance, for he was obviously uneasy about them.

The rest of the herd, a few dozen bucks, followed carelessly after. Halfway down the line, the leader stopped and browsed a little, then—suddenly aware that the stone men had been almost imperceptibly closing in on him—he broke into a trot. As his tail lifted, the other bucks caught the white flash which spells trouble, and they also ran.

Now the little herd was galloping over the stony trails and in a moment the long line of stone men came to an end, leaving a twenty-foot gap between the last of them and the lake. The herd bunched into the gap, heedless of anything now but escape from the Inukok on their flanks; and then, as they passed through into safety, Ohoto's rifle spoke from a well-concealed stone blind near the opening.

There were three shots, and the three largest bucks came crashing into the moss and the rocks, while the young leader led the survivors in a fantastic flight over the boulders and up the slope of the southern ridge that marked the end of the isthmus.

Ohoto jumped from his hiding place and ran over to the kills. We joined him quickly, and in a few minutes all three of us were hurrying back to camp and to a fire, laden with the meat for which our bellies yearned.

In the following days, the flow of deer over the isthmus grew heavier until it merged into one continuous stream, more concentrated and therefore more impressive than the herds I had seen crossing the Ghost Hills at Nueltin Lake. At the narrow isthmus they were so closely pressed together that even the "deer fence" of Inukok could no longer channel their flow, and from the main flood that followed the ambush road, other streams burst out between the guardian watchers.

With the coming of the deer there came to the land the transformation from death to life which I had seen on a much smaller scale at Windy Bay. The pallid skies that had been empty of living wings were now flecked across their endless breadth by the dark, labored flight of the ravens. The black birds did not come in ones and twos, but in long skeins of dozens and they shared the pale spaces with hawks that materialized suddenly out of the northern horizon. Three great gyrfalcons flew low over the isthmus one morning, barely clearing the huddled backs of the deer. After they had passed, a slow procession of rough-legged hawks beat lazily southward high over the tide of Tuktu. The flanks of the herds were whitened by the flocks of gulls that kept pace with the trek, waiting to play the carrion role of vultures.

On land, the yelping of dun-colored arctic foxes was a light echo of the voices of the white wolves moving wraithlike through the eddying masses of deer. Even the gaudy ground squirrels seemed to emerge suddenly out of the sandy drumlins, as if from a long hibernation, and their plaintive whistling resounded from the long ridges and from the hills. Terriganiak the weasel came to chatter his inane defiance from the rock piles near the shore; and Kakwik the wolverine plodded deliberately along in the van of the migrating herds.

But the transformation extended beyond the country itself, for it also came to the heart of Ohoto. On the first day of the deer, as we sat about the fire and hungrily waited for the blackening chunks of fresh meat to roast on the little red coals, Ohoto showed us the face that we knew—yes, and loved. And the change in him was not simply due to the prospect of gorging on meat. Rather it was as if the endless lines of the deer imparted to Ohoto something of their own immeasurable vitality. It was borne in upon me again that the affinity between the Ihalmiut and the deer was more than a merely physical tie. It was as if the People were required to eat of the spirit of Tuktu, the ephemeral presence which comes when the deer are in the land, and vanishes when the deer vanish.

Now that spirit was with us, and the bleak savagery of the lands we had seen no longer filled Ohoto with dread. When he and I stumbled on an old tent circle on the isthmus, Ohoto did not sink back into the mood of depression which had been his at the deserted camps on Angkuni Lake. He talked constantly now, of every subject under the sun, and when he was not talking he was laughing, or he was complaining that *I* did not laugh enough, but had too long a face. He spent hours clowning for our entertainment. With consummate cleverness he mimicked us white men, and the other men of the Ihalmiut, until we laughed so immoderately that the deer crossing the isthmus turned curious faces and stared in the direction of our camp. As for the ghosts—even Elaitutna and his dire predictions and warnings were not mentioned again.

One night Ohoto and I sat on a knoll near the camp. In the semidarkness of dusk we listened to the steady, monotonous, castanet clicking of the feet of the unseen beasts on the Deer's Way. I asked Ohoto if he would tell me some of those tales of the days of Elaitutna and the old ones. He was willing enough, and he let his mind lapse back into the days when Elaitutna, his father, was young.

During the youth of my father [he began], my family lived for a time on a river which flows north out of Tulemaliguak, the greatest of lakes. There on that river were our tents and they numbered more than threescore. Those who lived in that place were called *Kiktoriaktormiut*—People of the Mosquito Land—for in those times each camp had its own name, though all belonged to the Ihalmiut.

The Kiktoriaktormiut were the most north-dwelling ones of our race, and they were the only ones of the Ihalmiut who lived in contact with peoples who were not of our race. In those times there was no entry into the great plains except from the north. To the south, the Itkilit were strong and angry, and they closed their land to us; to the east lay the sea and its peoples, and these we never knew in those days. To the west there was another brood of Itkilit whom we feared greatly, for in ancient times they had driven us, with much bloodshed, out of the western plains.

So we had intercourse only with men to the north. The Kiktoriaktormiut sat at the gates of our land and my father's people were the keepers of the north gates to the plains.

That was also the land of Omingmuk the musk ox, and each winter hunters came from the southern camps of the Ihalmiut to the igloos of my father's people in order to join in the musk ox hunts. I have heard that in some winters a hundred sleds came up from the south, and the camps by the gates of the land were places of wonderful doings, of marvelous dances and games.

It usually happened that each hunter of the Kiktoriaktormiut would wait for one of his song-cousins to arrive from the south, so that the two men could make the winter hunt together. My father's song-cousin was Hekwaw—the same who still lives under the Little Hills of this land. And I have heard tales of their hunts from both Hekwaw and Elaitutna, my father.

Not until the middle of winter would Hekwaw arrive in the north camps. Then he would come, bringing his big sled laden high with gifts of deer meat and furs. Elaitutna would welcome his guest and send people out to the other igloos to announce a great song feast for his cousin.

That night the People would gather until the great house of Elaitutna was so crowded with men and with women that there was barely room in the center for the feet of the dancer. Elaitutna always began the dance by singing a song in praise of Hekwaw. And, at the end of his song, he made Hekwaw a gift—a valuable gift—and all who were present shouted in praise of that gift.

Then Hekwaw would dance, and his song would be of the great generosity of Elaitutna, and he too would end his song by making a gift to the hunter who was his song-cousin. So it would go, all through the night, as each of the two men sought to outdo the other in the giving of gifts, and the People in the igloo grew wild with excitement as the gifts mounted up.

The women kept busy. Though it was dark as death outside the igloos, nevertheless they kept special fires burning out in the snow, and they brought in the trays laden with steaming deer meat. New visitors would keep arriving from the outlying camps until at last the drum dance spread to the snow houses nearby. Elaitutna and Hekwaw went from igloo to igloo, and in each they sang new songs, and gave each other new and more wonderful gifts. By morning the excitement would have brought them to such a pitch that they had given away all things they owned, and by morning each would be in possession of all the belongings of his song-cousin!

Sometimes the dancing and singing went on for two or three days, and in the brief intervals when sleep was permitted Hekwaw slept with my mother, for this was the law. It was always the law that a hunter who came northward to seek Omingmuk would not bring his family on the hard trip. So when a man arrived at the gates of the land from farther south, he was permitted to sleep with the wife of his song-cousin, and to have refused him this hospitality would have been to set a terrible disgrace on the whole camp. Yet this you must understand: no man slept with the wife of another unless that woman was willing. It was always the woman who, in the end, made the decision. Of course, also, when Elaitutna journeyed south, in the summer, to the Little Hills country, he went by kayak and so there was no room for *his* wife. When he came to the tent of Hekwaw, he likewise naturally slept with the wife of his song-cousin, for he had no woman of his own in that place.

The festivities in the camp of Elaitutna continued for days, and often before they were ended, new hunters arriving from the South started the contest all over again. So the dancing and singing and gambling swelled and ebbed over most of the winter.

At last Hekwaw and Elaitutna would decide that the time for the hunt was upon them. Then they took their two sleds and their teams, and with only a light load of food set off into the wild land to the west of Tulemaliguak where no man has ever lived.

Sometimes they traveled through the broken rock hills for two weeks before they came on bare spots where the hard snow had been scraped up by the feet of the musk oxen searching for lichens and moss. When the men found these signs they made camp, a small travel igloo: then, taking only two or three hunting dogs with them, they went forward on foot.

It was night hunting then, for up in that land the winter days were only an hour or two long, and during daylight the musk oxen were hard to approach. So the hunters moved in the night, when the darkness was broken only by the long flames of the Lights in the Sky, or by the edge of Taktik the moon spirit's rising.

At last the dogs would go tense and strain at their leads—but in silence, for they had been taught not to cry at the scent of Omingmuk. As the men climbed a low hill, they might see a patch of black shadows against the deep blue of the snow in the valley ahead and they would know that these were musk oxen. Great hairy beasts these were, with their long fur hanging down to their feet and dragging like a great tail in the snow. Their heavy bodies were shaped like square rocks covered with long black lichens, and only their heads looked like the animal things we know.

After seeing where the Omingmuk were standing, the hunters would unleash their dogs from two places at once. Either Hekwaw or Elaitutna would make a great circle to the other side of the herd. The wavering bark of a fox was the signal they used, and when the circling man was in his position, he gave the signal and the dogs were let loose.

The dogs hunted in silence. Like wolves without voices they moved in on the herd and, at the first sign of their coming, the musk oxen formed a tightly closed ring, and the outer edge of the circle was a solid rampart of horns.

The bull musk oxen make a deadly rampart. No dog and no wolf can attack it and live. But Omingmuk knew little of man. They knew only that they were safe from most dangers when they formed their tight ring, and so they did not break and run as the two hunters cautiously approached from the hills. The men came like shadows themselves, and they saw to it that there were rock piles on their routes, where they could retreat if need be.

Now in the flickering dark of the night the man-fox barked once again and the dogs, knowing the signal, retreated and formed a wide circle which revolved far outside the circumference of the musk oxen herd. It was all done without sound—for sound may break up the herd and send it stampeding off over the hills. Only the whispering voices of the spirits who ride with the Lights in the Sky broke the stillness. Only that and the angry snorts of the musk oxen bulls.

Then suddenly there came the hard twang of a bow. Another—and arrows sped invisibly through the darkness. When they struck, the great shaggy beasts leaped with the pain—but while they still lived, the bulls did not break from their place in the ranks.

It was not until arrows began to strike the cows in the heart of the ring and these foolish ones gave way to panic that the ring broke. Then the bulls were pushed out of place by the frenzied lunging of the cows, and the impregnable defense of Omingmuk was broken. Now panic gripped the bulls also, for when the defenses were breached, the dogs leaped in amongst the milling beasts of the herd, and though they remained utterly silent, this made their attack more terrible still.

The hunters ran as swiftly as foxes, leaping in and out amongst the rock piles, stabbing with the short spears they used now instead of the bows, leaping for cover to avoid the blind charge of a great wounded bull, and running along the low ridges to cut off the escape of a cow. But after a short time it was all over.

The dogs were recalled, and they sat with grim patience waiting for the men to finish butchering the beasts which had been killed. Then, while the dogs fed, the men piled up the meat—cut off the precious horns of Omingmuk and rolled up the thick, woolly hides.

So the hunt ended, for it would take three or four weeks to carry the harvest of that one hunt back to the camps. This was the manner of the hunting of Omingmuk, and from his horns we made spoons, ladles and bowls, and best of all, the wonderful crossbows of the old days of my fathers. The meat of Omingmuk was as good as that of Tuktu, and richer, but the hides were not of much use for they were too heavy to wear, and so we used them only as mats under the sleeping robes of the igloos.

Only twice in my life have I, Ohoto, seen Omingmuk alive; for when the time came that the Kiktoriaktormiut were gone from the gates of the land, the musk oxen were already gone. The Itkilit to the westward had been armed with rifles by white men, and the Omingmuk vanished from the land about Tulemaliguak soon after that.

But I have heard of other happenings at Tulemaliguak, and of these I well remember the story of the *Angeoa*—the Great One—who lives in the lake.

One year Hekwaw did not return to his home by dog sled, but waited until spring, and then, with the help of my father, built a kayak for the return south by water. It was late July before the two men, accompanied by a third who was called Kahutna, set off in three kayaks. They drove their light craft up the river which leads to the lake, and at the great falls on the river where the water sinks deep into the earth through a dark gorge, they carried the kayaks up over the tundra into the waters above. When they reached the north bay of Tulemaliguak, they found the lake still covered with ice, though summer was half over then.

The three men found a passage along the east shore, and this they followed, though in other times men had always followed the west shore of the lake. The ice had broken free of the east shore and there was a channel between ice and land, and along this the three kayaks skimmed like the grayling that split the shining surface of rivers.

Tulemaliguak had always had a strange name with our People—the Lake of the Heaped-up Ribs, it is called. The name came to it in years faintly remembered when it was said men found the bones of a beast on its shores, and those bones were so great a man could not lift any one of them with both his arms! The greatest of lakes had more than that name, for there are many tales told of men, in times past, who ventured out on the breast of the lake and never returned to the land, because of the gigantic beast who dwelt in its depths.

In the days when Hekwaw and Elaitutna were young, it was the custom to travel close to the shores of Tulemaliguak; and for generations no man had crossed open water, and so the old tales had come to be thought of only as stories to tell to the children.

My father, Hekwaw and Kahutna made good time down the east shore. On their third day they came to a deep bay quite free of ice, and since they were anxious to escape from Tulemaliguak, they decided to cross that bay from headland to headland.

It was a clear summer day, so bright that the cold waters had absorbed all the blue from the sky, leaving it as white as new snow. But the blue shone in the waters which were so clear that even under the clouds of a storm a man could see downward for the depths of ten paddles.

Hekwaw was leading the three kayaks and all of the men were wielding their paddles with power, for they were anxious to make landfall at the still distant point to the south. Elaitutna was sweating and he felt thirsty, so he raised his paddle straight up in the air in order to catch the trickle which ran down it into his mouth. Then he plunged the paddle into the water again and his gaze followed it, and of a sudden he cried out in a voice shaken by fear—for beneath the hull of his kayak he saw a huge shape, a shadow as long as a hill, and the shadow was moving.

The other two men heard Elaitutna cry out and they rested until they caught the word that he shouted.

"Angeoa!" he cried.

Instantly all three men lifted their paddles and turned their kayaks to the shore, driving them so swiftly they hardly touched the still surface. But they had gone no more than a few dozen strokes when the water between Hekwaw and Kahutna began to boil up. The rush of that water caught the kayak of Kahutna and tilted it sideways so quickly that the man lost his balance. He flailed desperately with his long double paddle, but the kayak spun over and threw him out into the lake.

There was a roaring sound that rose like a whirlpool on a rapid, and above it the other two men could hear the screams of Kahutna—so they turned back to help him, for he was a good man. They turned back, but they had not taken a stroke toward him when, breaking the surface as a huge bubble breaks, there rose the sleek black length of a beast!

It was beyond the words of the People to tell you about, but my father who saw it said that it was as long as twenty kayaks and broader than five. It had a fin which stood up from one end, and that fin was as big as a tent. Neither my father nor Hekwaw saw its head, and did not believe the beast had a head.

As the Great One called Angeoa broke water, the two men in the kayaks turned once more for the shore and abandoned Kahutna, for it was plain neither arrows nor spears could defeat this monster from the depths of the lake.

Hekwaw and Elaitutna did not stop paddling until their kayaks crashed into the rocks of the shore. The thin skin of their craft was torn and ripped on the rocks, but the men did not care. So exhausted they could not stand, they crawled out of the cockpits and dragged themselves up the beach where they lay for a long time in the sun, unable to move from the weariness of their limbs.

My father was the first to recover himself. He staggered up from the beach, and, leaning against a big rock, he looked out over the blazing blue to the distant line of the ice. All was still on the greatest of lakes. The gray mist from the ice hung perfectly motionless over the floes. No breath of wind ruffled the blue of the water. Nothing moved—and nothing floated upon it! The kayak of Kahutna had vanished as had the man, and the beast that had risen out of the waters was also gone.

I can tell you that my father and Hekwaw abandoned their kayaks where they had landed, for neither would go again out on Tulemaliguak, even if it cost them their lives for refusing. And they nearly died too, for they were not prepared to walk for twenty days overland, when they had expected to have gone in seven by kayak, but they walked all the way to the present homes of the People, and this story is the one they told of Angeoa. And since that time no man of the Ihalmiut has ventured out on Tulemaliguak in a boat.

After that time, when men wished to travel north in the summer to their famous meeting place, called Akilingnea, beyond the north gates of the land, they took kayaks only to the south end of Tulemaliguak. Here they left their kayaks, and walked around the lake to the camps of the Kiktoriaktor-miut, where they borrowed kayaks to complete their journey northward.

Elaitutna often told me of these journeys to Akilingnea, and I have often wished I had gone to that place. It is a great ridge which lies by the Itkilit Ku—the Indian River (called Thelon by white men)—to the north and the west of our lands.

Itkilit Ku flows out of the distant southwest, out of the forests, up into the westernmost plains, and eastward until it comes at last to Kamaneruak Lake and goes hence to the sea. The River of Men also runs into Kamaneruak Lake, and so does the river which runs north out of Tulemaliguak, where the Kiktoriaktormiut lived.

Now from the shores of the ever-frozen salt sea, which is said to lie far to the north, there are rivers that stretch almost to the Itkilit Ku. And from the distant northwest there are many long chains of lakes that are said to lead to the Land of Copper, where a strange and fearsome race of men live.

It is because of the way these rivers run that the ridge on the lake near the mouth of Itkilit Ku came to be such a famous place in the world. For to the meeting place came the Quaernermiut, from Kamaneruak; and from the sea to the east, there came the Dhaeomiut; from the frozen sea to the north there came the Utkuhigjalingmiut; the Haningajormiut came also from northward, and our cousins the Harvaktor-miut and the Palelermiut came from the southeast. The many camps of the Ihalmiut sent men from southward, and from the seas to the northwest there came those we call the Ejaka—half men.

All of these people brought things to trade. The Ejaka brought the copper which is found in their land. We carried the soft stone that is made into pipes, bowls and cooking pots and we also brought certain furs and things made of wood. From the north sea the Innuit brought rare amulets and sealskins and the white bones which are the teeth of certain fish-beasts that live on the seas. From the east the Dhaeomiut brought iron, and things they had obtained from the white men at Churchill.

But not all came to trade. The men from the east, the west and the farthest north came there also for wood. All these men lived in lands where wood is not seen; but for a reason which we do not understand, Itkilit Ku carries great trees from somewhere far to the southwest, and leaves these big timbers along the shores of the lake at Akilingnea. The sea dwellers came here for this wood, and they spent the short summer months carving the dead trees into sled runners, spear handles, kayak ribs and many other valuable things. In the days of my father they cut these things from the solid trunks of the trees, using nothing but stones they had sharpened by pounding them against other stones.

Those who came to the ridge were our brothers, for all were Innuit except the Ejaka who came from the northwest. These were savage and treacherous men—and though they spoke a language that belongs to the Innuit, yet it was different and had many words we do not know. In some ways they were like the Itkilit, the Indians, for they were a dangerous people and their laws were not our laws. They quarreled often and when they were angry they would use their spears on each other and, often enough, on the men from the camps of our People.

Now all of these strangers came to Akilingnea in such a way that they approached from the south side of the lake— except only the Ejaka. These came always from the north of the hill, and this is how it is that to this day our greeting when we come to a camp is always, "Ai! I come from the right side! From the right side of the ridge!" For in the old days, this was to show that the visitor came from the south side of the ridge Akilingnea, and was not of the Ejaka, the dangerous ones who came in from its north.

Well, these are but a few of the tales I have heard from my father and Hekwaw. Often enough I have wished I had been a grown man in those times. Then there were great things to do and there were many camps to visit, and in the nights the Innuit of the plains had much time for dancing and singing. Those were wonderful times, and terrible times, at the ridge Akilingnea! Now that place is left alone to the ravens and gulls and there are no camps under its shores any more, for the time of my father is done. His time is done and mine will soon follow, so there is no more to tell you who are of the Kablunait and not of the world that I know.

XX

Last Days of the People

Toward the end of August we left the Inukok to their lonely vigil and turned back to Windy Bay. The forerunners of the herds had already preceded us and Andy's work at the Deer's Way was at an end. As for me, the strange lands about Angkuni had told me all they knew, for they could speak only with dead voices. I was ready to return to the living voices of the Ihalmiut.

The journey home was uneventful, and Ohoto was happy to find that his father's dire predictions had not yet been fulfilled. The People still lived, though they were hungry for they were without shells. We supplied them with what we could spare—and that was most of what we had, for our time in the land was almost at an end. There was a month still to run. This we spent with the deer and with the People, and, as always when these two are together, the time was happy and there was contentment in the hearts of all men. It is pleasant now to remember that those last days in the land were happy ones. . . .

In the time when the deer were hurrying south to the forests to evade the impending onslaught of winter, we too made our farewells to the Barrens. The nights had already grown long, the days had grown brief, and the season of Kaila's wrath was upon us. We saw little of sunlight or starlight. The gray cloud scud raced in from the east and the roof of the world was so close above us that we could stand on the dull moss of the ridges and feel the chill wraiths of the driven mists in our faces. The land was dying, and it was time for us to return to our own world.

Our canoe, old now with the weight of her journey, lay with her scrofulous sides on the shore. Beside her was the meager pile of supplies which must see us out of the land. It was raining. A fine penetrating haze as cold and dismal as the gray sweat on the face of a corpse hung over us.

Ohoto and Ootek came to help us stow our sparse dunnage against the rough, splintered ribs of the canoe.

Ohoto was smoking his little stone pipe, a tiny and shapely object of semi-translucent stone, neatly and artistically bound with the brass from an old cartridge case. I said good-by to him in the white man's way, and after we had shaken hands he took the pipe from his mouth and, without speaking, handed it to me. It was a trivial gift in farewell. And yet—how trivial was it? I knew how that pipe had come down from a century that is gone, for it was the pipe of Elaitutna, Ohoto's father. It had seen more of the land and more of the things in the land than any man living had seen or would see. It was to have gone with Ohoto into his grave, to remain with him as a familiar thing in the eternity he sought at the end of his days. Now it would go with me, instead, out of the land, to lie warm and smoldering in the palm of my hand as I remembered the things I needed to say if the voices of the Ihalmiut were to be heard in the world of the Kablunait.

I think Ootek, my song-cousin, was crying a little, but perhaps it was only the film of moisture which lay over all our faces as the cold east wind drove the spume low over the hills. Why, after all, should he cry? The white men were leaving the land, leaving it to the People. And we would not return, for in the time that can be measured in a handful of years nothing would remain to draw us back to the great plains.

The current gripped our canoe and as we passed down to the mouth of the river, I looked back. But I saw nothing worth remembering in that last glance. Thick mists obscured the Ghost Hills and the dark crest of the cabin by the shore. So I turned and looked forward as the old canoe made her way down the long arm of the bay and to the open waters of mighty Nueltin.

For nearly a week we coasted the shores of Nueltin, until we came to a maze of bleak little islands crowding the northernmost bay of the lake. Here, after much searching, we found the contorted passage which leads to the bay of Thlewiaza—the Great Fish River—which flows to the sea. Once on that river we were too busy to think again of the land of the Little Hills. The canoe leapt, shied and started like a frightened beast as she took the first rapid. We shot out at its foot and then paused to still our frightened hearts before we went on down this river that has been run by no more than three or four white men in all time. After the briefest of respites, the rapids roared at us again.

Thlewiaza is the only river running from the land of the People to the seacoast in the East. It barely tolerates men who try to descend it, and any man who tried to ascend it into the heart of the land would be brutally rebuffed. The river does not flow, but debouches insanely over a landscape which resembles a titanic slag heap spewed out by some tremendous subterranean smelter. It is a world which looks as hell might, if hell's fires were quenched. The river roars angrily over this chaos and spills its fury almost at will over the land, spreading out to envelop as much of the broken debris as it can reach.

In five days we covered a hundred miles. We had soon given up any attempt to count the rapids. They were often continuous for many miles at a stretch, and the interludes of calm water were so rare, and therefore so startling, that they impressed us more than the rapids would have done on any other rivers.

Although the season was too advanced for men in a canoe, we had no choice but to travel, whether through rain or into the hatred of sleet. At first we feared our slim load of food would not be enough, but soon we were thankful that we carried no more weight with us. Many times we were saved from destruction in the shallow violence of the rapids only because the canoe was so light that she could meet the hungry caress of the rocks without feeling their teeth.

I remember only two things out of that ordeal not connected with the hazardous confusion of rocks and boiling masses of water. The first of these is the memory of two great caribou bucks standing on the summit of a hill and facing each other defiantly with the silent challenge of the rut in their tense attitude. I saw them for only an instant before the ever-present storm scud whipped over our heads and blotted out the images of the two magnificent beasts.

The second thing I remember was a cairn of rocks on the shore which we mistook for a stone man. During our first five days on the river we had seen no sign that men had ever come down this torrent. When we saw the Inukok we fought our way free of the current and landed to inspect it more closely. It was no stone man, but only a little heap of flat stones piled over the grave of a child. Wolves or foxes had nosed aside some of the rocks and the white bones were scattered about in the gravel.

Only those two memories remain. The rest is a nightmare confusion of black, curling waves; of white, driven spray, and the half-seen glimpses of evil, dark rocks under the keel of the canoe.

Thlewiaza brought us out of the Barrens, but it did so with savagery and with the clear warning that it would tolerate no attempt at a return.

Late in September the canoe, shrunken now by the ponderous swells of Hudson Bay, began feeling the sting of salt spray in her wounds. It was almost the end. There remained a day and a night when we fought with an offshore gale and a blinding snow blizzard and, for a while, held onto the canoe, and to our lives, only because we found a reef and were able to stand waist-deep in the frigid green waters for the long hours until the tide changed and the wind dropped.

We turned north and at last found refuge behind the long yellow dunes of Eskimo Point. Our night on the reef had made it obvious that we could not hope to navigate a hundred-odd miles south to Churchill in our crippled canoe. After a week at Eskimo Point we were picked up by a wandering Royal Canadian Air Force plane, and then for the last time I looked down on the immutable face of the

Barrens and watched it recede from me, carrying with it the People I had known in its depths.

My journey was over, but I was still tied to the Barrens, not by the simple web of memories alone, but by something more powerful. There was, and is, an abiding affection in my heart for the men and women of the plains who lent me their eyes so that I was privileged to look backward through the dark void of dead years, and to see not only the relics of forgotten times, but also to see into the minds and the thoughts of the men of those times. It was a great gift I had from the People and one that deserved a repayment.

During the years which followed my return to cities I tried to keep myself informed of the Ihalmiut's progress. Avidly I searched for the stray scraps of news that trickled out of the Barrens, and I managed to piece these together so that I was able to trace the history of the People after my time. And what I discovered shocked me inexpressibly. When I left the Barrens I had naively believed that the Ihalmiut would know no more black days, nor be left to struggle with their dark fates unaided by us. I was sure that the work done by Franz, by Andy and myself, and our careful reports to the government, would have made it quite impossible for the monumental neglect of half a century to be continued. I was wrong.

Here is the epilogue to the story of the Ihalmiut.

During the winter and early spring of 1949–1950, starvation again struck at the People with undiminished ferocity. And that starvation would have been fatal but for one accident. It happened that a free-lance photographer and newspaper writer wandered into the northern Barrens in March of 1950, and he found the northern cousins of the Ihalmiut, the Padliermiut, in desperate straits from famine. His story was given screaming headlines in several influential newspapers, and in late April the R.C.A.F. was instructed to fly emergency supplies to the Ihalmiut and Padliermiut. Food was taken in, and shortly afterwards news releases from the authorities painted this humanitarian effort so brilliantly that no reader thought to ask why this dramatic rescue had been necessary. No one thought of the long winter when, once more abandoned, the Ihalmiut had struggled with death. No one asked why that agony had been allowed to repeat its brutal pattern once more.

That it should have been permitted to happen is even more incredible in view of the fact that during the summer of 1949 an epidemic of poliomyelitis struck the Ihalmiut and the authorities belatedly visited the Little Hills country—though not in time to prevent the disease from taking its toll.

First, the only child born to the People that year, a son of Miki, was dead. Itkut, the youngest wife of Kakumee, was dead. Howmik, the mother of young Inoti, and Hekwaw, the old masterhunter, were crippled; and Hekwaw's son, Ohotuk, was dead. Hekwaw and Howmik were evacuated to Churchill for treatment. They lived; but despite the fact that government agents had seen with their own eyes how bad things were, the Ihalmiut were once more abandoned.

Then, in the spring of 1950, a commercial fishing company, supplied by air from Churchill, moved to Nueltin Lake. This company needed only one thing to make its fishing venture a success (it had the fish, for Nueltin is an untouched reservoir of gigantic lake trout and whitefish), and that was cheap labor. Now the Canadian government is most anxious to encourage the spread of industries in the arctic, so what was more natural than to help out the new company by turning over to it the remaining Ihalmiut? In the summer the R.C.M.P flew to the Little Hills country, picked up the Ihalmiut, despite their efforts to resist, and delivered them into the benevolent hands of the fish company. A news release pointed out that this was done solely to benefit the Eskimos, who would now be able to protect themselves from future disasters by assisting the white men.

I have not been able to discover all the details of what followed,* but I know that the fish company failed and that the Ihalmiut, having once more given up their essential struggle with the land, were cast loose in a year's time to readjust, as best they might, to the old ways again. It was a repetition of the trader-Eskimo relationship of the '30's, but this time repeated under government sponsorship. In 1951 the Ihalmiut were again—and probably for the final and fatal time—forgotten in the depths of their land.

The official government statement covering the first part of this episode is so interesting that I have included it in full.

---

*The details are recorded in *The Desperate People*.

Starving Eskimos
May Be Evacuated
130 Miles by Air

Ottawa, April 25 (CP) — A band of primitive Eskimos facing starvation in the Lake Ennadai district in the Northwest Territories may be evacuated by air to Lake Nueltin 130 miles away.

Officials of the Northwest Territories Council in Ottawa said today plans are under consideration for the complete rehabilitation of the small band, believed to be the last surviving remnants of the caribou-eater Eskimos.

First reports of starvation among the Eskimos, estimated to number slightly more than 30, reached Ottawa a few weeks ago and a plane load of food was flown into the district by the RCAF.

At Churchill, Man., today, Major ———, army medical office at Fort Churchill, said the Eskimos are on the verge of starvation. He examined them after being flown into the district to return an Eskimo woman treated at Churchill for illness.

Major ——— said the Eskimos' inadequate diet has shown up in various ways, including skin diseases. Lacking the proper facilities to help them get food, he is sending in drugs to the district 300 miles northwest of Churchill as the next best thing.

The Eskimos are in a hard-to-get-at spot that lacks adequate facilities.

This report is typical of the publicity white men of this continent have given to our efforts to assist the arctic natives, and as such it deserves close examination. But such an examination quickly dispels the impression of our benevolent zeal as guardians and protectors of the Eskimos. It appears as a shameless effort to avoid the blame for a great and continuing evil, an effort to lay our conscience at rest.

The second paragraph of the release makes brave reading if you are not aware that the "plans" mentioned were those concerning the fishery at Nueltin . . . and if you are not aware that these plans came to nothing, and no further attempts to "rehabilitate" the Ihalmiut have been implemented as I write this, in December of 1951.

The third paragraph is even more startling, for it states that first reports of starvation amongst the Ihalmiut were not received until the spring of 1950. It is difficult to understand how the reports written by Andy and myself, and submitted in 1947 and 1948 directly to the government branch responsible for Eskimo administration, could have been forgotten. Nevertheless they must have been forgotten, as was Franz's report in the spring of 1947, and as was the action taken by the government itself in that year. Much has evidently been forgotten.

In the event of these discrepancies coming to light, however, the final paragraph provides an explanation, and an excuse. "The Eskimos are in a hard-to-get-at spot that lacks adequate facilities." It is not our fault, then, if all our good intentions fail. Our consciences may rest at ease—we've done our best.

Perhaps. But my conscience will not rest. I have spoken of the debt I owe the People, and this debt alone would prevent me from accepting oblivion as the answer to the problem of what fate awaits our native races. Refusing to accept this answer, I have written this book in an attempt to give form and substance to the voices which spoke to me from the graying rock heaps under Kinetua. The People lent me their eyes so that I might see what white men have tried not to see. Now I, in turn, have lent the People my voice so that white men shall hear the words the Ihalmiut cannot speak for themselves.

It may be that I have spoken too late and so have done no more than to remember the great days of a race which is gone. But the story of the Ihalmiut is not theirs alone, since much of what I have written about them holds true for many thousands of Indians and Eskimos across the whole length and breadth of the continent.

If I have only succeeded in writing an epitaph for the Ihalmiut, perhaps their tragedy can nevertheless be made to bear fruit—though it be bitter fruit. Perhaps it will help us to look, with a new honesty, into the lives of those who dwell by hidden rivers and by the frozen coasts, and in the depths of forests. If this should come to pass—then I will have paid my debt.

It is not enough to have chronicled the destruction of certain men. It is not enough to have been harshly critical of my own society and to have described the injustices and the crimes of stupidity and omission which must lie at our door. There remains the question of what can be done so that the tragedy of the Ihalmiut will not become the fatal pattern for all those who dwell within the cold sweep of the north. Solutions to this problem may be complex, but any solution must be based on one primary act.

We must first of all—and immediately—help the Eskimos and Indians escape from their now chronic condition of malnutrition and even outright starvation, and we must do this not as a dole, *but by helping them to feed themselves.* Charity is as fatal to a primitive people as it is to civilized ones. The continuous giving of basic sustenance brings about a dependency which is often mortal to the spirit. Furthermore, the kind of food we have so far provided for native peoples has not been food, but rather a slow poison which destroys the body through malnutrition almost as certainly as outright starvation would. No, we must not give "food." What we must do is to *give the natives the means of procuring their own food from the land which is theirs.*

It should be clear enough that flour and baking powder are no substitutes. The northern lands do not themselves provide foods of this nature. The kind of food they can provide is *meat.* The question is: how can we ensure that the northern people have meat—in plenty?

Let us see what has happened to the once abundant supplies of red meat in the north. The fate of the deer has been the fate of all. Some of the most important animals have already almost vanished: the musk oxen, the narwhals and right whales. As for the rest, they have all been terribly diminished so that the land and sea no longer raise their food crop for men as they once did. The land has been bled so freely that it now can lay just claim to that ominous name—the Barrens. The sea, too, has been bled, and is being bled. The sealing fleets along the eastern coasts have done yeoman work; the whalers have long since destroyed the great mammals which once came into Hudson Bay and into all the narrow waters at the top of the continent, and with the passing of the whales whole tribes of Eskimos have also vanished.

Nor is the bloodletting at an end. The walrus which were once the most important of the sea beasts to the coast Eskimos have been seriously reduced in numbers, largely by the R.C.M.P., by traders, and by missionaries who annually slaughter fantastic numbers of walrus in order to feed dog teams that are three or four times as big as they need to be. At Churchill a commercial plant to process white whales—"beluga" they are more often called—was established as recently as 1949 with full government approval. The meat of these beasts is to be shipped south to feed foxes on our fur ranches, or to provide fertilizer for our gardens. On the islands of the arctic many Eskimos have been forced to subsist largely on fish because of the disappearance of sea mammals, and now even the fish are being taken from them. In 1949 a new fishery was opened by Nova Scotian ships in an area where the Eskimos were almost completely dependent on fish. Had it not been for the presence of army personnel, who took a determined stand against this flagrant robbery, this fishery, which was also fully sanctioned by the government despite the outraged protests of several arctic specialists, would have brought famine to these Eskimos.

The picture is the same throughout the north. When any financial advantage can accrue to us through the destruction of the lifeblood of the northern people, we do not scruple to destroy. The authorities talk of "conservation" while at the same time one branch of government is accepting thousands of dollars from sportsmen to fly them—in government planes —to the heart of the caribou country where they can kill the people's food for sheer sport alone. The authorities enact game laws which reserve the dwindling numbers of meat-producing wild animals for "recreational" use by white men —for sport and trophy hunting—while effectively denying the use of these animals to the native people who need them for sheer physical survival.

In support of the decimation of the mammals in the north, certain experts claim that the Eskimos and Indians must, in the long run, learn to eat our food if they are ever to become part of our way of life. This justifies the wanton destruction of the arctic food. But does it? Eskimos and Indians will always live largely in the north, and so they will always be able to maintain their eating habits as they are, providing there is meat to eat. More important, they will always *need* the specific nutriments found in fat and meat. It is senseless to say the northern natives *must* change their diet—as senseless as suggesting that our race should abandon the basic products of our land in favor of strange foods to be imported from a far-distant region.

The question is, what can we do to restore the food we have stolen from the mouths of the northern peoples? And the answer is that we can do everything needful. The caribou provide a clear example of what might be done. If it were possible to overrule the selfish interests of white men, it would be relatively easy to make the Barrens plains again produce the food which men must have if they are to survive in that land. At the moment, and by the tacit admission of the government, the deer are close to the fatal level beyond which a further reduction in numbers will doom them to extinction. But they have not yet passed the point of no return. They could still be preserved, and I know this to be true, for I spent two years studying this problem in the field and as a scientist. There are enough deer left so that, if given full protection, the species could stage a quick comeback, and there is no good reason why this resurgence should not take place. The true value of the caribou lies not only in their contribution to the well-being of the Barrens Eskimos, but in the fact that they are of equal importance to the continued survival of about forty thousand high-forest Indians, and to the majority of the eight thousand surviving Eskimos across the whole Canadian arctic. All modern Eskimos are descended from caribou-hunting people, even though many Innuit now depend largely on the products of the sea. In fact, almost all Eskimos of our time would willingly and gratefully turn to the deer for their support, if the deer were available.

Unlike the buffalo who were fated to become extinct because they contended with us for lands we coveted, the deer live in a land no settler will ever wish to seize. The Barrens will never grow wheat or beef cattle. They will grow one food crop, and one alone—the deer. The Barrens can support a tremendous population of deer, perhaps as high as five million head. Once they were this numerous, and in order to return to this high level they need only protection. Not from wolves, not from the legitimate and normal appetites of the natives, but from us. Directly, they need protection from white trappers and hunters, and indirectly they need protection from the manufacturing companies who make a good part of their profits from the sale of astronomical amounts of ammunition, and from the sale of repeating rifles. If we were to place an absolute prohibition on the killing of deer by white men, and if we were to restrict the sale of ammunition and the types of weapons sold to the natives, the deer would do the rest. We should go farther and absolutely prohibit sport hunting of any species of animal in any region where these species could contribute to the well-being of native peoples. There might well be a period of increased hardship while the Indian and Eskimo hunters adjusted to a limited killing potential, but they are not fools, and they *would* adjust so that their kill became a valid one.

The futile and expensive stop-gaps that we now advocate would no longer be required. The idiotic system of paying bounty on wolves would not be needed. The periodic disease epidemics which wipe out overly large populations of natural predators in the north would do the job for us, as it has always done. Nature can, and does, manage this control very well. We are the one predator she cannot control. We must control ourselves.

Many agents of government have complained sadly that it seems impossible for the Indians and Eskimos to accommodate to the modern world.

The Aklavik Eskimos at the mouth of the Mackenzie River are an exception. Fortuitous circumstances (not any direct help from us) gave those people a fair chance to adapt themselves to our way of life—and they made the most of their opportunity. But why have not all the northern natives been as successful? Because men with starved bodies have starved minds as well. Starved intellects do not respond well to difficult tasks, and the adjustment of a primitive race to our civilization is exceedingly difficult. But well-fed men are capable of understanding, and of coping with new and unfamiliar problems. The Eskimos stand out as being particularly adaptable people with a remarkable aptitude for absorbing new ideas, mechanical and otherwise. Freed of the incubus of malnutrition and its hand-maiden, disease, our Eskimos are capable of quick and sane adjustment to the conditions of the white man's world, as the Aklavik people have abundantly demonstrated.

They cannot, of course, step from igloo into office overnight even supposing that this was what they wished to do. The northern natives as a whole can be *made* part of our scheme of things only by the expedient of employing them as brute labor—"slave labor" would be a better term—and in many cases this is what we have attempted. The better answer lies in a gradual transition, based on a solid foundation of economic independence of a sort that is compatible with the present knowledge and experience of the people.

It sounds like a tall order, yet *a solution to it has been known to the governments of Canada and the United States for the last thirty years,* and was actually developed *by* them! I am referring to the Reindeer Grazing Scheme, which was originally begun in Alaska, and which was copied by the Canadians. In brief the plan was to import Asiatic Reindeer —very similar to caribou—and to train natives to act as herdsmen. Each native village was to have its own herd, and these herds were to make the people independent as far as a supply of protein was concerned, while at the same time providing them with a salable cash crop.

The scheme developed rather strangely. In Alaska it fell into the hands of certain white men who exploited it for their own gain. In Canada it was begun purely as an experiment, and has remained no more than an experiment limited in its effects to a tiny handful of Eskimos near the Mackenzie Delta. Nevertheless it has shown that it could be an answer to the problem of economic independence for every Eskimo in Canada. There is only one really valid reason why it has not been extended. It has been strenuously opposed by important interests whose voices are clearly heard in high places. These opponents, the strongest of whom are connected with the beef industry, have held the field with their contention that Canada could not afford a reindeer industry. Yet it can be easily demonstrated that the initial cost of extending the reindeer industry—and "industry" it could well be—would be rapidly repaid, both in direct returns and in the indirect returns which would result from the money we might save, and which we now largely waste, in blind efforts to assist the Eskimos with charity.

There are approximately 2,000,000 square miles of the arctic which are completely, or largely, suitable for reindeer raising. The caribou occupy much, but not all, of this area; but the preservation of these wild deer would not provide a serious obstacle to the introduction of reindeer.

The introduction of reindeer herding as an industry throughout the arctic would accomplish two things. First, it would assist the caribou and the sea mammals in providing northern men with the kind of food they require. Secondly, it would provide a sound economic basis for the inevitable transition which the northern people must undergo—or perish. The Eskimos (and many northern Indians) would be producing salable commodities. The world today is a meat-hungry world, and will remain one for as far ahead as we can see. In Alaska, reindeer meat is widely used by white men, and was even shipped south to Seattle where it was distributed and sold as a luxury food until the pressure of the U.S. meat lobby forced the trade to be discontinued. The Eskimos of the Canadian arctic could do as well, or better, for they have access to a great ocean port (though one that is at present so little used as to be a serious financial embarrassment to us) at Churchill. From Churchill runs the shortest sea route to Europe, and in Europe animal protein is desperately needed. It might prove economically sound to establish a meat-packing plant at Churchill, not to prepare beluga for fox food, but to prepare reindeer and perhaps caribou meat, if the herds prosper, for shipment abroad. The plan seems reasonable, for at this moment we are canning horse meat in the central Canadian prairies, shipping it 1000 miles by rail, then transshipping it by lake and ocean freighter to Europe, where it is sold for human consumption at a good profit.

More than that, we could arrange to ship meat south from Churchill on the Hudson Bay Railway which operates its southbound trains at heavy loss, and make the refrigerated meat available throughout Canada.

Perhaps it would provide a certain amount of competition with our cattle-raising industry, but I hardly think this would cause much annoyance to our general population.

The interior Barrens on the west coast of Hudson Bay could support a minimum of 200,000 reindeer, and the annual crop of meat from such a herd would be quite large enough to bring a full measure of economic independence to the entire present Eskimo population of the Central Arctic.

Before I leave this point of economic stability I must mention the fact that the need for this condition is apparently accepted in principle by the authorities who have throughout the years suggested such ideas as an eiderduck industry or white-fox fur ranching on the Barrens. These suggestions, and others, have been put forward over the last two decades, but no serious attempt has been made to implement any one of them. They have been purely and simply "cover schemes." I cannot honestly guarantee that reindeer and caribou plans are certain of meeting all requirements. But they are a potentially effective method for achieving the results which the government has so frequently insisted it wishes to achieve.

With the establishment of a sound economy, the passageway from the world of the natives to our world would be open, and they could cross the void which now separates them from us, if they so desired. To date, we have tried only one method of bridging this gap, and that is to carry the northern peoples into our complex and unfamiliar life at one gigantic leap. Missionaries, for example, go to the arctic and suffer like martyrs so that in a year, or a decade, they can make professing Christians out of some heathen tribe. It is too great a leap. The so-called converts have no more idea of what lies behind the ideas they mouth than we have of what lies behind the eyes of God. Brave men, but dangerous men, the missionaries were also entrusted by the government with almost all the meager educational work being done in the North. In most of the church schools the Eskimos were taught the singing of hymns and the saying of prayers, but they learned little else and what they did learn was useless to them for it was not applicable to the physical realities of their present lives. Confused and baffled, they suffer for this attempt to "educate" them, since they learned only enough to make them feel vague dissatisfaction, without understanding how to bring about the changes which were needed. However, the missionary school system is advantageous to *us,* for it relieves the government of the need of spending tax money on the project, and it is beyond normal criticism, since few of us dare or wish to criticize the selfless efforts of the dedicated men who are our missionaries. Clearly what is required is to provide native teachers who have been rationally and intelligently trained and who can then go back to a healthy, unfettered people and teach what they have learned. The essence of the matter is to use no force. The northern natives should be in a position to embrace voluntarily and with understanding the white men's religious, economic and political creeds, *if they so desire.* Then the churches in the North could at least claim their new members were just that, and not the bemused dupes which native Christians now represent.

It seems to me that this is a sane point of view, but it is not shared by the Missions, for they have fought, and are fighting still, to keep the education of the Northern natives in their own hands. It is a fight which is made more dangerous to the Eskimos by the violent competition between opposing religious groups, who often engage in most un-Christian strife, using the souls—and bodies—of the natives as their pawns in their strange battles.

Certainly the Northern races can hope for little real opportunity to come to terms with our civilization until we extend to them the purely material facilities which are needed. Proper schools, proper medical facilities, preferably with native doctors, and a fair and honest economic treatment—these are the essentials.

To give a dying man a cup of water may be laudable; but to let that man die, when it is in our power to prevent it, is despicable. In effect we have been doling out cups of water to a dying people in the arctic, and have been free with self-praise of this benevolence. Surely we must possess a peculiarly facile turn of mind when we can virtuously condemn the cruelties perpetrated in other countries, while at the same time we avert our eyes from the cruelties we ourselves continue to condone in our own land. Certainly we are stupid and short-sighted, for the harm we do is not done alone to the Eskimos and Indians but it is done to ourselves as well

XXI
The Days to Come

The ideas I have put forward in the preceding chapter are by no means the nebulous and rosy visions of an idealistic dreamer. For the most part they are originally not even my own ideas, but have been propounded by men who are more competent than I am to understand the dilemmas which face us in the arctic. And, fortunately, I have the proof that these ideas are not only realistic, but can be implemented readily enough if we sincerely wish to see them realized. I can tell you of a place where all I have asked for the natives of the arctic has already been granted to an Eskimo people. This place is Greenland, the far eastern outpost of the Innuit, where the Danish government has for many years followed an enlightened policy of native administration, a policy which pitilessly exposes *our* blundering efforts for the thin shams they are.

In Greenland today there are no people called Eskimos. There are only Greenlanders. Some carry pure Eskimo blood

284

in their veins; some carry a mixture, and some are of pure Danish blood—but *all* are of one people. In that land there are men of Eskimo stock who teach in schoolrooms built for the children of all bloods. Native Greenlanders not only teach and are taught, but no limits are imposed upon their education. It is quite possible for a pure-blood Eskimo to pass through the Greenland school system, then go to Denmark (at government expense) to complete his education in a university. When such men return to Greenland they become the teachers of those who remain at home, and in this way the gap between the ancient past and our times is quickly bridged.

The descendants of men who speared seals on the ice packs of Baffin Bay now not only teach in schools but take an important, and increasing, part in industry—not as brute labor, but as men, of equal stature with all other men. They operate a large, efficient and lucrative fishing industry. They help operate the intricate scientific apparatus of weather stations. They assist in the operation of the trading posts, which are all government-owned and operated, and which deal with the people at no greater profit than is required to maintain the service. In effect the Greenlanders now own their own economy, though it is supervised by Danish administrators and will be until the native people have reached the point where they can take over full control.

The Greenlanders are rigidly protected from the commercial exploitation which has a stranglehold on our arctic regions. The type of white men who know how easy it is to make a rich living from the hearts' blood of a primitive race are forbidden to enter Greenland and they have no power there.

Natural food sources are protected with sane laws that are enforced, and it is seldom indeed that starvation comes even to the most remote areas inhabited by Greenland Eskimos. When a bad season, or other accident, brings hard times, the administration acts at once, and with full strength, nor does it wait to be shamed or frightened into taking action.

As in our part of the arctic, much of occupied Greenland is of a nature that is inimical to its habitation by Europeans. But the Greenlanders are a *part* of their land, for they possess the physical and mental heritages of the Eskimos, who long since learned how to live and prosper in that inhospitable region. Now, as a result, the Greenlanders are a race who can live in their own land and be happy there. They may well have something to contribute to the rest of the world in these sick times, and in the times which lie ahead.

And let me make this point clear: The Greenland natives are not serfs to white men's economic greed. They are not government wards, the voteless encumbrances of politicians. Instead they are a new people of increasing vigor, strength and understanding. Because one humane white race saw far into the future, the Eskimos of Greenland now belong to that future—and the future belongs to them.

So you see, it can be done.

Freed of the incubus which we have laid upon them, the Eskimos could become as valuable citizens of this world as we ourselves are. The future of the Eskimos need no longer be limited to the barren rocks of their own land. The terrible days of the Ihalmiut could be put out of men's minds and in many places, even along the River of Men, new voices would be raised in living laughter where now only the voices of the forgotten ghosts are heard.

All this can happen—and if it comes to pass, it will be our gain.

As for Inoti, the one-year-old son of Ootek—shall it come to pass that in the winters which still stretch ahead, there may be no need for him to place *his* children under the dark snows because there is no food for them? Shall it come to pass that Inoti's mother may rest secure in the knowledge that she will never be called upon to walk into the midwinter night and not return, so that Inoti's children may live for a little longer under the cold dome of the igloo?

In the days of Inoti, the son, the strength of a great people might be made to live once more. In time it would be *our* strength, and the people would be *our* people.

And then the dark stain which is the color of blood might at last be wiped from the record of the Kablunait in the place of the River of Men.

Author's Note

The subsequent story of the Ihalmiut from 1949 until 1958 is recorded in the sequel to this book, *The Desperate People,* published in 1959 by Atlantic–Little, Brown Books. It also records what is known of their history from the time of their first discovery by white men in 1893, until the period dealt with in *People of the Deer.*

ABOUT THE AUTHOR

FARLEY MOWAT is the possessor of celebrated propensities for travel and the outdoors. His librarian father moved a lot (from Belleville, Trenton and Windsor in Ontario to Saskatoon, Saskatchewan and back to Ontario's Toronto and Richmond Hill) —and the young Farley had little choice but to move with his family and the miniature menagerie that completed the Mowat household. As for the outdoors, Farley was tutored in its ways by an ornithologist uncle who introduced him to the Arctic in 1935. That introduction, which nurtured an already lively interest in nature and wildlife, led to a lengthy relationship between Farley Mowat and the Arctic, and inspired him to write such best-selling and widely translated books as *People of the Deer, The Desperate People, A Whale for the Killing* and *Sibir.*

Farley Mowat began writing for his living in 1949. Over thirty years (and almost as many books) later, he stands as one of the most popular authors and storytellers of the century, with books for adults and children, books of humor, drama and tragedy, including such perennial favorites as *The Boat Who Wouldn't Float, The Dog Who Wouldn't Be, The Top of the World Trilogy, Never Cry Wolf* and *The Snow Walker.*